The Character of Harms

How should we deal with societal ills such as crime, poverty, pollution, terrorism, and corruption? *The Character of Harms* argues that control or mitigation of "bad" things involves distinctive patterns of thought and action which turn out to be broadly applicable across a range of human endeavors, and which need to be better understood.

Malcolm Sparrow demonstrates that an explicit focus on the *bads*, rather than on the countervailing *goods* (safety, prosperity, environmental stewardship, etc.), can provide rich opportunities for surgically efficient and effective interventions – an operational approach which he terms "the sabotage of harms." The book explores the institutional arrangements and decision-frameworks necessary to support this emerging operational model.

Written for reflective practitioners charged with risk-control responsibilities across the public, private, and non-governmental sectors, *The Character of Harms* makes a powerful case for a new approach to tackling the complex problems facing society.

MALCOLM K. SPARROW is Professor of the Practice of Public Management at the John F. Kennedy School of Government, Harvard University. He is Faculty Chair of the Master of Public Policy Program, and of Executive Programs on regulatory and enforcement strategy, corruption control, and counter-terrorism. A mathematician by training, he joined the British Police Service in 1977, serving for ten years and rising to the rank of Detective Chief Inspector. He left the police to take up a faculty appointment at Harvard in 1988.

The Character of Harms

Operational Challenges in Control

MALCOLM K. SPARROW
Professor of the Practice of Public Management, John F. Kennedy School of Government, Harvard University

To Steve,

It has been a real pleasure working with you.

My very best wishes,

[signature]

CAMBRIDGE
UNIVERSITY PRESS

CAMBRIDGE UNIVERSITY PRESS
Cambridge, New York, Melbourne, Madrid, Cape Town, Singapore,
São Paulo, Delhi, Mexico City

Cambridge University Press
The Edinburgh Building, Cambridge CB2 8RU, UK

Published in the United States of America by Cambridge University Press, New York

www.cambridge.org
Information on this title: www.cambridge.org/9780521872102

First published 2008
5th printing 2012

Printed and bound by CPI Group (UK) Ltd, Croydon CR0 4YY

A catalogue record for this publication is available from the British Library

Library of Congress Cataloguing in Publication Data
Sparrow, Malcolm K.
The character of harms: operational challenges in control / Malcolm K. Sparrow.
    p.   cm.
Includes index.
ISBN 978-0-521-87210-2 (hardback)
1. Social problems – United States.   2. Social policy – United States.
3. Social conflict – United States.   I. Title.

HN59.2.S665   2008
361.10973 – dc22   2007050652

ISBN 978-0-521-87210-2 Hardback

Contents

Figures

Acknowledgments

My greatest debt is to the many practitioners, mostly public servants, who grapple daily with the task of harm reduction and who have shared with me both their accomplishments and their frustrations. In executive classrooms and workshops around the world, and through a variety of other collaborative explorations, they have taught me over the last fifteen years all I know about this subject, and thoroughly tested (at times ruthlessly) the relevance and value of any generalizations I may have drawn from their experiences.

I am also indebted to a number of colleagues who have helped me broaden the claims in this book by welcoming and facilitating my interest in areas I knew little about, providing expert guidance to relevant literatures as well as candid assessments of prevailing research traditions within their own fields. On the subject of poverty reduction, particular thanks to Mary Jo Bane and Merilee Grindle; on corruption control, Agnes Batory; on human trafficking, the Carr Center for Human Rights at the John F. Kennedy School of Government; on terrorism control, Graham Allison and the Belfer Center for Science and International Affairs, also at the Kennedy School. Thanks also to Tamar Miller for her encouragement to apply this analysis deliberately and energetically to the growing number of foundations, not-for-profit organizations, and international non-governmental organizations engaging in harm-mitigation projects of one kind or another; and for her expert and generous editorial advice.

I am also grateful to Amy Squires and Moira Smith for first rate research assistance, and to Chris Harrison (editor at Cambridge University Press) for his patience, support, and sage advice. Other colleagues have at various critical times, and probably without knowing it, spurred me on by reaffirming the value of this project. These include Mark Moore, John Braithwaite, Phil Heymann, Dutch Leonard, Allan Fels, David Ellwood, Tony Dean, Agnes Batory, David Herbster, Chris Daly, Chris Stone, and Jack Donahue.

Thanks also to my wife, Penny and daughter, Sophie, for their patience and support in dealing with me and my frustrations as I struggled, during the writing phase, to wrestle this amorphous abstraction into some tangible form.

Introduction

Much of the unfinished business for the human race seems to consist of harms, threats, or risks of one kind or another, insufficiently controlled. The United Nations Millennium Declaration, adopted by the UN General Assembly in September 2000,[1] lays out among its key objectives a daunting array of such harms to be controlled. The declaration lists, among others, hunger, war, genocide, weapons of mass destruction, international terrorism, the "world drug problem," transnational crime, smuggling of human beings, money laundering, illicit traffic in small arms and light weapons, anti-personnel mines, extreme poverty, child mortality, HIV/Aids, malaria, other emerging infectious diseases, natural and man-made disasters, violence and discrimination against women, involvement of children in armed conflict, the sale of children, child prostitution, child pornography, and loss of the world's environmental resources. Many other major policy challenges can be naturally labeled and described in similar terms. Societies seek in turn to reduce violence and crime, pollution, fraud, occupational hazards, transportation hazards, corruption, many forms of discrimination, product-safety risks, and so on.

This book examines the distinctive operational challenges that the task of *controlling harms* entails, pressing the claim that anyone involved at any level in the control or mitigation of harms (of any type) might benefit from understanding the distinctive character of this task, and mastering some distinctive patterns of thought and action that go with it.

The idea that this subject is worth addressing at such a high level of generality may seem ridiculous to some, and for a variety of reasons. Academics and practitioners who have spent significant portions of their careers delving deeply into one specific category of harms or another might argue that effectiveness in control depends only on domain-specific knowledge and analyses; that their specific domain is quite unlike anything else; and that it is therefore hard to imagine much value arising from a broader view.

Others might argue that controlling harms is ultimately no different from constructing goods: that one is merely the dual of the other. The task of controlling crime could equally be framed as *promoting public safety*. Instead of *pollution control* we should focus on *environmental stewardship*. Rather than declaring war on poverty, we should promote economic development and prosperity. Rather than focusing on gender discrimination, we should promote and advance *equality*. Rather than dwelling on the potentially embarrassing issue of *corruption control*, it would be better (certainly more comfortable) to focus on *promoting integrity*.

All of these harm-reduction challenges, apparently, can be described either way up: either the reduction of a *bad*, or the promotion of some countervailing *good*. Between the good and the bad is a surface to be moved, and it makes no difference whether we push from one side, or pull from the other. Thus the distinction, should we choose to draw one, might seem, for some, merely mathematical (seeking expansion of positives versus contraction of negatives), and they might say that in setting goals and measuring progress from one side of the boundary or the other we would only be playing with the mathematical signs (pursuing a "plus" times a "plus," or a "minus" times a "minus").

For others the distinction may appear a matter of social construction, stemming from differing ideological lenses and disciplinary traditions. Perhaps we'd imagine that law enforcement officials, if asked to wash a dirty frying pan, might launch into the task by aggressively attacking the burnt and blackest spots, followed progressively by the lesser evils, until "all the dirt had been properly dealt with." Social workers and educators – more accustomed to *bringing out the good* – might be more comfortable identifying relatively clean areas of the pan, and working away at the edges of those areas, progressively expanding them, until *cleanness* eventually covers the whole.

If the choice about which way up to describe such challenges is merely semantic, and has no operational consequence, then the subject of *controlling harms* is no different from the subject of *doing good*, or *constructing goods*; and doing good is surely so broad as to be no subject at all.

So one potential problem for this particular enterprise is the possibility that there might be no subject here – either because there are no useful higher level generalities that span the myriad domains of harm, or because the focus on harms rather than goods is of no consequence. I draw some hope, though, that neither is true – and I draw it principally from more than fifteen years of experience working with executives across the entire spectrum of regulatory or enforcement agencies. These public officials work in agencies, most of which have as their core mission the control or containment of some particular class of harms. Nevertheless these regulatory executives scarcely, if ever, have had the chance to converse across the lines that separate their respective regulatory fields, that is, until we put them together in a classroom or workshop setting and tell them that the agenda or curriculum is oriented precisely toward those managerial and organizational dilemmas which they all have in common. And, however skeptical they might be at the outset, they soon discover there are plenty of such issues.

In one recent executive program in Brisbane, Australia,[2] we brought together sixty-one regulatory executives spanning twenty-six different professions. The majority of the participants came from classic agencies of social regulation, with a predominant or substantial orientation toward harm reduction (even though virtually all such agencies deliver some services as well). These agencies included police, taxation, environment and natural resource management, fisheries protection, customs, financial regulation, consumer protection and fair trading, occupational safety, transportation safety, racing and gambling licensing, marine safety, mine safety, child safety, justice, and emergency services. The remaining participants came from agencies which were primarily providers of government services, but these participants represented sub-units within those service agencies that carried regulatory or risk-control responsibilities. These settings included the (Australian) Medicare program, disability services, education departments, and community service departments.

Despite the extraordinary range of their harm-reduction responsibilities, participants in such programs have no trouble at all understanding that their core tasks share the same fundamental nature, and that this common basis means they also share a set of rather complicated and troublesome organizational and operational puzzles. To discuss those puzzles, they merely have to learn each other's vocabulary; they already understand each other's issues. They soon discover that they all grapple with the challenge of integrating different kinds of work – some functional, some process-based, and some organized around specific concentrations of risk. They all seek clearer guidance on the awkward relationship between pursuing effectiveness in reducing harms on the one hand, and respecting the traditional regulatory values of fairness, consistency, proportionality, and predictability on the other. Everyone seems to want to understand the role analysis can play in systematic disaggregation of risks, and in the measurement of impact. And they very much want to understand what happens to the nature of managerial decision making, forms of organizational accountability, and the character of their relationships with the regulated community, when an agency tilts its focus towards the central purpose of harm reduction and away from functional, programmatic, or process-based traditions. As is usually the case, this particularly diverse class in Brisbane expressed their collective appreciation for the chance to spend a whole week together focused not on the generic challenges of government but on the specific challenges and consequences of having a harm-reduction mission.

Given the concentration of such issues within the regulatory aspects of governance, maybe the subject would be better termed *regulatory policy* than *harm-reduction*? For at least a decade, I thought so. My last book on this topic, aimed squarely at social regulators, was called *The Regulatory Craft*.[3] Here at the John F. Kennedy School of Government we advertised courses on this topic as being for regulators and enforcement officials. If others applied, we would advise them they probably did not belong, and should consider alternate programs. Over the last few years, however, the number of non-regulatory applicants seemed to rise. Applications came from officials in education and health; some from the private sector interested in corporate risk management; several from not-for-profit institutions who, while not regulators, were nevertheless committed to important causes of the harm-reduction type: anti-discrimination, protection of human rights, prevention of genocide, counter-terrorism, alleviation of poverty, and (of course) public health officials interested in disease control. Noticing the trend over time, I became a little slower to send them away and a little more eager to hear why they had applied. "Because," they said, "what you're teaching here is operational risk control, and we do that too." They were making, on my behalf, a claim I had been reluctant and deliberately slow to make: that the core elements of the art of harm-control didn't require the backdrop of regulatory policy, and that if we took away the restrictive setting of government regulation, and allowed in other players engaged in harm-reduction endeavors, that we would still all share a *subject;* and one with enough meaty challenges and important consequences to be worth formulating and developing.

A significant proportion of this book will examine an important phenomenon around which such an expanded audience might gather: that is, the emergence, across a very wide range of harm-reduction domains, of some very specific and distinctive patterns of operational and organizational behavior. These behaviors not only appear across a wide variety of harm-reduction endeavors; they also reflect a rather deliberate focus on the reduction of *bads* as opposed to the construction of *goods*.

The summary phrase I've used for the regulatory audience to label this operational approach is a beguilingly, and perhaps misleadingly, simple one: "Pick Important Problems, and Fix Them." However simple that sounds, it turns out that organizing around carefully selected and important pieces of a risk – rather than around traditional programmatic or functional tasks, or around core-high-volume operational processes – is extraordinarily difficult for agencies or institutions to do. Even if they manage to do it *once* for something special, many organizations have no place for such conduct within their routine operations.

Despite the difficulties involved, and the apparent novelty of the method, more and more organizations are learning to act this way, organizing around carefully delineated risk-concentrations or problem areas, and demonstrating specific *harms reduced* as a result. What sorts of harms do they address this way? All sorts; with many different shapes and sizes, and across a broad spectrum of professional areas. Here are a few miscellaneous examples of harms or problems which have been recently identified, analyzed, and then substantially reduced through the design and implementation of tailor-made interventions:[4]

- A pattern of unlawful filling of shorelines and unlawful removal of shoreline vegetation, associated with property owners installing sandy beaches, endangering the water quality in two outstanding surface water systems – the Butler and Clermont Chains of lakes in central Florida. The Florida Department of Environmental Protection carried out this "Environmental Problem Solving" project between October 1999 and September 2000. All ninety-four violations apparent at the outset were dealt with, ninety of them through voluntary

ion projects resulting from a carefully targeted public out-
nd information campaign, and the remaining four through
ment action.

ive piracy of copyrighted materials in Nigeria. The Nigerian
Copyright Commission launched a multi-party anti-piracy initiative
in 2005, aimed especially at organized industry groups engaged in
counterfeiting CDs, VCDs and DVDs. At the outset, an estimated
90 percent of such products circulating in Nigeria were pirated
copies, and Nigeria was regarded as a major supplier of pirated
materials for the region. The STRAP program ("Strategic Action
Against Piracy") involved as many as twenty national and international organizations at various phases, and focused significant
enforcement attention and a new monitoring regime on roughly fifty
optical disk plants that appeared to account for much of the high
volume production. As a result of the project, in May 2007, the US
Government removed Nigeria from the "301 list" of countries where
piracy and counterfeiting is regarded as pervasive. This delisting is
a landmark achievement for a developing country and a first in the
annals of Nigeria's anti-piracy efforts.

- A pattern of injuries and fatalities caused by poorly maintained or
  improperly operated fairground rides. This project was conducted by
  staff from the Department of Labor & Environment in Nova Scotia,
  Canada, and won that Department's annual prize for "regulatory
  excellence" in 2006.[5]
- Injuries to infants caused by falling down stairs whilst using baby-
  walkers. Emergency department injuries involving baby-walkers
  were reduced almost 90 percent from roughly 25,000 per year in
  the early 1990s to 2,600 in 2005. The US Consumer Product Safety
  Commission tackled this problem, accepting as a constraint the fact
  that they would not actually be able to justify a complete ban on
  baby-walkers. Their efforts instead focused on producing a revised
  voluntary standard for manufacturers with design modifications to
  limit baby-walkers' directional mobility and increase tip-over resistance once the walker stopped with one or more wheels over the edge
  of a stairway.[6]
- The illegal passing of red signals by trains. In the Netherlands, analysis of train derailments and collisions has shown that in nearly every
  case the accident is preceded by the illegal passing of a red signal.
  Authorities have therefore organized a collaborative effort to focus

attention on this particular precursor to rail disasters. The project involves railway companies, infrastructure administration, contractors, rail traffic control and environmental planners, all working together to pick apart the multiple human behavioral and technical contributors to this phenomenon, with the goal of substantially reducing the frequency with which red signals are passed.

- Dangerously high blood-lead concentrations for bridge painters in New Jersey resulting from constant exposure to lead-based paints. This was one of the very first projects conducted by a "Strategic Intervention Team" at OSHA's Area Office in Parsippany, New Jersey, under an organizational approach labeled "The Problem-Solving Approach to Hazard Mitigation in the Workplace."
- Severe underinsurance of homes (at levels below total replacement cost) which, when coupled with inflated rebuilding costs in the wake of a substantial disaster, imposes unmanageable financial burden on homeowners at a time of significant distress. A project to address this problem was launched by the Australian Securities and Investments Commission, which noted the particular misery caused by substantial underinsurance in the wake of the devastating Canberra bushfires in 2003.[7]
- A repeating pattern of fatalities and critical injuries to electricians while (a) working on 347 volt lighting systems, or (b) using certain types of multi-meters that have a tendency to explode. Ontario's Electrical Safety Authority launched two projects aimed at these hazards in 2005 following analysis of injuries and fatalities for electricians.
- Drug-smuggling across the Mexico/US border involving concealment of drug packages between the double-skinned walls of refrigerated trucks. The US Customs service tackled this problem under their "Strategic Problem Solving" initiative in drug interdiction, launched by the agency's Office of Enforcement in 1995.[8]

For many regulatory agencies, organizing around specific *bads* turns out to be a substantial departure from business as usual. Perhaps that helps explain why, when they do it well and significant harms get suppressed as a result, these agencies often win awards for *innovation*.[9] Why such behavior should be regarded as innovative has always intrigued me. One might imagine that identifying and controlling risk-concentrations that fall within an agency's purview should be regarded as a perfectly ordinary competence, central to achieving the agency's core mission. I'm not entirely sure whether the innovation awards, when they do come, are for the specific *solutions* that the agencies invented (which are invariably novel and uniquely crafted to the specific problem addressed), or for the *modes and patterns of thought* that enabled officials to focus on specific risk concentrations, understand their characteristics, and so invent effective solutions. I worry that the prizes are mostly for the former (the solutions), and I see many agencies falling into the trap of trying to replicate these specific solutions elsewhere, often in circumstances where the particular solutions don't quite fit. Surely it would be more valuable to understand and codify the latter – the modes of thought and action which make harm-reduction efforts effective – and to understand what it takes to replicate them; better still, to understand what it would take to make such conduct the new organizational norm.

The habits of mind which these "innovators" exhibit have something in common with the skills involved in a relatively mundane task: the undoing of knots. Give a knotted mass of string to an adult, who has developed all of the relevant cognitive skills (and maybe had some experience too), and watch how they behave. Notice how they hold the whole object up to the light, and look at it this way, then that way, turning it around and around, examining it diligently from all sides – careful all the time not to pull or tug or to make matters worse – until they begin to understand the *structure of the thing itself*. As the structure of the knot becomes clearer, so the components or stages of a plan begin to form in their minds ... "maybe if I can loosen this strand first, it will loosen that one ... in turn that will free up the main one – at which point I'll need to pass this tangled mass here through the opening that should develop ..." and so on. If they understood the structure correctly, and fashioned a plan accordingly, the knot eventually falls apart, and is no more.

By contrast, give the same knot to a child, who has yet to develop this particular set of cognitive skills, and observe their behavior. Witness their frustration as they tug and pull and generally make matters worse. Note the relative lack of attention to observation and discernment of the nature of the thing, or the particularities of its structure. Note the alacrity with which the child jumps into action, applying crude methods that usually fail.

In the regulatory field we have a growing list of harms undone, knots untied, risk-concentrations eliminated or substantially mitigated.

Invariably the knots undone by regulators, or others who act in this vein, are not broad, general phenomena (at the level of "air pollution," or "corruption," or "motor vehicle accidents.") Nor are they minutiae, representing single incidents (of crime, or injury, or death). These knots untied, these harms undone, all lie *in between*, where the object of study is larger than a single incident or event, but smaller than a general class of harms. It is in this *in-between* realm where much exciting work seems to take place, amid the complex and multi-layered texture that connects individual incidents at the bottom to entire classes of risk (with their one or two word descriptions) at the top. The operational work of control, for the most part, belongs neither at one extreme nor the other, but in this messy middle ground. It is in this middle ground, amongst the parts and the sub-parts of broader classes of harm, that we lack navigational guidance as well as established vocabulary. The knots addressed by these successful innovators are all clearly identified sub-components of a general class of harm, and they are referred to variously as *problems*, or *issues*, or *patterns of incidents*, or *risk-concentrations*, or *specific harms*, or sometimes as *trends*.

The crafters of these successful harm-reduction strategies, in each case, are somewhat slow to jump into action. They take time to engage in systematic but open-minded inquiry, seeking first to understand the dynamics and components of the harm. They slice and dice the overall risk, cutting it this way and that, exploring many different dimensions in which concentrations might be specified or become apparent. Then, as significant concentrations or parts of the risk come slowly into focus, and appear worthy of specific attention, these practitioners examine these intermediate objects (the knots, or concentrations) more closely still, molding and testing different problem-definitions and specifications, setting the scale of the overall endeavor, separating and enumerating the distinct knots they find, and discerning the structure of each one. All of this, even before any action-planning begins.

Analogies have their limitations, of course. Practitioners of risk control, whatever their field, might object that this analogy seems to undervalue preventive approaches. Why wait until you have a knot to untie? Why not work out in advance the rope handling disciplines or treatments that would prevent the knots from forming in the first place? Why not create a knot-free zone? Does this analogy not limit our attention to ex post remedial approaches?

This objection would be potent indeed if the knots related to *incidents* (e.g. specific crimes, or crashes, or calamities). In that case, accepting the very existence of a knot limits one's options to choosing among reactive treatments, and inhibits attention to earlier intervention or prevention. But the knots in this business do not represent individual incidents. They represent *patterns* of incidents, with frequencies and characteristics which develop, and which may repeat, over time. In choosing how to deal with a *pattern* of incidents (where the long term goal involves suppression of the entire pattern) preventive strategies are by no means precluded. In figuring out how to unpick the problem, we make sure to hold in mind the full range of technologies, tools and tactics for control. And, mindful of the chronological unfolding that precedes any one calamity, we should surely keep in mind the possibility of picking any one, or several, of the moments in that chronology at which to target an intervention. So long as one understands that the knots exist and are preferably addressed as higher level objects rather than specific incidents, then this particular analogy does not focus attention any more on reactive strategies than on preventive ones; nor vice versa. In the harm-reduction business we should seek lasting and resource-efficient strategies; and we should deliberately avoid any ideological preferences as to tools, tactics, or times for intervention. That's the essence of craftsmanship: the ability to pick the right methods and tools for the job. Selection of methods, and selection of the right moments for intervention, ought to remain tactical, problem-specific choices.[10]

Just as specific analogies have their limitations, so too do specific words. The financial sector laid an early claim to the phrase *risk-management*, by which they referred to the challenge of balancing risk and return in investment portfolios.[11] In more common and broader usage, there remains much overlap and ambiguity between the meaning of "risks" and other undesirable commodities like "problems" and "harms." In general, *risk* seems prospective and not very likely. *Problem* seems more current and certain. That could mean, for some, that a *problem* is merely a *risk* which did actually materialize; in which case *accidents* become "tangible ex post fact manifestations of risk."[12] The risk literature still focuses, for the most part, on exposures and outcomes which are probabilistic in nature, rather than deterministic or predictable.[13] Some scholars have used a distinction between *risks* – the by products of human decision making in adoption of technology – and *hazards*, which occur naturally.[14] Others choose to distinguish *danger* (meaning a recognized but actual risk) from *risk* (by which they mean a *perceived* risk).[15]

I prefer the word "harm" for its freshness and for its generality, and for the fact that scholars have not so far prescribed narrow ways to interpret it. I'd like to find one word that covers the broadest set of bad things, and so far *harm* seems less spoilt by particular usage and less monopolized by specific disciplines than the alternatives.[16] *Harms* is also the most general, provided it can be understood to include "potential harms" and "patterns of harm," as well as specific harms already done.

Whichever words or phrases different professions prefer to use, we still need to be clear whether we are talking here about *risks* (probabilistic in nature, looking forwards), or only *problems* (experienced in the past, or being experienced currently). Does it matter whether the knots are *actual* (with an established pattern of incidents observed) or merely *potential* (i.e. *plausible risks*, but not yet realized)?

My intention is to embrace both, deliberately and energetically, for two reasons. First, I believe that the patterns of thought and action relevant to the operational task of control are much the same whether applied to actual harms or to potential risks.[17] Second, the distinction between actual and potential is not as clear or clean as one might imagine at first. Often the distinction is tied only to different levels of aggregation. For example, the risk of being killed in a highway accident, for any one specific individual in any one year, might be 1 in 7,000[18] (on average, and assuming for a moment that there might be such a thing as an "average individual" in relation to this particular risk). From one such individual's perspective, therefore, the risk of dying in a car crash is both potential, unrealized, and quite small. But from the point of view of a state highway patrol department, responsible for containing and suppressing highway fatalities within their region, the fact that (say) 450 people died last year on their state's roadways is already *actual* – an established pattern of harm done. Even looking forward, there is not so much uncertainty from their point of view: they might predict with some confidence that, without a dramatic change in circumstances, between 400 and 500 people would die on the same roads next year. What they don't know yet, of course, is *which people*, even though they might know quite a lot about the characteristics and driving habits of the more likely victims.

So *potential risks* – whether it be the chance of dying in a road accident, or in a plane crash, or through terrorist attack, or from some rare form of cancer, or even by having a plane crash onto you from the sky (a somewhat quirky risk, apart from terrorism, which seems to get more than its fair share of mentions in the literature) – become *established patterns of harm* simply by sliding up the scale of aggregation. And as one slides up and down the scale of aggregation, so the modes of analysis that count, and the types of operational instruction that turn out to be most useful, vary considerably.

The recent growth of the *risk* literature does indeed seem to indicate the existence of a subject which we might broadly label *risk-control*[19] (incorporating *risk-analysis, risk-management*, and *risk-communication*); a subject many scholars have deemed worthy of serious attention, consequential for policy, and straddling multiple risk domains. But in terms of *levels*, this literature seems to have gravitated to the highest levels and to the lowest levels of aggregation, with less attention (so far) paid to the messy, complex, and textured layers in between.

At the lowest levels, we are concerned with individuals and the ways in which they perceive and assess risks, and the ways in which they behave as a result. With important contributions from the field of experimental psychology and behavioral economics, we have learned much about the implications of risks being familiar or unfamiliar, detectable or undetectable, voluntary or involuntary,[20] concentrated or dispersed,[21] and fairly or unfairly distributed.[22] And we know that people's levels of anxiety about risks can depend on many factors other than their actual chance of falling victim, including (for example) "the frequency and vividness of stimuli," and on whether the risk is constantly present or episodic.[23]

Thanks to the Nobel-prize winning work of Tversky and Kahneman,[24] amongst others, we understand how the non-expert human mind uses heuristics of various kinds (simple decision rules based on information available to the individual) in assessing and measuring risks.[25] We know quite a lot about the predictable ways in which humans get risk-assessments wrong (statistically speaking), often as a result of biases inherent in the use of such heuristics.

Much of the recent research on these questions has focused on risks where the underlying probabilities for a particular individual are small (less than 1 percent) and can be very small indeed (less than one in a billion); and where the risks emanate from natural or biological systems (as with diseases) or from complex technical systems[26] (as with accidents and "man-made disasters"). With such small probabilities in play, individuals can get probability assessments wrong by several orders of magnitude, or get comparative risk assessments seriously out of order.[27] Particular emotions, as well as an individual's overall emotional state, can affect or bias their evaluations of risks.[28] And an individual's willingness to accept certain risks and reject others can turn out to be based on social or psychological factors, such as their particular aversion to "fear of falling victim unfairly to uncompensated loss" even when the chances are miniscule,[29] or on personal evaluations that depart from scientific notions of hazard and exposure.[30] All of this research helps us understand how individuals think and therefore why they act in certain ways in response to certain risks.

At the opposite extreme – the highest levels of aggregation – risk analysis helps us navigate the complexities of macro-level resource allocations for risk-control, and helps us evaluate the costs and benefits of various macro-level interventions. In the fight against cancer, for instance, how best should society balance investments between environmental protection, industrial hygiene, food inspection, or public health services? The economist's instinct, operating at this macro level, is

to attempt to ensure that the values assigned to the preservation of the same life in different areas are constant. [The economist's] approach here may derive from the belief that if risk avoidance could somehow be packaged and sold to individuals, informed consumer sovereigns would reflect such constancy in their own purchases.[31]

So, across many potential risk-reduction investments, where should the marginal dollar go, and what will be the pay-off in terms of quality-adjusted-life-years?[32] Macro-level analysis has also taught us much about "risk-risk tradeoffs," where specific strategies for reducing one class of risks introduce or elevate other types of exposure.

At this, the highest, level – where one adopts the more paternalistic perspective of governments – the psychology of individual risk perception matters less, or matters for different reasons. An understanding of how and why people respond to different risks becomes instrumental in the context of assumed responsibility for protection of society at large. Policy interventions and risk-communications may deal deliberately with the class of "irrational individuals" who seem to persistently underestimate particular threats, and who therefore endanger themselves and others. Other interventions may focus on the group at the opposite end of the spectrum, prone to needless worry because they habitually overestimate risks.[33] This group of "worriers" may need special attention in order to alleviate irrational or excessive fears, which bring their own destructive consequences for health and community life.[34] Almost everyone in between will need a certain amount of information about risks, particularly emerging or unfamiliar ones. And the crafting of effective risk-communication strategies will have to take into account the range of behavioral responses that psychologists have helped us understand, because some of those responses might not best serve the interests of individuals or of the public.[35] The provision of understandable and usable information not only produces much sensible behavior, but promotes sympathy and tolerance for any necessary government interventions that affect citizens or businesses.

In the context of harm-reduction operations, psychological factors affecting degrees of fear (or "dread") matter not so much because they render the individuals' evaluations of risk – in the mind of the experts – more or less rational, but because they render governments' use of various risk-communication and behavior-modification strategies more or less effective.[36]

The *properties* of risks that count at these higher levels change also: from those that affect individual or psychological assessments of probabilities, to those that underlie societal, cultural, or political attitudes, and which need to be considered by legislatures.

The risk literature, so far, has paid somewhat less attention in between the highest and the lowest levels; and it is *in between* where the majority of practitioners operate. The literature has not illuminated so much the texture of risk-control operations, where the application of intelligence, analysis, creativity, and sensible use of discretion can make things go so much better, or much worse, without any change in the quality of national or macro-level policy frameworks. It has not made explicit the art of picking the right levels of aggregation at which to scan for concentrations, nor how to pick the dimensions by which to focus operational attention. It has not elaborated the tension between organizing around functional solutions, rather than around identifiable risk-concentrations, and the strengths and weaknesses of each approach. In fact, the risk literature so far has not given us a well-developed organizational theory for risk-control. Neither, conversely, has organizational theory paid explicit attention to the distinctive character of the harm-reduction task.

It is practitioners, not theorists, who need to know how to navigate the textured substructure of any general risk. It is they who have to know at what level of aggregation (how big or small) to define a new project, and how many knots (harm-reduction projects) to take on at any one time. It is they who have to construct the data gathering practices and analytic lenses that enable them to spot the knots (risk concentrations) that might, or might not, exist. It is they who have to know which ones they can or can't take on, and what to do when the knots turn out to have an awkward shape, failing to align with their programmatic divisions or jurisdictional boundaries.

It is often left to line managers in government agencies, as well as grant officers in the foundation world, to figure out the portfolio management aspects of the harm reduction task: whether to organize around programs, or methods, or risk-factors, or types of intervention, or times for intervention, or specific risk-concentrations, or all of these at once. Such practitioners face myriad decisions: how to define their market-niche and distinctive contributions, what competencies to seek out, what type of results to expect, and how to choose when and how to cooperate with others and around what aspects of the task.

Practitioners with operational responsibilities for harm reduction also have to worry about a different set of troublesome *qualities* or *properties* that some harms possess: not so much the qualities that affect the psychology of probability assessment (which the risk literature covers quite extensively); but rather qualities that alter the control challenge in material ways. Part II of this book sets out to explore some such properties, and their consequences, in greater detail. Let me mention here just a few of these especially troublesome categories:

- Some harms *have a brain behind them,* and therefore involve authorities in a game of intelligence and counter-intelligence, played against conscious opponents (e.g. terrorists, hackers, thieves, drug-smugglers, pirates). Many other risks do *not* have such a brain behind them (e.g. the majority of occupational hazards and environmental harms), and therefore fail to produce adaptive responses to control interventions.

- Some harms are essentially *invisible*, with low rates of reporting or detection (e.g. fraud, white-collar crimes, corruption, consensual drug-dealing, crimes within the family, date-rape, etc.) For these it is especially difficult to determine the true extent of the underlying problem, to peg investments in control at the right level, and to measure the effectiveness of interventions.
- Sometimes risk-control is a *peripheral* task within an institution, and may be dominated by the core purposes.[37] For example, consider the task of fraud control within health-care programs; or physical security and protection of information within an educational setting;[38] or the task of "compliance management" within a corporation committed to profit maximization. In such settings, the risk-control task may find itself culturally at odds with the organization's core purposes and culture.
- Sometimes improper or unlawful risk-taking is *performance-enhancing* for an organization, bringing opposing pressures to bear on the task of controlling the risk.
- Some risks exist at a *higher level or scale* than the available control apparatus, and thus require collaboration and coordination, without any overarching legislative or authority structure. The coordination task may be further complicated by disparate cultural attitudes and competing perspectives on the problem.
- Some risks are *catastrophic* in nature (representing calamities of high consequence, but which have never or seldom happened) – and for these the work of control consists of two decoupled segments – the work of *continued prevention*, and the work of *contingency planning* for response. For these, all the preventive work has to be defined, budgeted, divided, conducted, and measured early on in the chronological unfolding of the harm, among the precursors to the calamity itself.

Each of these properties transforms, or at least substantially complicates, the challenge of suppression or containment. Some harms exhibit multiple such properties simultaneously, compounding all the relevant operational difficulties. For example, political corruption belongs in the first and the second class above (involving conscious opponents, and invisible by its nature) and, if it reaches high up the political ladder (above the level of the investigative and judicial systems available to deal with it), then it may also bring in some of the complications of the fifth category (high-level harms) also.

Practitioners who confront these challenges often do so without any set of guiding principles or operational framework. They feel, not surprisingly, as if they are simply making it up as they go along, unaware that the quandaries they face and the apparently endless decisions that they confront (or avoid confronting) are in fact part of a craft that can be defined, and which probably can be learned. For many of them it comes as blessed relief to discover they are not alone, to sit down with others from entirely different risk-control or harm-reduction domains, and interpret their successes and their frustrations against a broader, common, conceptual framework.

This book seeks to help establish and clarify that common framework, hopefully in a way that is useful for anyone involved in risk-control or harm-reduction work, regardless of which sector they work in or what type of institution. The core claims of the book, to be tested and examined in the following pages, are as follows:

- The task of controlling bad things is usefully differentiated from the task of constructing good things.
- There are distinctive patterns of thought and action peculiar to controlling harms, which provide special opportunities for effective intervention.
- The fast growing risk literature so far provides least guidance where the majority of practitioners are required to operate – within the complex, multi-dimensional and textured layers that lie *between* high level policy decisions (based on macro- or national-level risk assessments), and low level incident-response (which is driven by established processes or protocols). Almost all the important operational decision making about harm-reduction lies somewhere in between these two extremes.
- Some professions (e.g. epidemiology, intelligence analysis, financial risk management) might have done better in learning the art and science of undoing harms than others, and have developed more sophisticated tools and approaches within their domains. Lessons drawn from best practice in such professions can usefully be codified and communicated more broadly.
- Advancing the art of harm reduction counts, not only for governments, but also for non-profit and business organizations, international non-governmental organizations, private citizens as they look out for themselves and their families, and for society as a whole. Clarifying the common aspects of this work might help reveal as

artificial some mental boundaries that seem to have separated different fields of application (corporate risk-control, regulatory risk-control, public health, law enforcement, etc.).

- Harms vary in terms of their characteristics, structure, texture, and dynamics. Certain properties of harms produce predictable and important consequences, not so much for the psychology of perception, but for the nature of the operational control challenge.

Just the slightest chance that these claims might turn out to be true would make this enterprise worthwhile; such a vast range of unpleasant things might be better contained or suppressed as a result.

Notes

1. United Nations Resolution A/RES/55/2, 55th session, September 18, 2000, pp. 1–8.
2. The Executive Program on Managing Regulation, Enforcement and Compliance, offered by the Australia and New Zealand School of Government (ANZSOG), Brisbane, Australia. December 3–8, 2006. This happens to be the most recent version of this program offered, as at the time of writing, and the largest number of distinct regulatory areas I had ever seen represented in one class.
3. Malcolm K. Sparrow, *The Regulatory Craft: Controlling Risks, Solving Problems & Managing Compliance* (Washington DC: Brookings Institution Press, 2000).
4. All of these examples were provided to me by alumni of executive programs on regulatory and enforcement strategy.
5. The department's annual prize for regulatory excellence is awarded to a project, program, or initiative:
   - which focused on a clearly defined, external problem, of significant public concern;
   - where, were it not for the initiative, attention to the problem would probably have remained diffuse, uncoordinated, and ineffective;
   - which incorporated a genuinely open-minded search for creative solutions;
   - wherein careful attention was paid to the measurement of outcomes, through the selection and monitoring of relevant metrics; and
   - which lead to the implementation of an effective and resource-efficient solution.

6. Gregory B. Rodgers and Elizabeth W. Leland, "An evaluation of the effectiveness of a baby walker safety standard to prevent stair-fall injuries," Journal of Safety Research, 36 (2005), 327–332.

7. This project is described in two reports, one written at the launch in 2005 and another in 2007 evaluating the results achieved by ASIC's intervention in the home insurance marketplace. "Getting home insurance right: A report on home building underinsurance," Australian Securities and Investments Commission, September 2005; "Making home insurance better: An ASIC report," January 2007. Information for homeowners, and the reports, available at: [www.asic.gov.au/fido/fido.nsf/byheadline/Is+your+home+underinsured?openDocument].

8. For details of the Strategic Problem Solving (SPS) program within US Customs, see: Sparrow, *The Regulatory Craft*, pp. 73, 124, 168, 227, 229.

9. Several of the programs described in this book have won awards under the Ford Foundation's "Innovations in American Government" program, an annual competition that has been running since 1986 and is now open to all levels of American government. The John F. Kennedy School of Government at Harvard administers the competition and manages the selection process under a grant from the Ford Foundation, but does not itself set any specific criteria or doctrine for selection.

10. In the field of crime control, one does find analyses of crime control opportunities, particularly relating to juvenile delinquency, which seem deliberately restrictive in the sense that they focus on early intervention and prevention, and make almost no mention of reactive or enforcement-centered strategies. Such deliberate incompleteness is in some cases the result of ideological preferences for prevention and for less-coercive tools, and in other cases arises from the conviction that policy gravitates so naturally to reactive strategies that a carefully reduced focus helps redress the imbalance. For an example of one such deliberately restrictive analysis, see: *Pathways to Prevention: Developmental and Early Intervention Approaches to Crime in Australia*, National Crime Prevention, Attorney-General's Department (Canberra, Australia, 1999). This particular analysis illustrates the complexity of delineating problems effectively years ahead of their realization.

11. One investment consultant defines risk management thus: "The basic foundation of risk management lies in setting clear investment objectives and formalizing a rational policy allocation across uncorrelated asset classes." Charles B. Grace Jr., "Understanding the Elements of Risk Control," *Trusts and Estates*, 137 (May 1998), 12.

12. Bridget M. Hutter, "Ways of seeing: understandings of risk in organizational settings," in Bridget Hutter and Michael Power (eds.),

Organizational Encounters with Risk (Cambridge: Cambridge University Press, 2005), p. 73.

13. The distinction is made clearly in: M. Granger Morgan, "Probing the question of technology-induced risk," *IEEE Spectrum,* 18 (November 1981), 58–64. The Canadian Treasury Board Secretariat, in developing guidelines for risk-management across all Canadian Federal agencies, has defined risk as "the uncertainty that surrounds future events and outcomes. It is the expression of the likelihood and impact of an event with the potential to influence an organization's achievement of objectives." "Integrated Risk Management Framework," Treasury Board Secretariat, (Ottawa, Canada, 2001); also, Stephen Hill and Geoff Dinsdale, *A Foundation for Developing Risk Management Learning Strategies in the Public Sector,* Canadian Centre for Management Development (Ottawa, Canada, 2001), p. 5.

14. For comments on Ulrich Beck's use of this distinction, and a broader examination of Beck's "World Risk Society" thesis, see: Darryl S. L. Jarvis, "Risk, Globalisation and the State: A Critical Appraisal of Ulrich Beck and the World Risk Society Thesis," *Global Society,* 21 (January 2007), 23–46.

15. Eugene A. Rosa, "The logical structure of the social amplification of risk framework (SARF); *Meta*theoretical foundations and policy implications,' in Nick Pidgeon, Roger E. Kasperson and Paul Slovic (eds.), *The Social Amplification of Risk* (Cambridge: Cambridge University Press, 2003), p. 64. Also, Niklas Luhmann, *Risk: A Sociological Perspective,* translated by Rhodes Barrett, Transaction Publishers (New Brunswick, NJ, 2005). First published, Aldine de Gruyter, New York, 1993.

16. The phrase "harm reduction" has in fact been used to describe a specific class of public health strategies in relation to HIV infection and drug abuse. The International Harm Reduction Development Program of the Open Society Institute defines *harm reduction* as a "pragmatic and humanistic approach to diminishing the individual and social harms associated with drug use, especially the risk of HIV infection. It seeks to lessen the problems associated with drug use through methodologies that safeguard the dignity, humanity and human rights of people who use drugs." OSI website, at: [www.soros.org/initiatives/health/focus/ihrd/about#whatis]. The use of this phrase within literature addressing HIV transmission among drug-users is quite specific to this particular set of public health problems, and quite specific regarding the choice of methods to be deployed. By contrast, *The Character of Harms* uses the phrase *harm-reduction* in the broadest sense, in line with its more common usage.

17. Although there are some special difficulties that arise in relation to risks that have seldom or never materialized. Chapter 10 examines these special difficulties in detail.

18. The number of road-accident-related fatalities in the US has remained within a narrow range, 41,500 to 43,500 deaths per year, from 1995 through 2005. Summary statistics available at: [www-fars.nhtsa.dot.gov/]

19. Some disciplines or professions, notably public health, prefer to avoid using the word "control" with its connotations of authority, coercion, and paternalism. *Risk-management* is often used, therefore as an umbrella term, encompassing all the others. The *Society for Risk Analysis* states on their website's welcome page that *risk-analysis* is the appropriate umbrella term, encompassing risk assessment, risk characterization, risk communication, risk management, and policy relating to risk.

20. Chauncey Starr explores public willingness to accept voluntary risks (such as those involved in hunting, skiing, smoking, or flying planes) and involuntary risks (such as those induced by natural disasters, disease, or drafting into the armed services), and concludes that public willingness to accept voluntary risks may be as much as 1,000 times greater than their willingness to accept involuntary risks which pose equivalent danger. Chauncey Starr, "Social benefit versus technological risk," *Science,* 165 (September 19, 1969), 1232–1238.

21. Baruch Fischhoff, Sarah Lichtenstein, Paul Slovic, Stephen L. Derby, and Ralph L. Keeney, *Acceptable Risk* (Cambridge: Cambridge University Press, 1981); M. Granger Morgan, "Probing the question of technology-induced risk," *IEEE Spectrum,* 18 (November 1981), 58–64.

22. Peter Sandman provides a list of ten such distinctions found to affect the acceptability of risks to citizens, and relevant to the siting of hazardous waste facilities. Peter M. Sandman, "Getting to maybe: some communications aspects of siting hazardous waste facilities," *Seton Hall Legislative Journal,* 9 (1985), 442–465.

23. Thomas C. Schelling, "The life you save may be your own," in S. B. Chase, ed., *Problems in Public Expenditure Analysis* (Washington DC: Brookings Institute, 1968), pp. 127–162.

24. The Nobel Memorial Prize in Economic Sciences was awarded to Daniel Kahneman in October 2002. Amos Tversky, his research colleague in the development of *Prospect Theory* had died in 1996 and was acknowledged in the announcement, but was not formally a recipient as Nobel prizes are not awarded posthumously.

25. Daniel Kahneman and Amos Tversky, "Prospect theory: an analysis of decision under risk," *Econometrica,* 47 (1979), 263–292; Daniel Kahneman, and Amos Tversky (eds.), *Choices, Values & Frames*

(Cambridge: Cambridge University Press, 2000); Amos Tversky and Daniel Kahneman, "Judgement under uncertainty: heuristics and biases," *Science,* New Series, 185 (27 Sept., 1974), 1124–1131; Daniel Kahneman, Paul Slovic, and Amos Tversky (eds.) *Judgement Under Uncertainty: Heuristics and Biases* (New York: Cambridge University Press, 1982), Dale Wesley, Dale Griffin, and Daniel Kahneman, *Heuristics and Biases: The Psychology of Intuitive Judgment* (Cambridge: Cambridge University Press, 2002).

26. For a discussion of technology-induced risks, see: Ulrich Beck, *World Risk Society* (Cambridge: Polity Press, 1999); Ulrich Beck, *Risk Society: Towards a New Modernity* (London: Sage, 2000); Anthony Giddens, *The Consequences of Modernity* (Cambridge: Polity Press, in association with Basil Blackwell, Oxford, 1990).

27. Paul Slovic, Baruch Fischhoff and Sarah Lichtenstein, "Rating the risks: the structure of expert and lay perceptions," *Environment,* 21 (April 1979), 14–20, 36–39.

28. Jennifer S. Lerner, Roxana M. Gonzalez, Deborah A. Small, and Baruch Fischhoff, "Effects of fear and anger on perceived risks of terrorism: a national field experiment," *Psychological Science,* 14 (March 2003), 144–150; Jennifer S. Lerner and Dacher Keltner, "Fear, anger & risk," *Journal of Personality and Social Psychology,* 81 (July 2001), 146–159; Cass R. Sunstein, *Laws of Fear: Beyond the Precautionary Principle* (Cambridge: Cambridge University Press, 2005), pp. 66–88.

29. William Leiss and Christine Chociolko, *Risk and Responsibility* (Montreal & Kingston, London, Buffalo: McGill-Queen's University Press, 1994), p. 4.

30. For example, where an individual feels that a precedent is being set, or that a small hazard may get worse over time. Baruch Fischhoff, Chris Hope, and Stephen R. Watson, "Defining Risk," *Policy Sciences,* 17 (1984), 123–139; reprinted and available within: Theodore S. Glickman and Michael Gough, eds., *Readings in Risk* (Washington DC, Resources for the Future, 1990), pp. 30–41. For a broader comparison of the expert and public views of risk see also: Douglas Powell and William Leiss, *Mad Cows and Mother's Milk: The Perils of Poor Risk Communication* (Montreal: McGill-Queen's University Press, 1997); Peter M. Sandman, *Responding to Community Outrage: Strategies for Effective Risk Communication* (Fairfax, Virginia: American Industrial Hygiene Assocation, 1993); "Integrated risk management framework" (Ottawa, Canada: Treasury Board Secretariat, 2001); Stephen Hill and Geoff Dinsdale, *A Foundation for Developing Risk Management Learning Strategies in the Public Sector* (Ottawa, Canada: Canadian Centre for Management Development, 2001), p. 15 and Appendix C.

31. Richard Zeckhauser, "Procedures for valuing lives," *Public Policy*, 23 (Fall 1975), 419–464 (p. 461).
32. For a recent defense of the practice of monetarizing benefits to enable such policy comparisons, see: W. Kip Viscusi, "Monetarizing the benefits of risk and environmental regulation" (Washington DC: American Enterprise Institute-Brookings Joint Center for Regulatory Studies, April 2006), Working Paper 06–09 available at www.aei-brookings.org. pp. 1–37.
33. A 2005 survey of Europeans' attitudes to risk, and to food-related risks in particular, does indicate the existence of a "worrier" profile. The study reports one third of the population demonstrating a pattern of being "very worried" (expressing worry about eleven or more risks out of list of fourteen possible concerns) with women and people with lower levels of education over-represented within this group. *Special Eurobarometer 238: Risk Issues* (Brussels: European Commission, February 2006), 3, 29–31.
34. For a discussion of the multiple types and purposes of risk-communication, see: Alonzo Plough and Sheldon Krimsky, "The emergence of risk communication studies: social and political context," *Science, Technology & Human Values,* 12, Summer/Fall 1987, 4–10.
35. Archon Fung, Mary Graham, and David Weil, *Full Disclosure: The Perils and Promise of Transparency* (Cambridge: Cambridge University Press, 2007), p. 34.
36. For an early example of deliberate experimentation with different risk-communication strategies to determine which best influenced the audience – in this case householders in New York State – to take appropriate radon-mitigation actions, see: F. Reed Johnson, Ann Fisher, V. Kerry Smith, and William H. Desvousges, "Informed choice or regulated risk? Lessons from a study in radon risk communication," *Environment,* 30 (May 1988), 0012–15, 30–35. For a discussion of the issue of whether and under what circumstances governments' risk-communications might stretch beyond the provision of reliable information into the realm of advocacy (e.g. for smokers to quit), see: *Improving Risk Communication*, Report of the Committee on Risk Perception and Communication, National Research Council (Washington DC: National Academy Press, 1989), 2–3, 16–23.
37. In the context of the Canadian Federal Government, the development of agency-wide risk management practices has focused heavily on control of threats *to the agencies themselves* (particularly threats of litigation) and to the public's trust in them, rather than as an operational method for controlling broader societal risks. The Treasury Board of Canada, which has promulgated this national approach, has

defined *risk-management* as "a logical step-by-step process to protect, and consequently minimize risks to, the government's property, interests and employees. Risk includes the chance of damage to or loss of government property, and the chance of incurring second- or third-party liability to non-government entities." See: "Risk management policy," Treasury Board of Canada, Preface, available at [www.tbs-sct.gc.ca/pubs_pol/dcgpubs/RiskManagement/riskmanagpol_e.asp]. The Australian Customs Risk Management Policy follows a similar vein, defining risk as "the chance of something happening that will have an [adverse] impact on [agency] objectives." [www.customs.gov.au/site/page.cfm?u=4576].

38. A survey of risks afflicting higher education in the Netherlands shows how effective control of such risks requires delicate trespass on the prevailing values of educational institutions, which include "unfettered transfer of knowledge" and relaxed and accessible physical environments. Ira Helsloot and W. Jong, "Risk management in higher education and research in the Netherlands," *Journal of Contingencies and Crisis Management,* 14 (September 2006), 142–159.

PART I

The nature of the control task

1 | *Which way up, and does it matter?*

From a purely mathematical or economic perspective, promoting good things and reducing the countervailing bad things look to be one and the same; conceptually identical, and with a difference only in vantage point. One might conclude, therefore, that it makes no practical difference which way up one looks at such things. From an operational point of view, however, it makes a considerable difference. Scrutinizing the harms themselves, and discovering their dynamics and dependencies, leads to the possibility of *sabotage*. Cleverly conceived acts of sabotage, exploiting identified vulnerabilities of the object under attack, can be not only effective, but extremely resource-efficient too.

Across the spectrum of harm-reduction tasks, we observe practitioners thinking and then acting like saboteurs. They may not use the language of sabotage, but they nevertheless engage in an analytical search for vulnerabilities of the harm itself: some critical commodity, a pivotal node in a network, an irreplaceable ingredient, or inescapable dependency of some kind. Finding such a vulnerability leads them quite naturally to an action plan which exploits that vulnerability with surgical precision.

One famous example involved the demise of the Alberto Larrain Maestre heroin-smuggling ring, otherwise known as the *French Connection*. A law enforcement analyst determined that the entire operation relied heavily on a small set of specialists, called *courier-recruiters*, operating in French airports. Their job was to select from among the passengers about to embark on flights to the United States those who could either be bribed, coerced, or blackmailed into carrying packages of heroin for collection by co-conspirators at their destination points. The recruiting task demanded considerable skill in making rapid psychological assessments, and some knowledge of the profiling methods used by customs officials at the far end. Ultimately this analysis proved correct: law enforcement officials focused attention on that one very specific role within the smuggling organization, making it impossible for the recruiters to continue operating. The whole organization was incapacitated. The specialized role represented a vulnerability for the criminal enterprise: a scarcity which law enforcement could produce, and which the smuggling organization could not readily cure.

Another drug control example also illustrates the search for an essential scarcity. Tampa, Florida, suffered an epidemic of street-level drug dealing during the late 1980s.[1] To begin with, Tampa police (with help from the Drug Enforcement Agency and the FBI) focused on mid- and upper-level traffickers. The familiar "King-Pin" theory suggested that removal of those at the top of a criminal organization would make it collapse. In fact, the trafficking organizations were able to adapt, promoting from within, and the King-Pin strategy was abandoned. A second strategy targeted street-level dealers, in the hope that a shortage of those could be created. However, more than 12,000 arrests in a three year period also failed to produce any appreciable decline, either in the level of street drug dealing, or in the level of community complaints relating to it. Apparently, even strenuous police efforts could not produce any shortage of street dealers.

What did work, in the end, was a focus on "dope-holes" – those specific street corners and locations which were convenient and relatively safe for drug-dealing. These spots had trees or bushes to provide cover, shade, and concealment for drugs and other paraphernalia if the police came by. These locations also offered convenient routes in and out, and places for customers to stop. And there were not so many of these dope-holes. A city-wide inventory revealed only sixty-one such places. The resulting intervention strategy assigned one police officer to each spot, each one tasked with closing down that location, one way or another. The officers were quite inventive and used a range of methods: simply parking a police car close by, arranging removal of bushes, or recruiting informants in neighboring apartment complexes who could report the dealers' actions and concealment locations. Under this strategy it took less than a year to reduce the number of active locations from sixty-one to nine. Another year later, street-level drug dealing in Tampa had virtually disappeared, and the number of related complaints had dropped to zero.

What makes sabotage efficient is the fact that one only needs to find a single point of vulnerability, not several. In this regard, acts of *destruction* differ from acts of *construction*. Constructing safety systems for, say, a commercial jetliner would require an enormous amount of engineering knowledge and experience. Such systems are multiple, constructed layer upon layer, with necessary redundancies and complex interactions. By contrast, the task of destroying a plane in flight would not need to involve or overcome all these systems – just a vital one or two. Sabotage requires analysis and imagination, and perhaps an element of surprise, but a lot less engineering complexity than the business of construction. We regret the efficiencies of sabotage when we consider them available to terrorists or enemies; but we should value them and embrace the opportunities they bring when they fall into our hands as *saboteurs of harms*.

Epidemiologists certainly think like saboteurs in seeking such efficiencies. To contain or suppress an infectious disease they might seek a way to stop it passing from generation to generation; or a way to stop it migrating from region to region; or a way to render the transmission process inoperative or inefficient by suppression of some relevant *vector* (such as mosquitoes). Again, they do not need to do all of these. They need just to find one vulnerability, within the operational reach of public health systems, vital to the disease itself, upon which they can put their finger.

President Bush, shortly after the terrorist hijackings of September 11, 2001, made an interesting public statement as the administration drew up plans to invade Afghanistan. He announced that his administration "does not distinguish between terrorists and those that harbor them." This statement itself indicates an important aspect of counter-terrorist strategy. The sense was not "we *cannot* distinguish . . . "; of course his administration could. Rather it was "we *choose not to* distinguish . . . " We hear this type of statement frequently from regulators, announcing how they will use their discretion, and which crimes they will regard as more or less serious – or, in this case, as *equivalent*. The practical effect of this statement is that it provides an important opportunity to create an effective scarcity. The prospects for creating a shortage of terrorists, motivated and willing to attack the US, seemed dim indeed, at least in the short run. More feasible, perhaps, would be to create through diplomatic and military means a shortage of safe havens and training grounds for terrorists. The hope was that accommodating countries, already finite in number, would turn out to be vital to the terrorist networks, and limiting their numbers further would therefore constitute an efficient method for controlling the terrorist threat.

In assessing the threat of nuclear terrorism, which he refers to as "the ultimate preventable catastrophe," Graham Allison works methodically through a list of possibilities, searching for one potential scarcity around which control efforts might be organized.[2] First Allison considers *who* might plan a nuclear terrorist attack on the US, and comes to the depressing conclusion that there are plenty of candidates with actual or potential nuclear aspirations: not just Al Qaeda, but a string of other existing terrorist organizations (Jemaah Islamiyah in Southeast Asia, Chechen insurgents, Hezbollah, Muttahida Majlis-e-Amal and other groups in Pakistan), and some of the more dangerous "doomsday cults" around the world.[3] Allison's conclusion is that no shift in American policies or activities would ever mollify every group, and that the availability of weapons of mass destruction makes any one disaffected group, even a small one, potentially dangerous. This is not, he concludes, a hopeful path toward reduction of the threat.

Allison in turn considers *nuclear expertise, potential targets,* and then *delivery mechanisms* (ways of moving a nuclear bomb to a target site) as possible ways of focusing attention. Expertise is by no means in short supply, as construction of a crude nuclear device, given the necessary materials, lies within the capabilities of many physics graduate students, and the necessary instructions are readily available on the internet.[4] There is also no shortage of available and attractive targets as any major American city would do, and no real possibility of reliably defending them all against attack at the last minute through the use of radiological detection technology. As for *methods of delivery,* moving a small nuclear device around the world turns out to be not much harder than shipping a bag of golf clubs.[5] So none of these three commodities, he concludes, could be made sufficiently scarce to negate the threat.

Allison settles eventually on the control of vital *nuclear materials* as the only seriously hopeful prospect. He notes that no terrorist, no matter how skilled, can make a nuclear weapon without either highly enriched uranium or plutonium, neither of which exist naturally. He therefore recommends an international effort to find and control "loose nukes" (such as those that went missing with the collapse of the former Soviet Union), round up existing fissile material from which bombs could be made (including materials generated from research reactors), and to prevent any new nations from developing the technical capacity to enrich uranium or reprocess plutonium.[6]

The events of September 11, 2001, coupled with the realization that terrorists operate more like *networks* than as *nation states,* produced a flurry of interest in what it took to control or suppress the operations of networks, particularly international and criminal ones. The conventional wisdom became, for a while, that "it takes a network to control a network." But that is no more logical nor true than "it takes a virus to control a virus," or "it takes vermin to control vermin." What it takes to control networks is an understanding of their potential vulnerabilities, and a willingness to investigate and exploit them.[7] Within a network, a unique *role* which can be removed and not easily replaced (e.g. the courier recruiters in the French Connection example), represents one kind of vulnerability. Nodes that are central or pivotal in a communication network represent another kind; their removal disrupts communications, or makes it less efficient by lengthening communication paths. Bridging nodes, or "liaisons" – the members of a network that connect otherwise disjoint parts – represent another important vulnerability; their removal effectively fragments the network. The discipline of *social network analysis*, in fact, presents a rather interesting collection of concepts of potential use to law enforcement and anti-terrorist operations. These ideas have mostly been studied by social scientists (and, more recently, organizational theorists) in rather more benign settings, generally motivated by a desire to understand what makes networks, formal or informal, work well. No-one took much notice of the possibilities for network destruction or incapacitation; at least, not before 9/11.[8]

All these examples show an attitude of mind, peculiar to the control of harms, intently focused on the harm itself. It seems unlikely, in any of these situations, that a focus on any of the countervailing goods (law-abiding behavior, abstinence from drug-use, sympathy for Americans and their values) would or could lead to the same type of inquiry, the search for weak spots, and surgically precise interventions.

Baruch Fischhoff, in 1995, describing the recent history of risk-communication, notes in passing the temptation and the tendency to relabel risks in their more positive light. He observes: "It will be interesting to see what effect, if any, is achieved by the current fad of relabeling probabilistic risk analysis as probabilistic *safety*[9] analysis. The change could put a happier face on the process or be seen as a disingenuous diversion."[10]

It seems unlikely that smallpox would have been eradicated worldwide if the focus had been on healthy living, or good diet, or even *infection control* more generally. Careful attention to the properties of smallpox itself enabled the World Health Organization to coordinate a global effort to eradicate the disease. The program, launched in 1967, consisted of a combination of mass vaccination campaigns, coupled with deployment of a ring-containment strategy to control any new observed outbreak.[11] This strategy only worked because of several *specific qualities of smallpox itself*, namely: no animal carries the disease; an effective, affordable and stable vaccine exists; and victims show a visible rash very soon after becoming infectious (which makes ring-containment feasible). By 1980 no instances of smallpox infection had been observed for two years, at which point the World Health Assembly declared eradication complete.

The SARS outbreak in 2005 was also contained, ultimately, by a similar strategy involving patient isolation and quarantining of their recent contacts, but without a vaccine in support. The containment of SARS by this method was only possible because of a relatively long "serial interval" of eight to ten days (the time between initial infection of a patient and that patient becoming infectious).[12] By contrast, influenza typically exhibits a much shorter serial interval of three to four days, and any new influenza epidemic would therefore not be controllable through such ring-containment strategies.

None of these examples, of course, should be interpreted as suggesting that broad constructive programs are valueless. That is not the point of these illustrations. They merely demonstrate a pattern of thinking that involves detailed scrutiny of a harm itself, and in many instances leads to the formulation of resource-efficient and remarkably effective interventions, exploiting the particular character of the harm to be undone.

We should be quite careful what we conclude from this, though. Does this mean, for instance, that we should turn every *good* upside down, focusing on the counterveiling *bad* in the hope of finding significant efficiencies through the application of sabotage? If so, then perhaps we would put aside a focus on *education*, and instead declare war on *ignorance*, attacking it piece by piece, knot by carefully identified knot? Are we to conclude – after appreciating some incisive acts of sabotage – that broader preventive programs, whose nature seems more constructive than destructive, are generally inefficient and therefore operationally inappropriate?

Emphatically no, to both. It clearly makes more sense to view education as an iterative and constructive process, each building block resting on others already in place. There might be very specific and important types of *ignorance* that one could identify later, but even these might better be described as *pieces of education missing* rather than as *specific forms of ignorance present*. It seems, in this case, that *education* is the more tangible object, and *ignorance* indicates the absence of it.

What about *crime* and *public safety*? Which one is more real, and which is better understood as the absence of the other? Ask a crime victim, and they will tell you for sure of a vivid, palpable experience – with a time and a date, and maybe it hurt – not at all, from their point of view, the mere absence of something else. What about *corruption* and *integrity*? We can witness both acts of corruption (e.g. giving or taking a bribe) and acts of integrity (e.g. refusing a bribe, or blowing the whistle on the corruption of others); but are not many identifiable acts of integrity in fact acts of resistance to corruption? If so, *corruption* seems the more tangible of the two, and *integrity* consists of attitudes and actions in opposition to it.

What about highway *accidents* and their flip side, highway *safety*? Which one should be regarded more naturally as the absence of the other? Certainly people experience accidents in a way that makes them seem real enough. They also experience near misses, even in the absence of a collision. After driving home from work, most of us can recall any scares we experienced along the way – the door of a parked car that swung open unexpectedly, the child who stepped off the kerb, the car alongside that suddenly emerges from your blind spot just when you were about to change lanes. We recall these events quite easily: real incidents, complete with adrenalin rush and evasive action. By contrast, one does not tend to arrive home and report an experience of *safety* along the route. Nor is one really aware even of *periods* of safety, except for occasions when a familiar threat is newly removed. "I'm so glad they put up the central divider along that stretch of road.... it used to terrify me." If one is aware of a specific moment of *safety* it usually involves a near miss of some kind, where some safety intervention kicked in and prevented a calamity: engagement of an anti-lock braking system, a conditioned driver reflex, or the comforting restraint of a seatbelt during braking or swerving. In these situations, we are arguably aware, not of the safety itself, but of some very real and bad thing (an accident), even though it didn't quite happen.

Poverty presents a more difficult and ambiguous case. Is poverty merely the absence of economic development and prosperity? Which is more real: the experience of poverty, or the experience of sufficiency? The experience of living in poverty seems vivid and miserable enough to those who suffer it; but the absence of poverty also involves specific tangibles like money, food, and health care. In this case the philosophical question – which one is more real – seems somewhat obtuse, and depends a lot on which definition of poverty one selects. The World Bank has traditionally defined poverty in the developing nations of Africa and Latin America in terms of threshold income levels of $1 to $2 (USD) per person per day, adjusted for purchasing power in different countries.[13] The definition of *extreme poverty*, used by the United Nations in tracking progress towards the Millennium goals, uses $1 (USD) as the threshold.[14] More complex definitions still rely on threshold income levels, either for individuals or families, but set the threshold rate by reference to the local cost of a carefully defined market basket of nutritious foods sufficient to sustain health.[15] Any definition centered on income thresholds, be they more or less sophisticated, neatly divides the population into two camps: those above the threshold and those below it.[16] Presumably the experiences of living on $2.10 per day or on $1.90 per day are equally real (and maybe not so different). Neither experience seems like the mere absence of the other.

Economic definitions of poverty usefully render the problem measurable through census and other data-gathering techniques. They also set the problem up for econometric analyses, typically involving regression analyses conducted at the level of nations. Such analysis can identify other factors significantly affecting levels of poverty and thereby indicate potential avenues for intervention. The factors that turn out to be most significant, not surprisingly, consist of broad measures of economic activity (e.g. GDP per capita), coupled with measures of income distribution across the population. Whether such analysis brings one any closer to knowing how to act in order to alleviate poverty depends on which factors turn out to count, and whether the giant levers they represent can in fact be pushed or pulled in the appropriate direction at the national level. One interesting consequence of conducting this type of analysis – and discovering that poverty goes down when economic activity goes up – is that it makes it seem all the more plausible that one challenge is merely the flip side of the other, and that there is no practical or operational value in making any analytical distinction between encouraging economic growth and alleviating poverty. If moving one represents the only method available for tackling the other, it matters not which one you focus upon; the policy consequences will be the same.

The advantage of employing ubiquitously applicable economic definitions for a problem such as poverty is that it renders the condition ubiquitously measurable, and susceptible to macro-level econometric analysis. The disadvantage is that this hides the underlying texture of the problem. Poverty researchers tell us there are many different types of poverty problems, with entirely different causes and manifestations, all conveniently but misleadingly lumped together under the same generic banner. Some kinds of poverty are really about material deprivation, others about malnutrition, some about lack of access to basic health care. Some are really issues of chronic disempowerment; as Amartya Sen termed it, *capability deprivation*.[17] The routes to poverty vary also: families find themselves in poverty as a result of natural disasters, chronic sickness in the family, death or departure of a wage-earner, or collapse of a local industry. Poverty for some is temporary; for others, permanent. Sometimes poverty has a *cycle* or dynamics that mean it can be passed from generation to generation.

Only once we climb down from the level of generic definitions and macro-level perspectives, immersing ourselves in the texture of the problem, can we begin to see specific knots, each with their own distinctive character, coming into focus. At lower levels, the vocabulary changes: we speak of *pockets* of poverty (usually concentrated in geographic terms), or *cycles* of poverty (a notion which invites a search for ways to break or interrupt that cycle). Specific concentrations, defined at these lower levels, seem more susceptible to scrutiny, analysis, and possible acts of sabotage. They seem unambiguously real: not merely a general absence of something else. These pieces of the problem involve specific sets of people, with their own story to tell about their specific experience of poverty. In operational terms, it seems more appropriate at these lower levels to imagine proceeding piece by piece, pocket by pocket, cycle by cycle, concentration by concentration – holding up each piece in turn, understanding what drives it and what it depends upon, searching for the artful intervention that might make it unravel completely.

In practical terms, distinguishing between harms to be controlled and goods to be constructed does seem to have some merit. Where the harm is real, the chances are that it has *parts*, and that the *parts,* once understood, can be *unpicked*. Where the harm is not real, trying to use such an approach would be quite frustrating, and possibly silly. So it is quite important to be able to tell where this approach applies and where it probably should not. Hence the usefulness of asking, given any countervailing pair, which is more real; and which is more the absence of the other? Clarity on this point might save the frustration of trying to use this approach on the wrong type of object. It does not seem useful to recast the process of education as the mitigation of ignorance, because it is awfully difficult to pick apart and identify the important components of an *absence*. It is difficult even to scrutinize an absence.

The fundamental claim of this book is that there are distinctive patterns of thought and action that accompany the reduction of harms; not that these patterns of thought and action can be applied to any kind of task. Stretching models to places they do not belong is worse than unproductive; it endangers the credibility of the model itself. This model is for the control of *bad things* – which I assert is a different type of work than the construction of good things.

Four possible confusions

The foregoing discussion seems quite likely to generate some predictable objections. Stating these objections and answering them might help clarify exactly what is being claimed at this point, and what is not.

Objection 1: Perhaps the most likely objection would be that focusing on the *bad*, as opposed to focusing on counterveiling *goods* limits one's choices in strategies for intervention. In particular, it would seem to de-emphasize the use of broad preventive programs. If we did sufficiently well in *promoting organizational integrity* perhaps we wouldn't have to dwell so much on *corruption control*, which surely equates to cleaning up the mess after a failure of prevention. And is this book claiming that encouraging healthy lifestyles is not worthwhile?

Should we always wait for disease to take hold before we consider intervening?

Answer: The reason for focusing on the existence of *bads* is that seeing them as such broadens, rather than narrows, the choices for intervention. In particular, it makes possible detailed scrutiny of specific parts of the harm, leading to the possibility of some resource-efficient and effective solutions. This opportunity is lost if one insists only on considering the positive and constructive view.

Nothing is lost by understanding the nature of the beast. No preventive strategy is precluded. No tool or technology is excluded. If, after examining the nature of the harm, broad preventive programs seem best, then use them. But it is surely a mistake to use broad preventive programs because of an *a priori* preference for them, especially a preference that obstructed open-minded examination of the harm itself.

The concepts of *integrity* and *wellness*, here, illustrate another important point. For most people the word *integrity* signifies more than a mere absence of dishonesty or corruption. The broader meaning includes a sense of moral wholeness, producing consistency in acting according to a set of moral values, rules or norms.[18] Similarly, the word *wellness* as a way of living brings benefits beyond the mere absence of disease. In both cases, these words represent positive goods which encompass, but seem larger than, the absence of a particular harm we have in mind. This is often so. A broad positive prescription accomplishes much in terms of the control of certain harms, and does more besides. It may have been designed in part to counter specific harms, and in part for the sake of its broader benefits. It might also have spillover benefits with respect to the control of a broad range of other harms.

But the usefulness of broad positive programs to the task of controlling harms does not make these equivalent. They are never fully aligned, and they are different types of object. One is a prescription, the other a task. From the perspective of the harm reduction task, a broad positive program represents one possible instrument, amongst many, and it may affect certain parts of the harm and leave others untouched. Promoting integrity or teaching health and wellness will have broad positive aspects which go beyond the control of corruption and disease. Accepting the usefulness and contributions of positive programs in no way alters the underlying nature of the harm-reduction task. Relying solely on positive programs usually leaves us far short of effective control. They make the harm no less real. They may simply contribute to the control of it.

Viruses are real enough. They have names and known behaviors. One can see them under a microscope and find their pictures in books. Granted, for some viruses the medical community might conclude (after careful study of the disease itself) that certain aspects of healthy living will help in countering the threat. For some diseases, such as common colds, we might conclude few other actions are necessary for most people may catch colds from time to time but their immune systems fight them off with minimal help, and public health systems can focus on the more dangerous cases that develop into bronchitis or pneumonia, or develop greater protections for specific populations at higher risk.

Having examined a specific illness and understood its characteristics, the response may well include, or might even consist solely of, a broad preventive program. With respect to the task of disease control, promotion of healthy living and broader wellness represents one potential intervention. But there are many others.

In general, preventive programs are always available as methods. They are means, not ends. They do not reconstitute the nature of the harm-control task. They remain available as options. In the control of crime, crime-prevention strategies will have their place. In the reduction of occupational hazards, promoting a "culture of safety" will always have some value. In order to reduce highway accidents, improved driver training will probably reduce some problems.

However, one kind of intervention should never be ideologically preferred to any other. Selection of tools and times for intervention ought surely to be seen as tactical, problem-specific choices. And interventions, however much they might contribute, ought not to be confused with the harm-reduction task itself. Advocating scrutiny of the harms never drives out any intervention options. But the converse is not true: advocating for specific intervention options, too early and without sufficient analysis, often drives out open-minded examination of the harm itself.

Objection 2: Another objection might be that focusing on the dark side constitutes a poor choice of communication strategy. Surely it is better to talk about "voluntary compliance" than "enforcement against violators." Would not industry react better if urged toward environmental stewardship, rather than threatened by an adversarial regulator? Do we not know, from studies of the psychology of compliance, that trusting people to do the right thing actually encourages better behavior? Talking too much about corruption, crime, or discrimination might drive away important partners and turn people off. Surely better to focus on integrity, safety, and promoting equality and opportunity.

Answer: This chapter has not discussed communication strategies, nor compliance psychology. Both of those belong in the general realm of *methods* for accomplishing harm-reduction, and do not alter the underlying nature of the task. The motivation for focusing on harms in this chapter is to clarify the distinctive character of that task, and thereby make available those special opportunities that go with it. Once practitioners have understood the underlying character of this task, and what is special about it, they can choose to present their purposes and plans, or communicate them publicly, any way they see fit. Indeed they would be wise, at that stage, to take seriously all that has been learned about different modes of risk-communication and the implications for behavioral response.[19] They would be wise also to frame their objectives publicly in ways that garner them support, resources, and partners sufficient to get the job done. That is all part of the *unpicking* strategy for any specific harm, which they need to design. The task at that stage involves political and strategic management as well as the design of a communications strategy. Having found the knots, practitioners may decide as a tactical matter to conceal their existence, or make only oblique references to them, or frame the challenge in other ways so as to avoid giving offense or inviting opposition. They have that choice. But it would be a huge mistake, because of any pre-existing preference about communication strategy, not to find or study the knots in the first place.

On compliance psychology: yes, we have learned a great deal – principally from Australian researchers on regulatory methods – about the importance of trust, the use of graduated sanctions, and the role of human psychology in the selection of compliance tools. All of that knowledge remains extremely useful when it comes time to select tools and tactics. But none of it changes the fundamental nature of the job.

Objection 3: A third objection might be that controlling one harm (or risk) produces or exacerbates another. In the risk literature, these effects are referred to as *risk-tradeoffs*, or *risk versus risk*. Does not this discussion paint a rather simple-minded black-and-white picture, which overlooks these subtleties?

Answer: There are actually two important situations in which a step forward in controlling one risk can mean a step back on another. In the first situation, the nature of the risks confronted differs. A much cited example shows that many Americans, in the months following 9/11 eschewed flying and drove their cars long distances instead. Between October and December 2001 the extra highway miles resulted in an estimated 1,000 additional road deaths.[20] Avoidance of one risk increased exposure to another. Such countervailing risks carry various labels: *side effects* in medicine; *collateral damage* in military operations, or *unintended consequences* in public policy.[21] Sometimes they affect the same set of victims (as in the case of people choosing whether to fly or drive), and sometimes different sets (as in the case of collateral damage).

Other examples abound. X-ray screening for cancers actually induces some new cancers. Banning the use of asbestos might increase the risks associated with the use of a range of substitute products.[22] Wearing seatbelts might save your life in some types of accident, but could conceivably trap you in a burning vehicle. Limiting truck-drivers' hours through regulation might improve highway safety, but could drive some truck companies out of business, forcing layoffs and hardship for many. The choice between building a coal-fired or a nuclear power plant involves a choice between contributing to global warming and facing the possibility of a radiological catastrophe. The literature is full of awkward choices involving such risk tradeoffs.[23]

Just because such harms are sometimes traded, it does not lessen in any way the importance of controlling them, each one. The existence of trade-offs does not change the underlying nature of the task, but does impose important obligations on those attempting to control any one of them. They need to evaluate as far as possible all foreseeable impacts of any action plan, including manifestations of different types of harm. They need also to define the knots they choose to tackle (specific harms to be addressed) at a high enough level to embrace any likely displacements or adaptations of the harm. In other words, they should take a sufficiently holistic or systemic view in unraveling any one knot to avoid creating new ones, and avoid making it more difficult for others to deal with surrounding knots. Graham and Wiener point to this as a practical challenge:

Our research indicates that risk tradeoffs are not an imagined inevitable perversity of life ... but rather a real consequence of incomplete decision-making, and that with attention and effort, individuals and society can wage the campaign to reduce risk with better tools that help to recognize and progressively reduce overall risk.[24]

Picking the right levels and defining problems in the right dimensions so as to avoid these traps is surely an integral part of the art of undoing harms. We shall examine the issues of scale and dimensions in considerable detail in Chapters 3 and 4, as these present critical operational choices.

The second type of situation where one harm might be traded against another occurs in settings where one person's gain is another person's loss. This applies in any harm-reduction setting involving adversaries or opponents. Any progress made by counter-terrorism agencies represents a loss for some terrorist organization. Progress against a pattern of drug-smuggling is a loss for the smugglers. So, also, with thieves, computer hackers, corrupt officials or organized crime. For any criminal, law-enforcement agencies and their operations represent a class of risk. The possibility of detection, for them, is a risk. For law-enforcement, detection is a benefit.

The existence of these cat-and-mouse games (or mouse-and-cat games, depending on which perspective one adopts) does not make the art of identifying and mitigating risks, piece by piece, any less relevant. It is simply relevant for both parties, and both may benefit by enhancing their understanding and performance of that task. Having greater sympathy for the cats than the mice, I devote a whole chapter later in this book to the special challenges that accompany harms involving conscious opponents. That chapter is intended to help public officials and other organizations engaged in the control of terrorism, smuggling, crime, corruption, or any other harm involving adaptive opponents.

Objection 4: A fourth objection might be that the focus on lower level knots, rather than higher level strategies, seems to undervalue macro-level analyses and the interventions they may suggest. If econometric analysis successfully identifies one variable that has significant impact on the overall level of a harm, would one not want to exploit that finding in policy formulation? And how is the identification of such a factor so different from finding one of those pivotal points of vulnerability that go with special opportunities for sabotage?

Answer: High-level analysis may well reveal important policy options. Where it does, and those policy options are feasible, they clearly should be exploited. If it turns out that overall levels of poverty in a country decline when GDP per capita increases, then by all means increase GDP per capita (assuming that particular lever can actually be moved!). If corruption is less likely where public servants are all paid well, then pay them all well, provided the nation can afford it.[25]

However valuable the higher level analyses turn out to be, there remain several compelling reasons to climb down into the lower level texture and grapple with the specific concentrations of harm that only then become apparent:

(a) The giant levers may in fact not be moveable at all, or moveable only so slowly that more urgent action seems preferable.

(b) By finding and addressing distinct concentrations of harm, at lower levels, one can often relieve considerable amounts of suffering in timeframes much shorter than it takes to produce any significant shifting of the giant levers.

(c) Higher level analysis is more familiar, and more available. Some harm-reduction domains (e.g. corruption control, and poverty reduction) have been dominated by traditions of economic analysis. Also, summary or aggregate data is more readily available. Hence any rewards available from macro-level econometric analysis are more likely to have been reaped already. Analysis and intervention at lower levels is less familiar in many disciplines, and therefore the marginal gains for additional effort at lower levels might be more impressive.

(d) Where macro-level policy solutions have been implemented, they leave behind pockets of harm, different in character, unaddressed. Dealing with the residual harms requires precisely this kind of more particular examination and carefully tailored interventions.

(e) Summary data hides many distinct phenomena beneath. High-level analysis will therefore likely fail to reveal the distinct phenomena, distinguish them, or show how best to unravel any one of them.

(f) Interventions based on a structural understanding of specific issues are often wonderfully effective, and particular bubbles of trouble either get eradicated or very substantially reduced. Finding points of structural vulnerability for specific objects is therefore quite different from finding high-level variables correlated with broad measures of a harm, and might be much more efficient. If a nation *could* increase the pay of all public servants by 2 percent, this might decrease the overall risk of corruption by some very small percentage. Moreover this would affect some types of corruption, but leave others untouched. By contrast, identifying and addressing a specific type of corruption opportunity (e.g. bribes taken by tax collectors relating to real-estate valuations) might eliminate that specific problem altogether, and within an attractively short time-frame.

One final illustration

It makes a difference which way up one describes a harm-control task. At the John F. Kennedy School of Government, we faced a recent dilemma over how to name a one-week executive program. The subject was corruption control, and the school's intention was that the audience would include officials who had a role in preventing corruption, as well as others (e.g. investigators and prosecutors) who had a role in dealing with it when it occurred. As Faculty Chair of the program, I advocated the course be plainly titled "Executive Program on Corruption Control." Our sponsors at the United Nations, however, who were planning to provide half the participants for each class as part of the Director General's new five-part Ethics program, preferred "Executive Program on Organizational Integrity." Understandably, they were mindful of potential embarrassment should the media seize upon the fact that training in corruption control had been deemed necessary for all senior UN managers. Even a compromise title – "Organizational Integrity & Corruption Control" – still gave them grounds for concern, and our marketing analysts confirmed this would be a problem for other organizations too. It seemed expedient, therefore, to drop the word corruption altogether, making it easier for organizations to send their staff on the course.

Within the school, we therefore had to consider carefully what would be lost by using the softer label. A number of things would be lost, for sure. First, the investigators and prosecutors would no longer regard the course as being for them. They would read the title as being solely about prevention, and not including response. Second, participants might self-select by reference to their professional roles, and we might end up with a class only containing officials whose functional responsibilities resonated with the phrase "promoting integrity." So we would attract *ethics officers*, maybe *compliance officers* from the corporate world, and training staff engaged in "inculcating values." We would be less likely to attract auditors, or financial controllers, and certainly no law enforcement agents, prosecutors, or judges.

Third, in selecting the curriculum, we might feel compelled to focus on certain types of corruption, namely those problems most naturally influenced by broad preventive methods such as clarification of rules, values-based training, and other organization-wide systems for promoting ethical conduct. Participants might be surprised if, under the positive label, we included discussion on how to undermine an established system of nepotism, how to expose and eliminate criminal networks embedded within organizations or professions, how to protect whistleblowers, or how to manage informants.

Insisting on using positive labels carries some predictable risks. It limits attention to a subset of tools, and that in turn limits attention to classes of harm for which those tools count. We should always reserve the right, for tactical or marketing purposes, to *present* a harm-reduction mission one way up or the other. But we should not deny the fundamental nature of the task. However gently we choose to portray it, the harm reduction task revolves around *bad* things, the possibility of them, or established concentrations of them. Denying that fundamental reality might mean missing important opportunities for effective sabotage.

Notes

1. David M. Kennedy, "*Closing the Market: Controlling the Drug Trade in Tampa, Florida*," John F. Kennedy School of Government, and the National Institute of Justice (Washington DC: US Department of Justice, 1991). For a discussion of this case within the context of problem-solving, see: Malcolm K. Sparrow, *Imposing Duties: Government's Changing Approach to Compliance* (Westport, Connecticut: Greenwood Press, 1994), pp. 49–52.
2. Graham Allison, *Nuclear Terrorism: The Ultimate Preventable Catastrophe* (New York: Times Books, 2004).
3. Ibid. Chapter 1.

4. Ibid. Chapter 4.
5. Ibid. Chapter 5.
6. Ibid. Chapter 7.
7. For a recent discussion of the adaptive behavior of international criminal and terrorist networks, and the resulting features of the control challenge, see: Jorg Raab & H. Brinton Milward, "Dark Networks as Problems," *Journal of Public Administration Research and Theory*, Vol. 13, no. 4, pp. 413–439.
8. For a discussion of methods for identifying structural weaknesses and vulnerabilities of criminal enterprise, see: Malcolm K. Sparrow, "Network Vulnerabilities and Strategic Intelligence in Law Enforcement," *International Journal of Intelligence and Counter-Intelligence*, 5 (1991), 255–274.
9. Author's emphasis.
10. Baruch Fischhoff, "Risk Perception and Communication Unplugged: Twenty Years of Process," *Risk Analysis*, 15 (1995), p. 138 (note 4).
11. Louise B. Russell, *Is Prevention Better than Cure* (Washington DC: Brookings Institution, 1986), pp. 19–20.
12. For a succinct narrative of the battle against SARS, see: Jonathan Shaw, "The SARS Scare: A Cautionary Tale of Emerging Disease Caught in the Act," *Harvard Magazine* (March–April 2007), 48–57, 93–95.
13. Gary Burtless & Timothy M. Smeeding, "The Level, Trend, and Composition of Poverty," in Sheldon H. Danziger & Robert H. Haveman (eds.), *Understanding Poverty* (Cambridge, Massachusetts and London: Russell Sage Foundation, New York, and Harvard University Press, 2001), p. 29.
14. *Millennium Development Goals Report* (New York: United Nations, 2005), p. 6.
15. Michael Hatfield, "*Constructing the Revised Market Basket Measure*," Applied Research Branch, Strategic Policy, T-01-1E (Hull, Quebec: Human Resources Development Canada, April 2002). Available at: [www11.sdc.gc.ca/en/cs/sp/sdc/pkrf/publications/research/2002-002379/it-01-1e.pdf].
16. For a detailed analysis of alternative measurement approaches, including a range of different threshold concepts, see: Constance F. Citro & Robert T. Michael (eds.), *Measuring Poverty: A New Approach* (Washington DC: National Academy Press, 1995).
17. Amartya Sen, *Development as Freedom* (New York: Random House, 1999), p. 85.
18. For a discussion of the relationship between the definitions of integrity and corruption, see: Leo Huberts, Karin Lasthuizen & Carel Peeters, "Measuring Corruption: Exploring the Iceberg," in Charles Sampford,

Arthur Shacklock, Carmel Connors & Fredrik Galtung, eds., *Measuring Corruption* (Aldershot, Hampshire, UK: Ashgate Publishing, 2005), pp. 265–294.

19. For a practical exposition of how to optimize the contribution of risk-communication as an operational instrument in risk-control, considering different qualities of risks, different types of audience, and differing contexts, see: "OECD Guidance Document on Risk Communication for Chemical Risk Management," OECD Environment, Health and Safety Publications, Series on Risk Management, No. 16. ENV/JM/MONO(2002)18, JT00129938 (Paris: OECD, 2002), pp. 17–26.

20. Jeffrey Kluger, "Why We Worry About the Wrong Things: The Psychology of Risk," *Time Magazine* (December 4, 2006, Australian Edition), 40–45.

21. John D. Graham & Jonathan Baert Wiener, eds., *Risk vs. Risk: Tradeoffs in Protecting Health and the Environment* (Cambridge, Massachusetts: Harvard University Press, 1995), p. 2.

22. Hahn and Sunstein argue that use of the increasingly popular "precautionary principle" with respect to one risk frequently involves neglect or underestimation of increases in ancillary or substitute risks. See: Robert W. Hahn & Cass R. Sunstein, "The Precautionary Principle as a Basis for Decision-Making," *The Economists' Voice*, Vol. 2, No. 2, Article 8, Berkeley Electronic Press (2005), 1–9.

23. W. Kip Viscusi, *Fatal Tradeoffs: Public & Private Responsibilities for Risk* (Oxford: Oxford University Press, 1992); Samuel J. Rascoff & Richard L. Resesz, "The Biases of Risk Tradeoff Analysis: Towards Parity in Environmental and Health-and-Safety Regulation," *University of Chicago Law Review,* 69 (2002), 1763–1836.

24. Graham & Wiener, eds., *Risk vs. Risk,* p. 4.

25. The extent of corruption among civil servants is negatively correlated with compensation levels, although the exact nature of the relationship remains unclear. Caroline Van Rijckeghem & Beatrice Weder "Corruption and the Rate of Temptation: Do Low Wages in the Civil Service Cause Corruption?," WP/97/73. A Working Paper of the International Monetary Fund (June 1997), [http://papers.ssrn.com.ezp1.harvard.edu/sol3/papers.cfm?abstract_id=882353].

2 | *A different type of work*

To do any type of work well, surely one would first have to *recognize* that type of work (perhaps distinguishing it from other types of work), then figure out how to *organize* it, how to *perform* it, and finally how to *explain* to your audience what you did. The acronym ROPE (recognize, organize, perform, explain) acts as a crude but useful starting point in diagnosing just how far any agency or institution has come in mastering the art of harm reduction. A few organizations do just fine all the way up to the end, but are stuck on "explain": they do terrific work but have not figured out how to tell the risk-control or harm-reduction performance story in a convincing manner. Others have not come so far, and – even though they recognize the form of work – have little idea how to organize it and conduct it on an ongoing basis. I find that these are the agencies that tend to ask for help, or send their executives on courses; they sense the significant opportunities that might result from mastering this art, even while they lack any formal systems to support it. These agencies, by the way, tend to be the pioneers, at least by comparison with the rest of the field. It seems many agencies and institutions have not even made it to the *recognition* stage yet. I certainly hope this book will help them get at least that far.

A host of institutions from the public, private, and not-for-profit sectors engage in or contribute towards harm reduction work. Where such tasks constitute an important piece of their work, one might expect them to be able to give a rather precise account of how that work was going. How many specific knots (concentrations of harm) have they identified? How many have they taken on? What progress have they made on each one? How many harm-reduction projects have they actually finished, and what exactly do they mean by "finished"? What systems have they established for monitoring the environment for new or emerging problems, and what forms of data gathering and analysis help with that task?

Having had the chance to look inside scores of regulatory agencies, whose core missions involve social harm control of one kind or another, it is stunning to find how little formality or structure there is, if any, around this task. Certainly these organizations are organized, but for the most part, not around *this*. It appears to be easier by far to organize around other types of work.

Functions

The most familiar mode of organization is *functional*, which is skills-based, and produces enclaves of specialists. Organizations group the lawyers together in the General Counsel's office; investigators in a centralized investigative unit; auditors in the audit department; educators in an education programs unit, media specialists in the public relations department, and so on. This organizational form serves some important purposes. We value functional expertise, and functional units act as incubators to help preserve and develop it. If the microbiologists (in environmental protection) or the industrial hygienists (in occupational safety) are co-located, they will encourage and challenge one another to be state-of-their-art. The magazines around the coffee machine reflect their disciplines. As a group they know what schools to draw recruits from, the nature of professional training and development, and what professional conferences to attend. Being professionals, no-one outside their discipline really has any business telling them what to do or how to do it. So they set their own agenda and schedule, and supervise and evaluate their own work. They tend to promote into management positions those who have climbed further up their own well-defined disciplinary ladders (not necessarily those with managerial skills!). The supervisors and managers who emerge through this system tend to be those well versed in the norms and mores of the discipline, and liable to protect the unit from "improper" outside interference.

Organizing around functions of course has its limitations. From the organization's perspective, functions represent tools, and tools ought to be organized around tasks. It proves unsatisfactory, ultimately, to tolerate a silo-mentality, allowing each tool to go off by itself, establishing its own agenda in isolation and without any type of coordinating framework.

Processes

But what type of task might it be that breaks open the functional silos? Not *harms* or *risk concentrations* or *problems* for the most part; but *processes*. Agencies set up core, high-volume processes to deal with *whatever flows in,* and it is these processes that break open the functional silos. Having set up processes, agencies have no choice but to operate them efficiently, otherwise the work piles up until it becomes a visible and embarrassing failure. *Customers* or *clients* on the outside, who can testify to any lack of timeliness, accuracy or coherence in the process, form a natural constituency for high-quality process management. Taxpayers dealing with the IRS might first deal with the *returns-processing* divisions, and later with the *examination* division, or even the *collections* division. From the taxpayer perspective, the agency should appear seamless. Hence cross-functional cooperation, organized around various client-related processes, emerges as an obviously desirable form of competence. Similarly, an environmental agency will look silly to the management of an industrial complex if one day it sends water engineers, the next day air quality experts, and the next day hazardous waste inspectors, without any of them knowing what the others have been doing. In order to iron out such obvious kinks and inefficiencies from the clients' perspective, the agency will probably invent a coordinated inspection regime, or deploy cross-trained field engineers, or produce some other single-point-of-contact or client-management scheme.

Even institutions whose principal purposes revolve around harm reduction have good reason to focus on process. First of all, operational processes, once established, acquire a power of their own. If police make the promise to respond to emergency calls, then the emergency calls for sure will come, and any failure to respond in a timely manner constitutes a visible failure. Once an environmental agency establishes permitting or licensing regimes, then it must deal with all the applications that flow in, often within timeframes established by regulation. Any agency that invites members of the public to submit to them reports or complaints (of discrimination, of defective products, of professional malpractice, etc.) has to deal with the resulting stream of work, no matter how significant or insignificant each item, and no matter the extent to which these process-loads relate to the harm-reduction priorities of the day. Processes tend to capture everything. They become all consuming. Process loads, in an era of static or dwindling resources for government agencies, can become overwhelming. It takes all day and every day, sometimes weekends and overtime too, just to keep up. Finding time to think about any *other* type of work becomes extremely difficult.

The second reason harm-reduction agencies focus on process is that much advice is available on how to improve or perfect processes, and how to utilize the perspective and insights of "customers" in so doing. For twenty years now, government agencies have been importing and incorporating process management methods originally developed within manufacturing industry. This wave of importation began in the early 1980s with *quality management,* followed during the late 1980s by *process management,* and then *continuous process improvement (CPI).* The early 1990s brought more radical approaches to the uprooting and redesign of processes, including *process re-engineering.*[1] At the federal level in the United States, Clinton and Gore's *Reinventing Government* movement pressed hard on customer-based reform of government operations, driven by the notion that government agencies should be as professional in their customer-service operations as the very best of private industry.

As a result of this focus, we have witnessed some impressive gains in recent years in terms of process efficiencies, timeliness, service-quality, and customer satisfaction. The Food and Drug Administration has significantly accelerated the drug approval process. US Customs has worked with the Immigration & Naturalization Service to completely redesign the passenger screening and admission process at international airports, reducing average wait times by more than 80 percent and using advance passenger information to focus inspection efforts more effectively. And the IRS has made significant strides in improving the accuracy and timeliness of its returns processing operations, and gives much better taxpayer advice in response to telephone queries and letters, and through its website.

Twenty years of experience with various forms of process management have driven home the basic lessons: functional organization is important but not sufficient. It leaves no-one in charge of processes that straddle multiple functions. External customers and clients experience the organization through processes, not functions. Therefore the organization must understand the client perspective and provide integrated management of complete processes. In other words, organizations must put someone in charge of the processes. And they do. These people, in the language of CPI, are now called *process owners*.

Putting someone in charge of processes, however, is not the same as putting someone in charge of specific harms or problems. Processes are a creation of the agency, a piece of machinery to operate. The relationship between process improvements and any increased effectiveness in harm-reduction is complicated.

One might assume process-based competence to have a generally positive effect on the attitudes of clients, which might lead them to behave better and cooperate more. Giving taxpayers easier access to more accurate information should surely improve compliance – at least, for those taxpayers motivated to comply but unsure of the rules. But other forms of non-compliance – in fact all forms involving willful tax evasion – might not be touched at all by such services, no matter how professionally delivered. Willful evasion could even be facilitated by increased transparency and predictability.

The relationship between process improvements and the task of controlling non-compliance appears to bear an uncanny resemblance to the relationship between *wellness* and *disease control*. Broad positive *customer-service* programs might eliminate or mitigate some types of *non-compliance* (the tax world's equivalent of disease), but leave some types completely unaddressed. They might also produce a range of broader benefits beyond their impact on non-compliance, such as establishing a relationship of trust, giving citizens confidence in their government, and raising morale within the agency.

We should not let the mention of *non-compliance* – as if it were a real *harm*, and to be treated as such – pass without comment. Surely it is, by definition, a *"non,"* which means an absence (of compliance). Does it make any sense at all to regard *patterns of non-compliance* as analogous to real harms, with parts to be identified and untangled? I think it does, even though the term *non-compliance* itself might suggest otherwise. One can get rid of the "non-" by substituting more concrete terms, such as *tax evasion* or *tax avoidance strategies*. Clearly one can identify patterns of non-compliance, defined in terms of specific behaviors (whether deliberate or not) and concentrated within identifiable segments of the population. Clearly such patterns can be studied and measured and understood, and specific tailor-made interventions invented which might deflate or eliminate them. Many tax agencies can

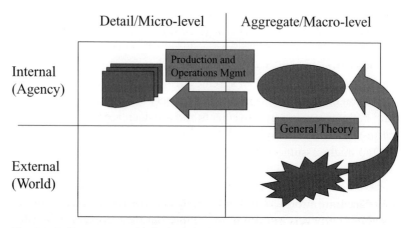

Fig. 2.1 Reliance on established methods

produce some examples of such problems which they have identified and tackled and solved. I believe it does therefore make sense to think of patterns or concentrations of non-compliance as objects for scrutiny and unpicking, even though tax agencies might also strive to develop a broad culture of compliance across the population as a whole. The overall task of *compliance-management* would surely encompass both, just as the practice of medicine involves both the promotion of wellness and the control of specific diseases.

Understanding these two forms of work, *functional* and *process-based*, goes a long way towards explaining how agencies with harm-reduction missions organize and conduct their business. Organizational charts reveal many functional enclaves. The existence of these helps determine where various functional experts hang their coat, and whose office is next door. What they spend their time working on, though, is largely determined by their process responsibilities. Once an organization has assembled the right set of functional capabilities, and organized them around its core operational processes, the bulk of its routine operational practice is determined.

Figure 2.1 presents a simple schematic that captures these ordinary forms of organizational behavior. The horizontal dividing line separates the external world (below the line) from the internal workings of the agency (above the line). The vertical divider crudely distinguishes macro-level or high scale considerations (on the right) from micro-level or detailed ones (on the left).[2] The ugly blob in the bottom right hand cell represents some rather broad category of harm (such as pollution, corruption, crime, or occupational hazards), at some point in time determined by society to be insufficiently controlled. In response to concerns about this general set of harms, government creates an agency or program designed to counter them, which is represented by the more pleasant looking object in the top right cell.

The nature of the harm-control operation then depends on formulating some idea about what might be done – which I shall refer to as the *theory of operations*. To control pollution, an environmental agency might establish and monitor a system of permits for industrial facilities. To reduce occupational hazards, OSHA might choose to conduct unannounced on-site inspections followed up with heavy fines for any violations found, relying on specific and general deterrence to make this and other workplaces safer in the future. Police might depend on rapid response to calls for service, coupled with investigation of reported crimes, as major planks in their approach to crime control. Tax agencies might establish a system for receiving, selecting and auditing tax returns as their principal method for managing compliance.

Sometimes the general method of operations is prescribed by an agency's authorizing legislation – but not as often as bureaucrats tend to believe. More often the theory of operations reflects a tradition that has developed over time, eventually becoming an entrenched part of the agency's behavior. Some theories of operation, appropriate for the problems of the day when the agency was first established, outlive their relevance.

On certain occasions we can observe different theories clashing or competing with one another. Of course it is not the theories themselves that compete, but their human champions. The competition manifests itself in battles for credit, for managerial and political attention, and for resources. The most obvious clashes occur in two specific situations. The first involves organizational mergers, where constituent pieces arrive with differing traditions and self-images. Perhaps one of the merged departments comes as a traditional regulator, heavily reliant on enforcement. Another comes with a tradition of providing technical consulting to industry, and with staff who view themselves as service-providers and advisers. Two such groups may well have trouble appreciating each other; they represent different theories of operation.

The second situation involves overlapping jurisdictions, where two or more agencies share responsibility for control of certain harms, but have sharply differing views on how best to proceed. The FBI and DEA, for example, have overlapping jurisdiction for some aspects of drug control, even though the DEA formally answers to the Director of the FBI. In the US, the task of intelligence gathering and analysis for counter-terrorism is likewise distributed across a host of different intelligence agencies – hence the various attempts post September 11, 2001 to break down cultural differences between these agencies and facilitate or enforce better collaboration.

The possibility of clashing theories at least indicates some scope for choice. For a brand new agency, the choice can be quite daunting. The transition to the new Financial Services Authority in Britain, launched in 1997, involved the eventual merger of twelve previously existing regulatory bodies, each with their own operating tradition. Each one had supervised a specific segment of the financial services industry. As the boundaries between the segments of the industry became increasingly blurred, so the need for integrated regulation increased. In the year 2000, all the precursor sector-specific regulatory statutes were replaced with a new umbrella statute which governed the new, merged agency – the FSA.[3] The governing statute stipulated the FSA's goals in broad terms – to identify and control risks to markets and investors – and specified some aspects of how this new mega-regulator would be held accountable. But it said very little at all about operational methods. The executives of the FSA faced quite a task . . . to invent *what to do*, and to produce some kind of operational coherence, despite the disparate sets of players, methods, and skills.

The invention of new theories of operations is rare. Most harm-reduction work is conducted under theories established years ago, with functional mixes codified in budgetary structures and allocations, and with established processes dominating both operational practice and organizational reporting.

No matter how old or new an organization's *theory of operations*, nor where it came from: management still has to determine what each of the field agents will do *tomorrow*. Such detailed prescriptions for action belong in the top left hand cell of Figure 2.1, and derive from parsing the desired agency output (top right) into smaller pieces. Organizational structures and methods for dividing the work involve both geographic and functional structures, which produce matrix-style reporting relationships. For example, a drinking water specialist in the regional office of an environmental agency answers both to the local geographic commander, but also to the drinking water program chief at central office. The degree to which the geographic form of reporting dominates the functional, or vice versa, shifts back and forth over time, sometimes due to the assertiveness of specific managers, but also due to the natural tension between functional-coherence and geographic responsiveness. Despite these complexities, the work gets divided, handed out to the field, and performed. The net product is a collection of functional outputs, and of processes operated, which can now be aggregated and described at the level of the agency. This "performance" therefore sits in the top right hand cell – and it looks like a collection of organizational outputs. In order to claim any effect on the overall level of harms (bottom right cell), the organization asks the public to accept its theory of operations; that all this work, and efficient operation of all these processes, *ought* to have made the world a better, cleaner, healthier, or safer place. If aggregate or general levels of observed harm decline over time (measures which would belong in the bottom right hand cell), that is of course good news. But the agency's claim to have *caused* the decline, or contributed to it in a meaningful way, still depends on the credibility and acceptance by others of its high-level and general theory of operations.

A different type of organizational behavior

When institutions organize around specific concentrations of harm, rather than around functions or processes, they engage in a very different form of organizational behavior. When they spot the *knots*, study them, and unpick them one by one, they depart from business as usual. Figure 2.2 shows the alternate path they follow, as well as the original one. Work still needs to be allocated, eventually, to field agents – so the arrows (that represent definition and division of work) still have to lead eventually into the top left hand corner, so the individual field agents can receive their specific assignments. But the method by which the work is defined, divided, and handed out is quite different. Rather than specifying the overall agency performance, and dividing that up, the big broad and rather general harm (in the bottom right) is studied instead, and significant parts of the harm itself are identified first. The parts identified come in all kinds of different shapes and sizes, and they all belong in the previously empty cell in the bottom left hand corner. They represent specific concentrations of harm, or problems,

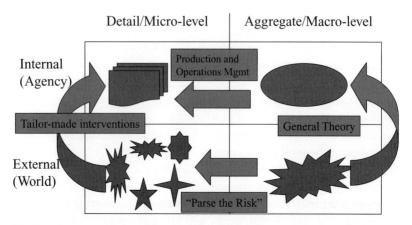

Fig. 2.2 Alternate forms of organizational behavior

or issues, or patterns. These objects exist in the outside world, and exist independently of the agency's structure, processes or traditions. Paying attention to them, one by one, quite naturally seems to result in the production of specific tailor-made responses, and those tailor-made responses are nowhere described either in legislative prescriptions or in the agency's routine policy manuals. In this sense, each *unpicking* represents a departure from normal practice.

The circumstances under which different institutions discover and engage in this new form of behavior vary considerably.

An early and unsettling experience for the IRS came in 1991, when Commissioner Fred Goldberg challenged his management team during an executive retreat to consider non-compliance issues directly, rather than focusing on existing agency processes and methods. His executive team rank-ordered the non-compliance issues of the day, and top of the list was what they referred to as the *non-filer* problem.[4] Various tax gap studies had estimated that roughly 11 million individuals and businesses, mostly self-employed individuals or small cash-based businesses, failed to file returns even though they were obliged to do so. Worse, these entities had *never* filed, which rendered them invisible to IRS data systems and therefore outside the normal scope of IRS analysis and operations. The managerial tools of the day (in the early 1990s) stressed process management and process re-engineering. The distressing property of the *non-filer* issue was that this problem was completely unrepresented in all of the agency's core processes.

Non-filers obviously did not show up under returns-processing. Not surprisingly, non-filers also did not write letters, or call, or initiate any other contact with the agency. Hence process-improvement, no matter how professionally done, would not have touched this problem – the agency's leading non-compliance issue – at all. Meanwhile the agency creaked under its process loads, struggling to keep up, and executives could only find a moment to consider such a problem amid the rare luxury of an executive retreat.

The *non-filer* problem may be an extreme case, but it is an extremely instructive one. Usually, any regulatory or harm-reduction organizations might expect, or even assume, that all the major problems within their scope of responsibility are properly represented and dealt with by the processes they have established. If the reporting or submission mechanisms that feed the processes turn out to be biased or selective in some way, then the process-loads might give only biased or partial views of the problems. But at least the process loads usually provide *some* view. In the case of the non-filer problem, the process loads provided no view at all. The misalignment between major processes and leading problems was extreme.

Even the possibility of such misalignment should nag constantly at the minds of regulatory executives. At a minimum, it should drive home the fact that focusing on *processes* and focusing on *problems* produces two quite different patterns of thought and action.

The US Customs service learned a great deal about this type of work from one specific problem they just had to tackle, even before they developed any formalized apparatus or protocols for this form of work. The problem arose during the period 1994 to 1996, when drug smuggling organizations employed a particularly violent and offensive drug-running method at various Mexico/US border crossing points. Termed *port-running*, the practice involved small but powerful trucks, loaded with up to 500 pounds of contraband.[5] The driver of the truck would stop at the inspection booth, but would be uncooperative. If the inspector detained them with questioning, or tried to pull them over for secondary examination, the *port-runner* would simply put their foot down, smash other cars out of the way, run over any inspector foolish enough to stand in the way, and speed away. For port-running, the smugglers selected ports of entry that provided rapid escape into densely populated urban areas, making pursuit difficult or impossible.

In 1994 Customs had recorded 824 port-running incidents, with gunfire exchanged during more than a dozen of them. Many more incidents might have passed unrecorded, where inspectors felt so intimidated that they simply waved the smugglers through and said nothing.[6] In January of 1995 Deputy Commissioner Mike Lane, responding to public concern and congressional pressure, formed a task force to address the port-running issue directly.

Customs, like most other major regulatory bureaucracies, had a matrix-style functional and geographic organizational structure. It also operated a set of core processes. The port-running problem was a very awkward shape, and did not align neatly with any one function, or port, or region, or process. It clearly involved the inspection-at-the-land-border process... but the task of controlling it didn't look or feel like a *process improvement* task, because those normally revolved around facilitation, customer-service, and efficiency. This was more about stopping a specific bad thing from happening in the context of that broader process.

Geographically, the problem was an awkward shape and size. It was not a national problem, as it only occurred on the southwest land border of the US, yet it straddled two different federal regions (Texas and California) and several different ports (a *port* is the US Customs' lowest-level geographic unit). The task did not obviously belong with any one of Customs' three major functional divisions – Inspection, Intelligence, and Special Agents – as dealing with these smuggling organizations clearly required the involvement of all three. Hence the need for a task force, or something like it, as the shape of the task did not align with any previously existing organizational unit.[7] The task force the Deputy Commissioner created brought together representatives of the two regions, several ports and three functions, and their assigned task was to *eliminate port-running*. And so they did, at about the fifth attempt. First, they tried pursuit strategies, using cars. These failed to control the problem, because the smugglers would send through "clean" cars first to reconnoiter and report back on pursuit capabilities and readiness. Second, they tried pursuit strategies involving Black Hawk helicopters. These turned out to be too expensive to hold constantly in readiness, and hard to hide in the desert. Third, they tried installing pneumatic bollards in the roadway, giving the inspectors handheld remote control devices. After several months of use, and several million dollars of investment, these were eventually abandoned as too costly, too inflexible and too dangerous. If the bollard was activated by mistake they could seriously injure innocent civilians or the inspectors themselves. And trapping port-runners right there in the middle of a crowded bustling entry port did not seem particularly safe either. Certainly not the best place to have a gun battle. Fourth, they tried closing down lanes deliberately to lengthen the waiting queues, and deploying drug sniffing dogs out among the queues, where they could identify and apprehend port runners while they still had too many cars in front of them to "run." Unfortunately the dogs could not work for more than a few minutes at a time in the heat of the day, on the boiling tarmac, and surrounded by exhaust fumes.

The fifth idea the team had worked like a charm. Thinking like saboteurs, they exploited a particular vulnerability of the port-running method itself. Port-running depended on *rapid escape*. If the team could take away rapid escape, port-running would fail as a strategy. Eventually they invented a way, placing Jersey barriers (the heavy concrete barriers used on highway construction sites) in a zig-zag formation *behind* the inspection points. With the barriers in place, any perpetrator that did barge through had then to negotiate a chicane, and their escape could be closed off at the far end, and away from the crowds. Wherever the zig-zag configuration was placed, the port-runners stopped coming. Within six months of the formation of the team, and very soon after settling on the Jersey barrier strategy, the rate of port-running incidents dropped by more than half. The intelligence officers also reported that the prevailing price being paid to the drivers to "run a load" had suddenly risen from $5,000 to $7,500, suggesting that port-running, from the perspective of the smugglers, had become more difficult and dangerous.

For Customs, this early experience contributed substantially to their understanding of the need to recognize forms of work other than function and process. By the summer of 1995 the agency formally launched its *Strategic Problem Solving* program (or SPS), through which it would identify, analyze and tackle *specific drug smuggling concentrations*. It took some time to sort out staff confusion between process-improvement and problem-solving. Even though the agency had learned process-improvement first, that was still relatively new to the agency. Moreover, the terminology of *problem-solving* had already popped up as part of the process-improvement lexicon. Eventually they figured out the difference, realizing that process-improvement is a *managerial* method for improving the agency's *processes*; whereas *problem-solving* was an *operational method* for working on external harms. The *problems* for their process improvement teams were things like glitches, bottlenecks and inefficiencies within the agency's high-volume processes. The problems for the SPS program were smugglers, their concentrations, their patterns of behavior, and specific smuggling methods. These *harms* existed in the outside world, and could be scrutinized in their own right without any reference to what Customs already had, or did, or the way it was organized. Another distinction – one the staff appreciated – was that the two methods produced quite different types of results: process improvement projects aimed to produce efficiency and public satisfaction, whereas *strategic problem solving* aimed to reduce drug smuggling.

The Occupational Safety and Health Administration (OSHA) also learned about the problem-solving approach (which they called *the problem-solving approach to hazard-mitigation in the workplace*) during the mid 1990s. In the spring of 1995 the agency was fighting for survival, under fierce assault from the newly Republican Congress led by Newt Gingrich. The Republicans targeted the EPA and the FDA also, but proposed elimination of OSHA altogether. "Replace OSHA with a brochure" was their motto; their platform "get regulators off the back of industry." Industry can be trusted, the Republican line claimed; just give them the right information so they can do the right thing.

Executives at OSHA were relieved, and to a degree surprised, when the *Washington Post* came to their defense.[8] Before we do away with this agency, this one article proposed, it would be prudent to consider what OSHA had accomplished. The article then listed a range of hazards that showed measurable declines after OSHA's intervention: 58% fewer deaths in grain-handling,[9] 35% fewer deaths in trench cave-ins in the construction industry, the rate of brown-lung disease amongst textile workers dropping from 20% of the workforce to 1% within a seven-year time period, and so on. Hazard by hazard, visible and significant reductions.

But in 1995, what managerial methods did OSHA have available in order to do better? Process improvement, of course. Consequently, like almost every other federal agency at the time, they had launched into process improvement, designing new response procedures for complaints and industrial accidents that significantly reduced response times and, as a result of the efficiencies gained, freed up significant internal resources. If that is all OSHA had done, the chances are they would have lost any personnel and resources these new efficiencies had freed up, and their gains would mostly have been limited to timeliness, productivity, and efficiency. What counted – judging by the *Washington Post's* defense – was *effectiveness* measured in terms of lives saved and hazards mitigated. It wasn't obvious that process improvements necessarily translated into lives saved. Realizing this, and grasping the difference between process-improvement and hazard-reduction, they advanced both ideas at the same time, taking the efficiency gains that came from process improvement, and reinvesting resources and personnel to address specific hazards. Under the OSHA "Redesign Strategy" that resulted from this combination, the improved processes were rolled out Area Office by Area Office, freeing up between one third and one half of all the personnel. These staff members were immediately formed into *Strategic Intervention Teams*, trained in problem-solving methodology, and given the job of identifying specific concentrations of risk at the local level, and inventing methods to reduce the corresponding injury or illness rates.[10]

OSHA's Area Office in Parsippany, New Jersey, was the very first to go through this transition, and they set the tone for the rest of OSHA with two very successful early projects. One of these focused on contractors who paint New Jersey's bridges, whose workers were exposed all day long to lead-based paints. The goal of that project was to bring these painters' blood-lead concentrations down to safe levels. Progress would be monitored through the introduction of routine blood testing within the industry.

The Parsippany office's second project focused on deaths and injuries on highway construction sites, many of which were caused by inadequate separation of construction workers from traffic passing through. Noticing that all such sites already had state Highway Patrol Officers on site, the Parsippany team decided to engage the State Highway Patrol as partners in the enterprise, and provided training for police officers in how to spot occupational and construction hazards, even though these were not normally police business.

This mode of organizational behavior – focusing directly on the harms themselves, and on very specific pieces of the harms – shows up frequently in almost any discussion of regulatory innovations. The connection to *innovations* is mostly explained because this type of behavior produces interventions which are tailor-made (being crafted around specific knots), and which therefore appear novel, or innovative. The more important innovation is surely the pattern of organizational behavior that produces such fruits, rather than the fruits themselves. Organizations that recognize this distinction are less likely to fall into the trap of celebrating and replicating individual *solutions*, and more likely to develop problem-solving as an operational approach relevant to a vast array of different harms.

In previous work, I have analyzed the different types of innovations surfacing within the regulatory (social risk control) side of government. Data regarding these innovations was available from the Ford Foundation's annual "Innovations in American Government" competition. This competition, launched in 1986, is open to federal, state and local agencies, and routinely receives more than a thousand applications per year, wherein agencies can present a summary of programs they consider innovative.[11] My analysis of this data put aside all the initiatives that primarily concerned the delivery of government services, and focused on those that had to do with control of some harm or another. Most of these submissions came from agencies of social regulation, or from law enforcement.

Taking thirteen years of the competition's history (1986–1998), I restricted attention to applications that were judged sufficiently noteworthy and valuable to make it to the pool of finalists. Twenty-five entries per year make it to the finals, with ten of them ultimately selected as winners. Each of the ten winners receives a good deal of publicity, as well as $100,000 to support further replication and diffusion of the idea.

Focusing on the collection of finalists across the history of the awards program, a rather interesting picture of innovations regarded as valuable emerged.[12] Despite the fact that the dominant managerial tools of this period involved process improvement, and the political pressures for reform emphasized easing regulatory burdens and enhancing client service, only three of the applications within this particular pool reflected those themes. The IRS was selected as one of the ten winners in 1997 for their Telefile Program (which allowed certain taxpayers with relatively simple and straightforward tax returns to submit them via keypad entry on a telephone). The Food and Drug Administration won in 1997 for implementing an accelerated drug-approval process. Also, the City of Chicago reached the finals in 1991 for an automated system integrating the various stages of parking ticket issuance, adjudication, and collection.

These three were classic process improvement projects, done well, each producing benefits in terms of efficiency, accuracy, and timeliness. None of them altered the underlying business models of the agencies involved.

A larger group of innovations finalists, eight in total, reflected quite a different type of work. They each involved a quite specific concentration of harm, which was demonstrably reduced through the thoughtful design and successful implementation of a tailor-made solution. Eight knots, spotted, and then unpicked.

One of these knots was an extremely disturbing pattern of juvenile homicide in the city of Boston. During the early 1990s the rate at which kids were killing kids rose to alarming levels. With grant support from the National Institute of Justice, a multi-agency task force was formed, with analytical support from some criminal justice experts at Harvard University. The intervention, since replicated to varying degrees in other cities around the US, became known as the *Boston Gun Control Project*.[13] The project team's incoming assumptions – that the heart of the problem involved easy gun-supply routes up the eastern seaboard to Massachusetts from southern states – were examined and then soundly rejected. Gun-trace data for guns used in past homicides showed quite the opposite: guns used were mostly fairly new, and first purchased in Massachusetts. So the knot was turned this way and that, through a sequence of analytical explorations, seeking alternate perspectives and insights into the nature of the thing. Eventually the team established that the bulk of the homicides lay along the lines of established "gang beefs" (hostilities between various pairings of Boston's sixty-one gangs). Important dynamics of the problem included the fact that most gang-involved youths carried weapons, they believed, for the purposes of self defense. Also, by committing an act of violence, gang members gained respect among their peers – for them a powerful motivation. Once the project team understood the dynamics of the problem, they developed a strategy ("Operation Ceasefire") to reverse the effects of peer-pressure within the gangs by making any gang member who committed an act of violence the mechanism of downfall for the whole gang. Through a series of meetings which gang members were obliged to attend as a condition of probation or parole, the project team delivered a stern warning to the gangs. From that day forward, any gang member who committed an act of violence would bring the concerted attention of federal, state and city police agencies down not just upon themselves, but upon their entire gang. The task force promised law enforcement attention so focused and intense that they said they could remove any one gang from the streets entirely. They would use outstanding arrest warrants, parole violations, whatever they had. They would bring the most severe charges possible, using federal indictments where necessary, to put the whole gang behind bars. Once the strategy was fully communicated the team did have to deliver on its promise, twice, with respect to two different gangs. At that point, the rest were apparently convinced the threat was serious, and gang violence dropped off dramatically. The homicide rate for victims under age 25 dropped by 68% in the first year after Operation Ceasefire began, and continued to decline thereafter.

Another of the specific knots unpicked involved prostitutes in San Francisco. The District Attorney's office, working with law enforcement and public health agencies, devised a plan to rescue young women from a life of prostitution. Analyzing the pressures through which women are first drawn into the trade and subsequently trapped within it, the team decided to focus on the moment of first arrest as an important opportunity for intervention. The first arrest, unlike the fifteenth one, came as a shock, and maybe represented the best opportunity to intervene before the cycle of offending and re-offending became entrenched. Hoping this was, for young prostitutes, a "teachable moment" the team devised a program including elements of counseling, life skills training, treatment, and case management. They offered an eight-hour seminar on the risks and impacts of prostitution as an alternative to prosecution. Instituted in 1995, the program reached the finals of the innovations competition in 1997, and was selected a winner the following year (the 1998 cycle). The reason for the difference, with essentially the same innovation presented two years running, was that the project had more results to show a year later: that is, more women extracted from the profession.

These two examples both exhibit four important properties typical of this whole class of innovations. First, they addressed specific, tightly defined concentrations of harm, rather than generalities or broad classes of harm. The Boston project did not target all violence, nor all "Part 1 crimes," not even all homicides. Once the analysis had identified gang-related violence as a significant and discrete component of the overall homicide rate, the collaborating agencies then honed in on that piece of the puzzle. Similarly, the San Francisco First-Offender Prostitution program did not tackle all sex crimes in the Bay area, nor even the whole problem of prostitution and its societal impacts. Rather it picked apart the dynamics and development of a life of prostitution, searching for a point of leverage where targeted resources could make a real difference.

Second, these projects involved a prolonged period of analysis and inspection, before any new action was initiated. In the Boston project, several different hypotheses about *what the problem really was* were tested and discarded before the relationship between juvenile homicides and gang-hostilities was finally established.

Third, having understood the problem and defined it precisely, the interventions that resulted were not merely a mixture of existing functions or methods; they were qualitatively new. And the methods were not novel for the sake of being novel (entry in the competition invariably came as an afterthought); they were novel because the problems to be addressed had not responded to the standard treatments, and therefore required novel ones.

Fourth, these projects involved multiple agencies and organizations working in collaboration. Why? Not because cross-agency or multi-functional collaboration is inherently desirable for its own sake. Rather, multiple agencies were involved because the problems addressed straddled jurisdictional and programmatic boundaries, making collaboration essential.[14] The partnerships involved in these projects formed around the shape of the knots themselves, rather than recasting the problem to conform to existing institutional structures or trying to divide it along traditional functional or programmatic lines.

Even this group of eight innovations finalists, representing *specific problems identified and solved,* was not the most significant category. The analysis showed another, yet larger, grouping of innovations finalists. This set, comprising thirteen different projects, followed similar lines to the previous set but went beyond the identification and solution of one specific problem. These thirteen projects involved setting up analytic systems of one kind or another designed to enable an agency to spot problems – not once or twice, but on a continuing basis. The majority of these analytic systems involve pattern recognition methods (some crude, some quite sophisticated), as well as the adoption of operational procedures to address whatever patterns the systems revealed.

This set includes New York City's Compstat program (which became a competition winner in 1996). This program established routine precinct-level analysis of reported crime data, and then held precinct commanders accountable for addressing any patterns of crime identified through the analysis. The Pension Benefit Guaranty Corporation (winner, 1995) devised an early warning system for pension plans at risk of insolvency. This set of innovations also included a range of other technical analysis and survey systems used by law-enforcement to identify patterns of crime, road accidents, and other community concerns. Florida's Department of Environmental Protection reached the finals in 1994 with a system for analyzing marine spills of oil and other contaminants, so that repeat sources and causes could be addressed.

Where do these types of innovations belong on the chart? I would suggest they belong in the middle, and at the bottom, under the label "parse the risk." These systems use various data sources, and various ways of slicing and dicing that data, to make visible any knots that might exist, with the presumption that they can then be addressed. These projects show a range of agencies moving beyond the untying of a single knot. Here they are getting into the *knot-spotting* and *knot-untying* business, and building some pieces of organizational infrastructure to sustain it as a part of ongoing operations.

Why innovative?

At first it seems somewhat ironic that such programs should win *innovations* awards. If a police agency could not spot crime problems and successfully address them, what use would they be? Surely citizens would expect environmental agencies to be able to recognize specific environmental problems, tax agencies to spot important patterns of non-compliance, and OSHA to deal with specific patterns of death and injury in the workplace? Is that not the core of their mission? Yet when they do precisely this, they win prizes for innovation, and society celebrates both their brilliance and their courage. But why should such behavior represent a departure from business as usual? Why should it require brilliance, or courage? Should it not be utterly routine? Should it not be, in fact, the core of normal operations?

Perhaps it should. But the truth of the matter, sadly, is that functions and processes take over; and it pays to understand why. Functions are *comfortable*. They group employees together with others who share common training, celebrate a common set of skills and knowledge, share a specific professional culture, and climb a well-established disciplinary ladder.

Processes are *inescapable*. Process loads are tangible and voluminous. Related timelines are mandatory.

By contrast, the business of organizing around specific harms, and devising solutions for one piece or another, seems vague, amorphous, and entirely optional. It is never clear who's job that is, if anybody's, because job responsibilities are not framed that way. If an agency should address problems of this type, it is not clear how many, or how big, or for how long. It is certainly not obvious how this type of work – if and when an organization chooses to engage in it – fits with the other kinds of work, which still need to be done, nor what priority it might take. Absent any system for driving this type of work, and connecting it properly with everything else an agency does, whoever chooses to tackle a knot often has to invent the whole methodology for themselves, provide all the energy and all the ideas, and enlist all the necessary partners. Many of the award winners who did this work had no authority to do it, and certainly no mandate. Many of them received no support from their agency, nor recognition – until after the fact when the rest of the world took notice. From talking to staff members who have engaged in this type of work, one does begin to understand the need for courage and determination. The solutions they generate look like a slap-in-the-face for the prevailing *theories of operation*. Focusing attention on a particular harm in the first place (and therefore distracting attention from routine business) seems to carry some professional risk.

Even in institutions that have declared their commitment to a problem-solving strategy and promised managerial support for it, practitioners report a host of reasons why this type of work remains absurdly difficult: This is *extra* work, and every other kind of work has a formal structure, and deadlines, and a legal mandate; this has none of those. This type of work brings unfamiliar degrees of discretion, and involves endless subjective judgments – what to take on, how big, how small, how the problem is best defined, what partners, what methods, how much to spend. Problems straddle organizational boundaries, and other agencies bring sharply conflicting perspectives to bear on them.[15] We have no established protocol for this type of work. We have no *forms* for this type of work. Half the agency does not believe this type of work is different, or needs organizing. The problems do not fit our system of job definitions, so it is not clear where they belong.

Once one hears all these complaints, time and again, across many different professions one does begin to understand why the people that actually manage to do this type of work – to focus on a harm, devise a solution, and stick with it long enough to make a real difference – deserve to be celebrated and rewarded. It takes heroism, and acts of organizational subversion, to overcome the institutional pressures stacked against them.

There is nothing particularly complicated about the basic notion of picking harms apart, identifying critical components, and unraveling them one by one. We often use quite plain and straightforward phrases to describe this practice: "Pick Important Problems & Fix Them." "Oh, that's just the problem-solving approach, applied to risks." Hearing this language, one could be forgiven for assuming this approach was not new; or if it were new, that it was nevertheless straightforward. Neither of these turns out to be true. For many organizations it is new. When they do it once, everyone celebrates. When they try to do it more often, or routinely, they discover they do not know how to organize or support it. If they do manage to establish it as a part of operational practice, it often turns out subsequently to be fragile and short-lived.

When staff gather in functional units, they gather around their shared past, their shared training, their shared skills. When staff gather around processes, they gather around a visible and tangible flow of calls, files, transactions or reports. Little imagination is required, in either case, to understand the nature of the work.

But when people gather around a specific identified harm (one of those objects in the bottom left hand cell of Figure 2.2) what is it exactly that they are gathering around? Some piece of a more general harm, to be reduced? Who says which piece, and how best to define it? Who decides which component of a risk to address? Who decides if the focus should be on reducing the probability of some class of events, or changing their distribution, or limiting their consequences? When we look at a general class of harms (in the bottom right hand cell) we have in mind a condition in the world that we would like to be different. The specific harms (bottom left) represent select pieces, subjectively chosen, of the general conditions we would like to be different. No wonder this practice seems abstract, vague and elusive; and no wonder most activity gets organized some other way.

When practitioners do recognize this form of work and determine to operate this way, they confront a host of subjective decisions: how many pieces to identify, in what dimensions, and at what scale. And that is just the work of *defining* the task. *Performing* the task brings another round of choices: what methods to use, what partners to enlist, how much of a reduction to set as the goal. On every one of these questions, all the other interested parties are free to disagree. This type of work might proceed more naturally on odd occasions when a specific harm stares everyone in the face, demanding attention, and where the shape and nature of the problem is reasonably plain to everyone. But these are the exceptions. The rest of the time practitioners need some guidance to help them navigate the endless choices involved. Without such guidance, the most attractive choice is not to do this type of work at all, and to revert to forms of work that are more familiar, comfortable, and straightforward.

Notes

1. See: Michael Hammer & James Champy, *Reengineering the Corporation: A Manifesto for Business Revolution*, HarperBusiness Books (New York: HarperCollins Publishers, 1993).
2. I am grateful to my colleague Mark H. Moore for this framework. He proposed it as a device for categorizing performance metrics. It is also useful as a way of understanding different organizational behaviors.
3. Transition to the new mega-regulator happened in stages between 1997 and 2000. Ultimately the Financial Services and Market Act, 2000, provided an integrated statutory umbrella, replacing all the sector specific statutes upon which the prior multi-agency supervisory system had been based.
4. For a fuller discussion of the non-filer issue, and IRS analysis of it, see Malcolm K. Sparrow, *The Regulatory Craft: Controlling Risks, Solving Problems & Managing Compliance* (Washington DC: Brookings Institution Press, 2000), pp. 73–75.
5. Ibid., pp. 124–129.

6. Such failures do not result simply from laziness on the part of inspectors. The smuggling organizations are violent and ruthless. They target specific inspectors, find out where they live, and threaten their spouses and children. Systematic intimidation of inspectors is part of the smuggling strategy. They also use "spotters" overlooking the inspection areas, equipped with binoculars and radios, to direct the load-carrying vehicles to lanes manned by inspectors who are compromised, vulnerable, or inexperienced.

7. Archon Fung comments on the complexity and awkwardness of "problems that lie between the core competencies and responsibilities of several agencies..." given the fact that a bureaucracy "...develops a stock of procedures and techniques to address the canonical problems that arise in [their] arena." This comment applies equally well across functional units *within* large bureaucracies as well as *across* agencies. Archon Fung, *Empowered Participation: Reinventing Urban Democracy* (Princeton, New Jersey: Princeton University Press, 2004), p. 21.

8. "OSHA's Enemies Find Themselves in High Places," *Washington Post,* July 24, 1995.

9. The most common method of death involves drowning (i.e. asphyxiation) in grain silos.

10. OSHA had eighty-six Area Offices at the time, covering the twenty-nine states in which OSHA operated. In the remaining twenty-one states, occupational safety is the responsibility of state agencies.

11. The John F. Kennedy School of Government helps to administer the program, under grant from the Ford Foundation, and is thus in an especially good position to gather and analyze data from the program.

12. For a full description of this analysis, and for a brief description of all of the regulatory and enforcement innovations which have been selected as finalists during the first thirteen years of the competition's history, see: Sparrow, *The Regulatory Craft*, Ch. 6.

13. For a fuller account of this project, see: David M. Kennedy, "Pulling Levers: Chronic Offenders, High Crime Settings, and a Theory of Prevention," *Valparaiso University Law Review,* 31 (1997), 1–53; Sparrow, *The Regulatory Craft*, Ch. 12.

14. Jorg Raab & H. Brinton Milward, "Dark Networks as Problems," *Journal of Public Administration Research and Theory,* 13 (2003) 413–439 p. 414; Benny Hjern, "Illegitimate Democracy: A Case for Multi-Organizational Policy Analysis," *Policy Currents,* 2 (1992), 1–5.

15. The Department of Environment & Labour in Nova Scotia, Canada, recently launched a project focused on the risk of *workplace violence* in the province, because data on workplace injuries pointed to

violence as a growing source of concern. The problem awkwardly straddles the jurisdictions of multiple departments, including the department
of labour (accustomed to developing systems for *hazard mitigation*
and *accident prevention*), and police (more accustomed to dealing
with *crimes*). To complicate things further in terms of defining the
problem to be addressed, significant subsets of violence-related workplace injuries occur in prisons and in health care delivery settings,
involving a broader range of institutions and operating norms. One
of the early challenges for this project, therefore, involves awkward
decisions about how much of the overall problem to take on, and
which parts; and how to frame the issues in a way which energizes
rather than alienates important partners. A list of public information
resources regarding the project is available on the agency's website
at: [www.gov.ns.ca/enla/healthandsafety/violenceintheworkplace.asp].
See, particularly: *A Workplace Violence Prevention Strategy for Nova
Scotia: Promoting Greater Awareness of Workplace Violence Prevention* (Halifax, Nova Scotia: Department of Environment & Labour,
April 2007).

3 | Defining problems: setting the scale

The US Environmental Protection Agency (EPA), eager to make the best possible use of innovative programs, set up an Innovations Action Council (IAC) in the fall of 1996.[1] The Council comprised all the senior managers of the agency from national and regional offices, gathered together once every quarter to focus on the EPA's use of innovative methods. The express purpose around which the Council gathered was framed this way:

The IAC's goal is to develop an innovations strategy that *deploys innovative approaches and tools that make measurable progress on important environmental problems.*[2]

As a focal point for the IAC's discussions, this single sentence reflects both an appreciation of the need for innovative methods, and a conviction that innovation is not for its own sake but counts only when it makes a difference on problems that matter. Despite these positive ingredients, the sentence remains quite ambiguous about which of two quite different modes of organizational behavior it might produce. It can be read either forwards or backwards, and this simple choice significantly affects the operational consequences.

Reading the sentence forwards, the agency would begin by listing the *innovative approaches and tools* in its repertoire. Then, with these tools in mind, managers would proceed to search for *important environmental problems* where those tools might offer *measurable progress.* The starting point for such deliberation, therefore, is an expanded toolkit filled with tools the agency has already learned how to use. Referring back to Figure 2.2, this deliberation sits most naturally in the top right cell, where the agency, mindful of specific innovative tools, adds them to its functional and programmatic repertoire along with more traditional methods. Equipped with an expanded toolkit, the question then becomes "what else can we find to do with them?"

This approach seems perfectly legitimate. It is the same question asked in product development when industry *has* a specific technology (e.g. a glue so weak it does not even leave a mark on paper), and searches for *product innovations* that exploit it (e.g. the now ubiquitous "Post-it Note"). At the time the Innovations Action Council was set up, the EPA had a substantial list of new tools to think about. These included negotiated rulemaking, permit trading systems, the use of *supplemental environmental projects* in settlements, ecosystem management, place-based management, the *common-sense initiative* (which addressed issues specific to six particular industry groupings), and Project XL (a system for allowing an industrial facility to do worse in one area of pollution if it did much better in some other area, for an overall "net environmental benefit").

Reading the IAC's statement back to front, however, produces quite different organizational behaviors. The first job for the agency in this case would be to create a list of *environmental problems*. Presumably that might involve some type of scanning for new or emerging problems, as well as considering familiar ones. The next step would involve deciding which of these problems were more *important* than others, assuming the agency had inadequate resources to work on everything. To make those choices, the agency would need to develop some list of criteria to be weighed in making such choices. Having determined which were the *important environmental problems* the next step would be to define *measurable progress* for those specific problems; that is, establish metrics by which one could tell if the situation improved. Last of all, having selected specific problems and established relevant metrics for each one, then (and only then) would staff consider *which innovative approaches and tools* might have some impact.

In fact, at this last stage, one would hope the EPA would keep a completely open mind about relevant methods. Perhaps some recent additions to the toolkit – the fashionable innovations of the day – might be relevant. But a renewed application of traditional methods or a different combination of them might work instead. Quite likely, with the task clearly established, and the goals and metrics set, the agency might discover that nothing they did or had done before would deal with a particular problem. At such a moment, they would share an experience common for craftsmen or craftswomen working on a task: the sudden realization: "*I don't have a tool for this.*" Such realization comes (along with the associated sinking feeling) when a craftsperson is immersed in a task, and has a clear sense of what they want to accomplish. At that moment, the craftsman leaves the task bench for a while, and either moves to a different bench to fashion the new tool they need, or takes a quick trip to the local hardware store in the hope of finding something suitable. Either way, they are searching for a *technology innovation*, where you know what you want to achieve but do not yet have the technical means. This is quite different from a *product innovation*, where you have a technology and are trying to figure out what else you could do with it.

Reading the IAC's sentence backwards moves the whole discussion into the bottom left hand cell of the matrix, rather than the top right. The landscape in this cell comprises a host of environmental problems of one type or another, of many different shapes and sizes, whose existence and nature is independent of the agency and its capabilities. Life in the bottom left cell starts in the *field,* even though the business of *spotting* these problems and working out how to navigate this terrain is very much a question of agency capability. By contrast, life in the top right hand cell starts in the *toolshed,* where discussion focuses on the internal workings and established capabilities of the agency.

Each of these two approaches produces distinctive language and phraseology reflecting the different organizational consequences. Should researchers and practitioners choose to focus their attention in the top right cell, where the organizing principle is tools-based, then the resulting tasks or research projects would exhibit two characteristics. They would be relatively precise with respect to methods, and rather general or vague in terms of the harms to be addressed. Consider the following task definitions, for example:

- extending the use of negotiated rulemaking in environmental protection;
- exploring the role of civil society in corruption control;
- evaluating the effect of "three-strikes and you're out" policies on crime levels;
- reducing drug abuse by expanding drug awareness resistance programs in schools;
- decreasing worker injury rates through the use of experience-rated premium-setting for employers in workers' compensation insurance;
- developing education and information campaigns that would help reduce international trafficking in women and children;

- developing broader international cooperation among law enforcement and intelligence agencies in combating money laundering.

The simple fact of considering multiple tools, rather than just one, does not necessarily get you out of the toolshed. Here are some further task descriptions, each of which involves shifting resources or emphasis among different functional or programmatic areas, or establishing an optimum distribution or balance between two or more of them. All of these task definitions still inhabit the toolshed more than they do the task environment, and speak of the harm to be controlled only in broad and general terms:

- (in tax administration) determining the optimal mix of audit, enforcement, and taxpayer assistance that would improve overall compliance rates;
- (in environmental protection) developing partnerships with industry associations as an alternative to increased enforcement;
- (in drug control) shifting attention and resources from controlling smuggling to reducing levels of domestic demand;
- (in terrorism control) focusing less on undermining the operations of terrorist groups and focusing more on technologies for defending high-value targets;
- exploring opportunities to make greater use of "alternatives to enforcement" (the prevailing political imperative of the mid and late 1990s in US regulatory agencies).

In calculating an optimal mixture among a given set of tools, some organizations employ quite sophisticated mathematical and econometric techniques, yet remain quite narrow in the range of tools considered. Such analyses can only lead to a redistribution among existing methods, without the possibility of creating new ones nor indicating the need for them.

By contrast, even rather unsophisticated analyses conducted at lower levels of the task environment can show quite quickly where "we don't have a tool for this," and provide insights into the nature of new tailor-made methods that might be suitable. Explicit task and project definitions that belong more naturally in the bottom left cell of Figure 2.2 show relative precision in specifying the harm to be addressed, and remain wide open with respect to relevant methods and potential innovation. For example, consider the following:

- dealing with domestic burglaries being committed by high-school kids on their way home from school in mid-afternoon, when many parents leave their homes unattended and unlocked;
- reducing the frequency of serious or fatal spinal and head injuries caused when roofers fall from roofs in the course of their work;
- reducing the incidence of repetitive back-strain injuries in the nursing profession, caused by lifting patients without proper equipment or in awkward circumstances;
- eliminating the forms of corruption in real-estate development involving the infiltration of local development boards and manipulation of land prices (by either granting or denying development permissions) by organized crime groups;
- reducing excessive concentrations of arsenic in surface waters on golf courses resulting from over-use of certain pesticides and fertilizers;
- eliminating the practice of port-running, used by drug smugglers at land-border crossing points between Mexico and the United States;
- reducing the threat of commercial airplane hijacking by terrorists willing to commit suicide;
- combating the trafficking of Nepalese girls for prostitution in eastern European countries by smuggling organizations deceptively offering modeling careers as enticements.

One more important difference between the tool-based and task-based approaches involves the type of performance story available at the end of the day. Programmatic projects most obviously produce programmatic outputs: "we delivered two thousand hours of education programs," "we provided five million inoculations," "we convicted and incarcerated 150 offenders," "we enlisted 32 companies in Project XL." How much these programmatic outputs contributed to the reduction of harm is open to speculation, and rests on the credibility of the prevailing *theory of operations*. It can be very frustrating for anyone running or promoting tool-based projects when they find they *cannot* draw any direct connection between the program outputs and any resulting change in field conditions. The inability to prove a causal linkage frustrates political champions of particular methods, as well as not-for-profit foundations funding or using specific methods for which they have some ideological preference.

The EPA has struggled for many years to link various innovative programs to specific environmental results. Likewise one sees philanthropic foundations demanding accountability for *outcomes* from grantees, even though the grants were for deployment of particular methods as opposed to the solution of particular problems. The lack of connection is not so much a failure of evaluative methods after the fact; the damage is done right up front, in the way the project – or grant – was specified at the outset. If the project is specified in terms of the methods it employs rather than the target it addresses, then it belongs in the top right hand cell of Figure 2.2. In most cases, projects conceived and conducted in that cell produce highly specific outputs, but cannot be connected directly to specific outcomes. Specific outcomes belong in the bottom left hand cell. Projects conceived and conducted there may end up employing a range of methods, some novel, some not, and thus involve a range of outputs; but because they were structured at the outset in terms of specific harms to be reduced, then – if successful – that is exactly what they will produce: specific harms reduced.

I am not suggesting here that technology innovations are necessarily better than product innovations. They are merely quite different. Industry benefits from both. Surely the task of harm-reduction can similarly benefit from finding new targets for known methods, as well as tackling specific concentrations of harm. Nobody should imagine that one of these organizational behaviors is good, and the other bad. Society would certainly benefit, though, from some more appropriate mixture of these two forms of activity. For now, almost everything is tool-based, and falls in the top right cell, for all the reasons discussed in the previous chapter. It is just so much easier to organize work that way. Judging by the celebration that accompanies departures from this norm, we know for sure which way the underlying balance needs to shift. While I appreciate the courage and creativity of innovators, I would like the types of behavior so far regarded as heroic and celebrated as innovative to become a little less exceptional. This would surely begin to happen more broadly if institutions learned to structure investments more often around pieces of the problem, and less often around pieces of the toolkit.

That means asking people to spend more time operating within the texture of the task environment, focusing attention, energy and (for grant programs) funding on selected problems, rather than on preferred methods. Those who choose to make this shift might appreciate some guidance and navigational aids, because they will discover soon enough that the terrain in the task environment is considerably more complex, messier and harder to navigate than the neatly organized toolshed.

Setting the size, and picking the dimensions

Navigating the texture of harms is distressingly complicated. Who is to decide how big or how small a problem to take on? Who should decide in what dimensions a problem should best be defined? Answer: practitioners! It is they who must decide these things, as a part of ordinary operational practice. In so doing, they confront an extraordinary range of choices.

In terms of setting the size, I would like to clarify two extremes between which the most fruitful work lies. At the lowest level, attention might be focused on a problem so small and so particular that it really represents one incident or violation, and is really not a pattern at all. An incident may be part of a pattern, but is not a pattern by itself. The right way to think about individual incidents is from the point of view of incident response; and the chances are an organization already has processes and procedures established to handle such work. So focusing attention at the finest level of granularity, moves practitioners *below* the level for effective problem-solving, and back into a reactive case-by-case processing mode. Figure 3.1 shows this incident-response capacity as the "lowest" level (i.e. addressing the smallest objects in the task environment) that might normally be considered, and refers to it as level 1.

Level 5 reflects the opposite extreme, where the problems being addressed are not specific at all, but are bundles of disparate objects, all lumped together under a common title, and usually a rather brief title – like poverty, corruption, or crime. Figure 3.1 shows this as the "highest" level that might be considered. At this level, one considers generalized classes of problems and weighs the merits of generalized classes of response. Through analyses conducted at this macro-level, organizations revise from time to time their general theories of operation, or add or subtract major programmatic elements from their prescriptive repertoires. (Referring back to the structure of Figure 2.2, this type of analysis and thinking belongs at the macro-level, and therefore aligns with the right hand half of that diagram.)

This, level 5, is also the level at which econometric analysis most often appears, and where the unit of analysis (in studying phenomena

Scale:	Works on What?	Comments:
Highest (Level 5)	Broad categories of harm, addressed at the level of *nations*.	■ Studied through macro-level analyses, which seek to determine the relationship between one summary indicator (of the level of the harm) and a collection of other macro-level variables. ■ The level at which 'general theories of operation' compete for attention and acceptance. ■ Many parties are ideologically committed to one macro-level approach or another. ■ New analyses may produce adjustments in portfolios of major programmatic or functional approaches. ■ Lower level texture is not visible at this level.
High (Level 4)	Specific harms which have escalated to crisis proportions.	■ Problem is visible to the public, obviously urgent, and getting attention at the political level. ■ Existence of the problem is evident to all, and failure to control it would be readily observed. ■ Continued failure to control it would produce inescapable embarrassment for responsible authorities. ■ Visibility and urgency are sufficient to produce concerted action.
Medium (Level 3)	Anything in between!	■ Problem is small enough to appear 'optional.' ■ Problem is large enough to require organizational systems and structures. ■ Many agencies lack any system for formulating or conducting harm-reduction work at these 'in-between' levels.
Low (Level 2)	Problems or patterns sufficiently small to be addressed by highly motivated individuals or small teams.	■ Not large enough to require formal support systems and structures. ■ Tailor-made solutions represent departures from normal operational practice. ■ Successful interventions often heralded as innovative and heroic.
Lowest (Level 1)	One specific case or incident.	■ Handled through routine processes. ■ This unit of work is the normal basis for workload recording and reporting. ■ 'Quality' issues concern the adequacy, timeliness and professionalism of response. ■ The object of attention (an *incident*) is not a collection or pattern of lower level objects.

Fig. 3.1 Levels at which harms can be defined and addressed

such as corruption, poverty, or disease rates) is quite large; most often *nations*. So nations are compared, one with another, in terms of their overall levels of corruption[3] (as indicated, for example, by the Transparency International Corruptions Perceptions Index), or in terms of their overall poverty rates, or (for the purposes of comparing health systems) in terms of their mortality rates for various age ranges. Analysis at this level may generate prescriptions for action, applicable at the level of nations. Such prescriptions may be broadly useful, but necessarily miss important textural elements only visible at lower levels of granularity. Moreover, such analyses tend to assume that the underlying character of poverty, or of corruption, or of crime in any one country is the same as it is in another.

This point is made forcefully by Jeffrey Sachs in relation to traditional approaches to poverty reduction.[4] In *The End of Poverty* he includes a chapter introducing what he terms "clinical economics." In it he criticizes the blandness and generality of prior approaches:

"The IMF-World Bank programs of the structural adjustment era were designed to address the four maladies assumed to underlie all economic ills: poor governance, excessive government intervention in the markets, excessive government spending, and too much state ownership. Belt tightening, privatization, liberalization, and good governance became the order of the day.[5]

Sachs points out that – even at the level of nations – the nature of poverty problems can vary substantially. "Clinical economics," he suggests, "should train the development practitioner to hone in much more effectively on the key underlying causes of economic distress, and to prescribe appropriate remedies that are well tailored to each country's specific conditions. When in Afghanistan or Bolivia, the IMF should think automatically about transport costs; when in Senegal, attention should turn to Malaria."[6]

Other poverty experts point out that careful characterization of a nation's poverty problem might still not properly reflect the miscellany of problems to be found at regional or lower levels. In a discussion of *poverty traps*, Stephen Smith points out "sometimes the idea of poverty traps is applied to problems of national stagnation, and local poverty traps in regions, villages and families are much more common."[7] Smith stresses the importance of listening to the poor describe their own experience as a way of preventing researchers and policy-makers plugging diverse experiences into familiar buckets or higher-level categories. To illustrate the potential diversity of poverty experience, he lists sixteen distinct types of *poverty trap*, each with a different essential ingredient: mental health traps, powerlessness traps, common property mismanagement traps, criminality traps, farm erosion and overuse traps, under-nutrition and illness traps, high-fertility traps, family child labor traps, illiteracy traps, and more.[8] Despite their differences, he calls all of these poverty conditions *traps* because they not only describe today's experience but also involve some dynamic which tends to guarantee persistence of the condition over time.

As with poverty, so with corruption. Studies at the level of nations have provided us with lists of things which, in general, help to lower overall rates of corruption.[9] These include freedom of speech, media with unfettered access to information, an independent judiciary, free and fair elections, a clear set of conflict of interest rules for public servants, an enforceable set of anti-corruption laws, and effective international cooperation on legal and judicial matters.[10]

From time to time new analyses, similarly conducted at the level of nations, will add more factors to the list of things deemed influential upon, or at least correlated to, overall levels of corruption. Such analyses add one more giant lever to the set already potentially available to policy makers. For example, one recent study tested the hypothesis that "the more a country is tied into international networks of exchange, communication, and organization, the lower its level of corruption is likely to be."[11] The authors of that study report that "the analysis of data from approximately 150 countries strongly confirms our expectation."[12] Whether the new lever (in this case, the extent to which a country is tied into international networks) could actually be shifted over time, and, if so, whether moving it would constitute an efficient operational method for addressing corruption, remains unclear. Nevertheless, another potentially useful macro-level relationship has been established.

Meanwhile, at lower levels, myriad different corruption problems of all shapes and sizes might exist. Some might involve corrupt administrations or political systems in particular cities or municipalities, rather than at the national level. Other problems might involve specific forms of corruption exercised by certain professions, such as protection and extortion rackets run by police, bribe-taking by tax officials for adjusting audit assessments downwards, or cartel-based bid-rigging in public construction projects. Even where corrupt networks extend high up the political chain and span multiple areas of government, they might – as in the case of Vladimiro Montesinos in Peru (President Fujimori's

Intelligence Chief) revolve around one orchestrating genius;[13] or they might have no such central node or point of vulnerability.

Just as Stephen Smith exhorts poverty researchers to open their minds and *listen to the poor,* anti-corruption researchers might be urged to *examine how corruption works,* paying particular attention to the dynamics that make individual patterns of corruption persist over time.[14] Just like the poverty researchers, corruption researchers should expect to discover countless different versions, many of them unexpected and unfamiliar. Then, as the structure and dynamics of the knots themselves begin to come into focus, a vast range of possible interventions quite naturally begin to emerge, tailored to the specific problems themselves. Very few of the specific solutions to specific corruption problems can be found on the standard lists of generic, macro-level prescriptions.

Narrowing the range

Even putting aside the two extremes – incident response at the lowest level, and macro-level prescriptions for general categories of problems at the highest level – the range of levels or sizes at which one might choose to define and address problems remains vast.

As a practical matter, early experiences in project-based problem-solving work, for most agencies, sit towards the extremes of the remaining, slightly narrowed, range. Figure 3.1 shows these as levels 2 and 4. At the high end, publicly visible problems grow to embarrassing proportions (e.g. port-running for US. Customs, or the juvenile homicide rate for Boston Police), and the need for a concerted and novel response becomes obvious to everyone. The organization or organizations responsible have little choice but to put their heads together and find a solution, because they would suffer considerable embarrassment if they did not. At the opposite end (level 2) lie rather small projects, tackled by a few energetic individuals acting on their own initiative, on their own time, and without any formal support from their agencies. These happen readily enough where staff are highly motivated and creative, and where the agency itself does not have to do anything other than tolerate their initiative.

Almost anything in between these two sizes (a vast range, which Figure 3.1 broadly captures as level 3, *medium,* or *in-between*) needs a *system* for supporting projects (because they are too large to be conducted by individuals without support), and a method for launching such projects as a part of ordinary operational practice rather than waiting for embarrassing failures to grow to crisis proportions. Of course, without any compelling crises, working in this domain seems optional. And if the agency lacks the managerial systems to organize and support such work, then the chances are that it will not get done. A great many institutions do seem to lack such apparatus, and therefore end up unable (or, at least, insufficiently motivated) to do any harm-control work that lies between levels 2 and 4. That does not necessarily mean that these institutions are unaware of, or are deliberately ignoring, the multitude of problems that do indeed sit in this middle range. It just means that they do not organize around them in the same deliberate way. Instead, they rely on existing programs and established processes, assuming or hoping that will take care of them all. The alternate form of organizational behavior – identifying and directly addressing specific harms – peeks out of the institutional woodwork only for problems which are inescapable (level 4), or for those within the reach of highly-motivated individuals (level 2).

If practitioners want to operate on specific harms as a matter of ordinary operational practice, they have to conquer all the territory at level 3, deciding at what level to define and address all the problems that fall awkwardly *in between*. The range available is still quite wide. Clearly one might find plenty of problems, above the level of individual incidents, which are still way too small to be important – where success, even if it came, would be insignificant. Similarly, one can find problems below the level of nations, and not yet in the realm of crises, that would still seem huge or overwhelming, and where prospects for progress within reasonable timeframes might seem slim indeed.

If practitioners bite off too much, chances are they will choke. Bite off too little, and nobody will much care. Obviously an agency can take bigger bites than an individual or a department; and a consortium of institutions can presumably take even bigger bites without being overwhelmed. So what makes one level better than another? Can we just pick *any* level, for *any* problem, and then simply fit the level of resources and number of partners to the size we chose? Or is there one *correct* level at which certain problems should best be tackled? Are some levels better than others?

Important clues about this can be gleaned from the successes and frustrations of agencies who have tried to operate this way. Some have picked little problems, and solved them quite quickly, only to have critics write these successes off as meaningless or anecdotal. Some have picked huge problems, and the resulting projects have ground to a halt, either because the problem definitions were so vague that there really was no practical way to proceed, or because the demands of the project far exceeded the capacity and authority of the team committed to it. But many projects, including examples already cited in this book, have succeeded handsomely, picking problems at once big enough to count and small enough to be feasible. By getting the size right – at least, right *enough* – these teams have been able to produce demonstrable and publicly valuable results, surprisingly quickly.

So, what rules did they follow? None at all, as far as we know, because none of their agencies *had* any rules for this. Looking back on what they did, however, and from a variety of experiences in helping others to act similarly, I would suggest the cognitive processes employed by these enterprising practitioners took into account three factors.

The natural size and shape of the harms themselves

Why did Customs put together a multi-port, bi-regional, multi-functional, but not-as-big-as-national team to tackle the port-running problem? Because that was the shape of the port-running problem itself. Why did Operation Ceasefire end up focusing on gang-related violence in Boston? Because the phenomenon of gang-related violence, in the domain of harms, appeared to be *one object*. Not two or more objects lumped together, and not half an object (where the other half would have to be tackled later, or by others), but *one natural whole*.

In both cases, these projects could have been rolled up or down to another level, or even defined in different dimensions. The port-running problem could have been subdivided further, in a variety of ways. Customs could have formed two different regional teams, or several port-based teams instead of one task force. They could have launched a separate project for each of the major smuggling organizations that used the port-running method, with different groups focused on disrupting each organization and free to do it anyway they chose.

The Boston Gun project could have gone further and tackled a much broader spectrum of crimes. But even with the focus narrowed to gangs, the project focused quite specifically on *violence*. Why not their drug-dealing too? And why not the rest of Massachusetts, or inclusion of other cities? In both of these cases practitioners seemed instinctively drawn to the level where the harm to be addressed:

- consists of a single, coherent object in the task environment;
- captures the whole of that one object;
- does not appear to be a collection of lower-level *unlike* objects.

The effect of focusing on a *single coherent object* is that the scrutiny and analysis can embrace all aspects of the harm, but aims in the end to produce just one successful intervention. *Capturing the whole* means that once the job is done, it does not have to be repeated, or done elsewhere, to cover other parts of the problem. As for the third criterion: if the harm in one's sights looks like a collection of lower-level, unlike objects, then it would probably be better to approach it with a *portfolio of unlike projects*, which could then produce suitably different interventions for each of the constituent parts.[15]

Boundaries of jurisdiction and access to tools

Clearly our celebrated practitioners were mindful of the limits of their jurisdictions in setting the scope for their projects. The District Attorney in San Francisco had no jurisdiction outside his area, and thus the project to intervene in the lives of prostitutes only dealt with prostitutes in one jurisdiction. Such limitations conflict, of course, with the notion of *capturing the whole of the object* (second bullet point, above). Prostitution is a global issue, and the interventions any one District Attorney might invent should likely have national relevance at least. Nevertheless, the District Attorney takes on *less than the whole*, because of jurisdictional limits.

Notice, however, that the DA enlists several other agencies as partners, thereby enlarging the toolkit available in the design of an intervention. It might have been possible, also, to enlist neighboring jurisdictions, in order to get a little closer to *capturing the whole*.

So *limitations of jurisdiction* tug at, or conflict with, the efficiencies that accompany dealing with *a coherent whole*. From a practical standpoint, nevertheless, they act as serious constraints and must obviously be considered. They might be overcome through extensive use of partnerships straddling all the jurisdictions relevant to any one problem. But that could make the whole project completely unwieldy and impossible to operate. Moreover, localized experiments driven by individuals committed to their own plans are more likely to demonstrate quickly and without enormous investment whether a particular idea works or not.

The limits of human capacity

Does the task definition pass the "crush test"? In setting the scope for harm reduction projects managers should always bear in mind ordinary human limitations. The "crush test" says, basically, "how would I feel, as an individual, or as part of a small team, if I were made responsible for solving this problem?" Would it feel overwhelming and hopeless? Or would it feel challenging, but possible? Can I imagine coming up with something that might make a real difference within a reasonable timeframe, even if I can't think of it now? Is this something I could wrap my head around? Which is more likely: that the possibility of success would make my job more rewarding and exciting; or would I give up in despair, duck for cover, or look for another job?

Give one team the responsibility for all aspects of water quality in the Great Lakes, and they will most likely feel overwhelmed. Break it down further, into some of the more critical constituent pieces, and all of a sudden it seems doable, even if the staff do not know the particular solution yet. Being asked to figure out "how to stop discharge from ballast tanks of ocean going vessels in the Great Lakes introducing exotic species (such as the zebra mussel)" seems both important, challenging, and possible.

Tensions

As practitioners grapple with these different considerations, they will inevitably discover tension between them. Limitations of jurisdiction and of capacity will always tend to roll the size of a project downward. Trying to take on the whole of a problem will tend to roll the size back up again. Finding a suitable level requires a compromise between these ideas, without allowing either one to completely dominate the other. If the various limitations (of jurisdiction, tools, and capacity) become the dominant consideration, then the problems end up finely sliced along the lines of existing control structures. Shying

away from the complexities of enlisting and engaging relevant partners, practitioners' sights can shift from the problem itself back to their
own familiar contributions and comfortable structures; and they end
up taking responsibility only for programmatic outputs, not for solving
the problem. Unfortunately, very few problems worth addressing conform nicely to jurisdictional and functional boundaries. (The pollution
problems of rivers, whose courses may run thousands of miles, provide
an obvious and potent example).[16] That is why so many of the successful projects already witnessed involve coalitions and partnerships that
straddle functional, agency, and jurisdictional lines. The right combination of players coalescing around the task can take responsibility for the
problem as a coherent whole, and have a hope of solving it. The important successes arise, it seems, when practitioners pay more regard to the
notion of *tackling a coherent whole,* and overcome at least some of
the restrictions of jurisdiction and capability by enlisting partners to the
cause.

From the perspective of Figure 2.2, this means *holding attention
below the line* (i.e. keeping attention focused on the outside world) for
longer. It requires practitioners to identify objects in the bottom left
hand cell in terms dependent only on the structure of the harm itself;
not in terms derived from structures or divisions of responsibility above
the line. Overall, we need practitioners to *respect the natural shape and
size of the problems themselves,* and to heed less the structures of the
existing control apparatus.

One caveat: The role of experimentation

I should mention one caveat to the principle of *capturing the whole,*
which in certain circumstances can have the effect of rendering limitations of jurisdiction somewhat less regrettable. This caveat relates to
the value of experimentation.

Many harms exist at a level which is broader or larger than the level
at which one would first want to try any novel treatment. As Granger
Morgan has pointed out,

Most risk-management systems seem committed to providing immediate
global solutions. We have not learned how to encourage different approaches
to the same problem so we can go slowly and select the one found to work
best, or so a broad approach can be adapted to local circumstances.[17]

There may be value in testing treatments on a smaller scale, or in testing a number of different interventions in different locations at the same time. Effective interventions, once identified, can then be applied wherever else they might apply.

Thus, even though the San Francisco DA's plan might have relevance for young women drawn into prostitution all across America, there is certainly some value in testing an intervention locally, rather than launching unproven programs at a wider scale. Similarly, the control of gang-violence in Boston might produce many lessons of value to other cities with violence problems of similar character.

It is important, though, to understand why this division-for-the-sake-of-experimentation does not undermine the notion of a dealing with a *coherent whole*. The reason is related to the fact that the life of a prostitute in San Francisco is not dependent upon or connected to the lives of prostitutes in other cities. Likewise, gang violence in Boston was not dependent on the dynamics or realities of life in other cities. In that sense, gang-violence in Boston was not a part of a larger problem, even though it might belong in a larger group of *similar* problems. Dealing with one problem, even if there are other copies or versions of it elsewhere, is not the same as dealing with part of a problem. Thus both of these problems addressed had some coherence and completeness, even though they were not unique.

At the end of the day, picking the right scale for a harm-reduction project is likely to remain an inherently subjective choice. For any particular harm, there are several different scales at which it might reasonably be tackled. Picking among them will necessarily involve some artful, intuitive, or even arbitrary choice. Nevertheless, from this discussion (and from watching many agencies' attempts to systematize this approach) I can suggest some clear pointers that help show when the level selected might lie *outside* the best range. Potential clues that the level selected might be *too low* include:

- the project is so small that, even if successful, the accomplishment would seem insignificant;
- the project has been defined so that it falls comfortably within the jurisdiction and functional capabilities of one unit;
- the scope of the project has been set below the level at which it requires recognition and support from the organization;

- there exists an easy or obvious adaptation or displacement of the harm, which would render success on this project, as currently defined, of little value. (In this case, officials might want to consider enlarging the scope in order to cover or mitigate any such displacements, making the overarching accomplishment more worthwhile.)

Potential clues that the level selected might be *too high* include:

- the *crush-test*: no-one in their right mind would want to be made responsible for tackling this;
- the object of attention is a collective term or broad category of harms, rather than one *knot* carefully identified at a lower level;
- the description of the problem is very short. Useful problem definitions usually consist of at least one or two sentences, not one or two words;
- the object of attention seems to be a collection of two or more unlike objects, dissimilar enough that each seems worthy of separate analysis and intervention;
- the project straddles many jurisdictions making collaboration unwieldy, and experimentation on a more localized level could proceed more quickly and easily, and without any loss of coherence or completeness in terms of the harm being addressed;
- relevant performance metrics seem elusive. This is often a symptom of the fact that the problem definition remains vague. Once a problem is defined more carefully, relevant metrics become more apparent. In fact, the ways in which one would know if the problem were reduced or eliminated are closely related to the data indicating the existence of the problem at the outset.

Getting the size right (or sufficiently right) is only half the job when it comes to defining problems. The other half, equally artful, is to understand the *shape* of the problem, and to pick the most appropriate dimensions in which to describe and address it.

Notes

1. For details of the composition and history of the IAC, see: [www.epa.gov/innovation/action.htm].
2. Author's italic emphasis added.

3. The most frequently used measure of corruption at national levels is Transparency International's Corruptions Perceptions Index, published annually by Transparency International, headquartered in Berlin. Available at: [www.transparency.org/policy_research/surveys_indices/cpi].

4. Jeffrey D. Sachs, *The End of Poverty: Economic Possibilities for Our Time* (New York: Penguin Books, 2005).

5. Ibid. p. 81.

6. Ibid. p. 79.

7. Stephen C. Smith, "Poverty Traps: Why the Poor Stay Poor," *World Ark* (Little Rock, Arkansas: Heifer International, July/August 2006), 8–15. p. 8.

8. Stephen C. Smith, *Ending Global Poverty: A Guide to What Works* (New York and Basingstoke, England: Palgrave Macmillan, 2005), pp. 12–17.

9. See, for instance, "*The TI Sourcebook 2000: Confronting Corruption: The Elements of a National Integrity System*" (Berlin & London, Transparency International, 2000). Available at: [www.transparency.org/publications/sourcebook]; Rick Stapenhurst & Sahr J. Kpundeh (eds.), *Curbing Corruption: Towards a Model for Building National Integrity*, EDI Development Series (Washington DC: Economic Development Institute of the World Bank, 1999).

10. Ibid. Chapter 4, pp. 35–37.

11. Wayne Sandholtz & Mark M. Gray, "International Integration and National Corruption," *Cambridge Journals,* International Organization, 57 (2003), 761–800.

12. Ibid. Abstract.

13. For an account of the methods used and corrupt network of influence established by Vladimiro Montesinos, Intelligence Chief for President Fujimori, see: "*Robust Web of Corruption: Peru's Intelligence Chief Vladimiro Montesino*s," John F. Kennedy School of Government, Harvard University, Case draft: November 4, 2003. For a briefer synopsis, see: "The Government is Missing: Fujimori and Montesinos vanished amidst strange stories of soothsayers," *The New Yorker* (March 5, 2001), 58–73.

14. Angela Gorta stresses the importance of breaking down or classifying different types of corrupt conduct as a prerequisite for development of effective controls. See: Angela Gorta, "Minimizing Corruption: Applying Lessons from the Crime Prevention Literature," *Crime, Law & Social Change,* 30 (1998), 67–87, (p. 73).

15. The practical process of choosing the right size and shape for a "problem" to be addressed might be regarded by some risk scholars as a part of *risk characterization*, which is recognized as a "complex and

controversial activity," the aim of which is ". . . to describe a potentially hazardous situation in as accurate, thorough, and decision-relevant a manner as possible." See: Paul C. Stern & Harvey V. Fineberg (eds.), *Understanding Risk: Informing Decisions in a Democratic Society*, National Research Council (Washington DC: National Academy Press, 1996), pp. x–xi, 2.

16. For a discussion of multi-jurisdiction institutional arrangements for the management of rivers, and the ways in which similar structures might be developed for flood control, see: J. Wessel, "Institutional Frameworks for Flood Management," *Physics and Chemistry of the Earth*, 20 (1995), 503–506.

17. M. Granger Morgan, "Choosing and Managing Technology-Induced Risk," *IEEE Spectrum*, 18 (December 1981), 53–60.

4 | *Defining problems: picking the dimensions*

The discipline of paying more attention to the harm itself, and less attention to existing control structures, counts in picking the dimensions as much as in choosing the size. One wants to find dimensions which properly reflect the essence of the harm itself, not those that reflect the essence of existing control structures.

There is a rather different but more familiar sense in which risks are understood to be *multi-dimensional*. That idea, already familiar within the risk literature, concerns the *consequences* of a harm, and the fact that one event might have several different types of consequence associated with it.[1] An occupational injury, for example, brings both economic costs (for the worker and for the company) and consequences in terms of health and suffering. The same is equally true for terrorist attacks and natural disasters, although the list of consequence categories for such major events is much longer. For corruption, harmful consequences can include loss of efficiency, misallocation of public resources, deliberate official neglect of public protections, damage to democracy through the production of public cynicism about politics, and even the possibility of leading to regime instability.[2] Certainly, in tackling harms or risks, one ought to be mindful of all the foreseeable consequences, especially where losses are experienced by multiple classes of victim and in different ways.

But the issue of how best to define a problem in the first place is quite different. This idea is not so much about the dimensionality of consequences, but about the shape of the problem itself, and the dimensions that best show how it is concentrated. To illustrate the distinction, consider one of OSHA's early problem-solving projects. In the Atlanta region of Georgia, OSHA identified *lacerations to hands and forearms* as a very high rate hazard on poultry production lines (where manual workers use sharp knives all day long, preparing and segmenting chickens for market). The OSHA team launched a project to analyze and remedy the related workplace practices in this particular class of

93

production facilities. Workplace accidents of this type certainly have consequences in multiple dimensions: pain and suffering; economic loss for the worker; interruption to production processes for the company; and the risk of spreading blood-borne infections to fellow workers. However, these categories of consequence are quite different from *the shape of the problem itself*, which is more about a concentration of causes. In this example, understanding the shape of the problem involves combining multiple delineators: the problem involves a specific class of injuries, specific parts of the body at risk, specific tools in use, specific work-practices as context, the presence or absence of relevant protections, and one narrow segment of the workforce. These delineators do not align much at all with the categories of consequence for accidents that happen in this setting.

In general, there is no reason to assume that the dimensionality of the causes is necessarily related to the dimensionality of the consequences. Moreover, in considering any one particular type of harm, practitioners have no choice over the dimensionality of the consequences; merely the obligation to consider them all. But in choosing how to define a problem, and therefore how best to organize around it, they have considerable discretion.

Harms do come in a multitude of different shapes. In introducing and formalizing the concept of *problem-oriented policing* for law enforcement, Herman Goldstein devoted considerable time and energy persuading the profession to use analytic methods beyond the traditional "hot-spot" analysis. Pin-maps, showing crime locations, had long decorated precinct commanders' office walls. Clusters of pins represented hot-spots, and hot-spots showed police where to pay special attention. With the advent of computers, the pin-maps morphed into analytic software packages for "spatial and temporal analysis of crime." The medium was different, and the analytic methods more sophisticated, but the basic idea was the same. Goldstein decried the narrowness of this one analytic approach.[3] He pointed out that not only did police tend to rely on one analytic approach; worse, they relied on one standard tactical response – termed *directed patrol* – whenever this analysis showed them a concentration. Directed patrol meant flooding the particular area at the relevant times with uniformed patrols in order to suppress the "crime problem."

Goldstein sought to jolt the profession into a broader analytic versatility, pointing out that crime problems come in many different shapes and sizes, and geography and time represent only two of at least a dozen relevant dimensions. Some crime problems revolve around repeat offenders, even though the crime locations are dispersed. Other crime problems result from competition or conflict between rival criminal enterprises in the same business. Some patterns involve particularly vulnerable classes of victims (e.g. single-manned convenience stores as targets for robberies), or repeat victims, or methods of attack, or specific behaviors (e.g. glue-sniffing in the schools), or specific commodities (e.g. OxyContin-related pharmacy break-ins), or features of architectural design that create opportunities for crime, and so on.

In urging poverty researchers to adopt *clinical economics*, Geoffrey Sachs' argument also suggests the need for a broader analytic versatility. He describes how traditional macro-level assumptions about the nature and causes of poverty provide only a bland and insufficiently differentiated understanding of poverty problems. If *poverty* is not one thing, but a collection of unlike objects, then immediately poverty analysts would have to ask "well then, what shape and what size might they be?" Only by having some idea about the possibilities would anyone know at what levels and in what dimensions to look, and what types of searches to perform in order to spot the constituent pieces of the overall problem.

Sachs suggests a host of possibly relevant dimensions. Extreme poverty problems, he says, might be spatially concentrated, and could be special to urban or rural regions. They could be related to demographic conditions of households, asset ownership and economic activities, demographic trends, environmental shocks, climate shocks, changes in infectious disease incidence, costs of doing business, limitations of the coverage of key infrastructures, trade policy frameworks, incentives for investment (domestic and international), budget structures, transportation conditions, agronomic conditions, ecosystem conditions and changes, animal diseases, plant pests and diseases, patterns of governance, the nature and extent of corruption, cultural barriers to economic development, discrimination against women and girls, interethnic tension or violence, national security and economic relations with the rest of the world, refugee movements, terrorism or cross-border warfare. Quite a list! And the purpose of such lists is not primarily academic, nor merely a demonstration of complexity in the world we inhabit. The purpose is practical and operational: to promote awareness of the many potential shapes that problems might take, and thereby increase the chance of them being recognized for what they are, rather than being mistaken for something else. Such recognition is a pre-cursor for effective action. As Sachs puts it, "The checklist is long... A differential diagnosis is the beginning, not the end, of the process. The next steps, of course, are to design programs and institutions to address the critical barriers to poverty reduction that are identified through the differential diagnosis."[4]

Environmental problems, similarly, come in a multitude of different shapes. Some are best defined in media-specific and familiar terms, such as repeat discharges from industrial facilities into air or surface waters in excess of permitted levels. Other problems might involve repeat offenders (particularly irresponsible facility management) even though the violations relate to different media. Some environmental problems relate more closely to watershed areas, or air basins, or other topographical features where contaminants accumulate. Some relate to endangered species, or ecosystems thrown out of balance. Some are industry specific (gypsum stacks as a by product of the phosphorus industry, heavy metals from the printing industry, pesticide run-off from farmland, etc.). Some have to do with domestic products sold in supermarkets, such as household bleach or lead batteries. Some are about other household threats, such as radon gas, lead paint, asbestos, or mold.

Similarly occupational problems can be defined by reference to specific bad actors, classes of victim, types of injury or illness, specific chemicals, types of machinery, patterns of non-compliance, geographic concentrations, seasonal concentrations, or industry specific issues. Corruption problems could be concentrated around one sector of government, or one set of economic incentives, or the operations of one criminal network, repeat offenders, corrupt methods, vulnerable enterprises (procurement, cash handling, valuable commodities), or specific opportunities for corruption.[5]

For almost any broad category of harms, one could quickly generate a list of at least ten wholly different dimensions by which different classes of problems might be defined. The problems that are easiest to see, of course, are the ones that reflect the existing structure of the control apparatus. Many organizations create analytic lenses, through which to view the world, that reflect their own structures. If a police agency has a precinct structure, it is perfectly natural to perform precinct-based crime analysis. If a tax agency organizes by region or by class of taxpayer (individual, small business, large business, international, etc.) then it will be perfectly natural for them to analyze non-compliance patterns in these dimensions. If a police agency does manage to spot a problem which is dispersed across precincts but concentrated in other ways (e.g. high levels of domestic violence incidents on particular days of the year), it is much less obvious to whom the concentration belongs... because the problem's own dimensionality does not align with their organizational structure. If a tax-agency spots a non-compliance issue which relates to one specific tax deduction, but has no regional concentration, then they would need something other than the regional structure to address it.

So then, how best should an agency organize itself for this kind of work? Should an environmental agency re-organize itself around ecosystems, or watershed areas, or around industry groups? Which form would put them in the best position with respect to the important problems of the day? The answer, somewhat disturbing at first, is that whatever form of organization one selects, it will be the wrong one most of the time.[6] If an agency organizes around ecosystems, one might predict that the next problem requiring attention would not be ecosystem-shaped; it would concern one industrial group, or an invasive species, or a drinking water problem. But if the agency organized by industry group, that would not help them deal effectively with radon in homes, or airborne deposition from other countries, or endangered species. If, for any particular category of harms, there really are at least ten different dimensions in which problems might be concentrated and defined, then choosing any one of them as a permanent basis for the organization would render the agency more effective in dealing with problems of that particular shape, and less effective at dealing with everything else. Worse, heavy reliance on particular dimensions might even blind the organization to the very existence of other types of problems, or tempt it (when it does see them) to smash them into conformity with its own structures, losing sight of the essence of the thing, and missing the chance to tackle it as a *coherent whole*.

Let me make two other practical observations about the selection of dimensions in which to describe a problem. First, this is an inherently messy business, involving artful choice and instinct as much as analysis and science. Goldstein, having listed numerous dimensions in which crime problems might be described, comments:

The typologies [of problems] that emerge are not mutually exclusive or even tidy. A problem defined primarily in terms of territory could often just as easily be defined in behavioral terms. It is not yet clear what significance, if any, there may be to the way in which problems are naturally defined.

Nor is it clear if, for purposes of analysis, one way of defining problems is preferable to another. It may be that none of this matters: that the primary concern ought to be to define the problem in terms that have meaning to both the community and the police.[7]

Clearly Goldstein, widely considered to be the founding father of *problem-oriented policing*, was unwilling to set rules or propose firm guidelines on this question. Nevertheless he recognized that the question "*how is a problem to be defined*," which others might consider purely philosophical, has to be settled in each case as a practical matter with operational consequences. And, in moving towards some answer, he acknowledges that problems themselves have a *natural* dimension or dimensions; that there is seldom only one possible choice; and that the choice may involve some accommodation to modes of description that will help to engage relevant actors.

Second, one's view about how best to define a problem may well change over time. Scrutiny leads to better understanding, and reveals that the problem *is not what you thought it was* at the outset.[8] This was palpably true for the Boston gun control project. The initial focus was guns, not gangs; and the initial hypothesis was that the homicide problem was strongly connected to patterns of gun supply from southern states. That hypothesis, and several more in turn, were all rejected before the real pattern was uncovered, and the boundaries of the resulting project established.

Respecting the natural shape and size of harms themselves does not sit easily with traditional forms of organization. Most institutions in the harm-control business have organizational structures established many years ago. The basis for those structures might be functional, or process-based; or they might employ the dimensions which best captured the priority problems during the time the organization was formed. In order to tackle the full range of knots effectively, institutions need a much higher level of analytic versatility and organizational fluidity.[9] They also need to understand the ways in which the forms of analysis conducted affect organizational responses. Harm-reduction work, in practical terms, ought not to be a hopeless mess. So practitioners need some clarity about what they want from analysis, and from their organizations, in order to make the undoing of knots a routine and sustainable practice over time; and to prevent this work from producing intolerable levels of uncertainty and stress.

Notes

1. This version of multiple dimensionality of risk is discussed in: Baruch Fischhoff, Chris Hope & Stephen R. Watson, "Defining Risk," *Policy Sciences*, 17 (1984), 123–139; Paul C. Stern & Harvey V. Fineberg (eds.), *Understanding Risk: Informing Decisions in a Democratic Society*, National Research Council (Washington DC: National Academy Press, 1996), pp. 61–66.
2. Robert Klitgaard, *Controlling Corruption* (Berkeley, California: University of California Press, 1988), p. 46.
3. Herman Goldstein, *Problem-Oriented Policing* (New York: McGraw-Hill Publishing Company, 1990), pp. 34–35, 66–68.
4. Jeffrey D. Sachs, *The End of Poverty: Economic Possibilities for Our Time* (New York: Penguin Books, 2005), p. 88.
5. The literature on control of corruption has not demonstrated much versatility with respect to the use of different dimensions in the analysis of specific corruption problems. The most commonly used delineators are by type of *agency* (e.g. police, taxation, customs administration, etc.), with some attention to specific *functions* (e.g. procurement operations, humanitarian relief, post-conflict reconstruction). For analysis based on varieties of *modus operandi* see: Klitgaard, *Controlling Corruption*, p. 50. For a breakdown by *modus operandi* within the context of procurement, see: Robert Klitgaard, Ronald Maclean-Abaroa & H. Lindsey Parris, *Corrupt Cities: A Practical Guide to Cure and Prevention* (Washington DC: World Bank Institute, 2000), pp. 120–122.
6. Bridget Hutter and Michael Power (eds.), *Organizational Encounters with Risk* (Cambridge: Cambridge University Press, 2005), pp. 25–30.
7. Goldstein, *Problem-Oriented Policing*, p. 68.
8. This echoes concerns expressed by others that *risk characterization* involves "careful diagnosis of the decision situation to arrive at preliminary judgments and openness to reconsider those judgments as the process moves along." Stern & Fineberg (eds.), *Understanding Risk*, p. 2.
9. Susan Gates stresses the necessity of fluid organizational forms as the composition of the work changes over time, and provides a critique of the Volcker Commission's recommendations for a one-time reorganization of government agencies into "mission-driven" departments. Susan M. Gates, "Organizing for Reorganizing," in Robert Klitgaard & Paul Light (eds.), *High-Performance Government: Structures, Leadership, Incentives* (Santa Monica, California: Rand Corporation, 2005), pp. 139–159.

5 | *Patterns of thought and action*

I n the harm-reduction business, one source of stress for practitioners is ambiguity. *Something* should be done, because some set of
harms is not sufficiently controlled. *Somebody* should act, and
yet there is no system or protocol that specifies whose job it is, nor
how much discretion they have, nor what range of methods anyone is
authorized to consider.

A very different form of stress results when practitioners find themselves unambiguously accountable for results that matter. In the harm-
reduction business, that most often involves accountability for *harms
reduced*. People responsible and accountable for reducing harms are
motivated to action or driven to despair depending, of course, on
whether they have any real possibility of success. Rigidity in the organization, lack of support from necessary partners, and lack of power
to reallocate resources or adopt new techniques can minimize the
prospects for success of any kind.

Executives, temporarily removed from the constraints of their own
organizations, can explore together how they would *like* to behave in
response to unambiguous pressure for results, if only it were possible.
It doesn't take long in an executive classroom setting for practitioners to work out together how they think their organizations *ought* to
approach a harm-reduction task. Once that discussion is done, the serious work for them then is to figure out what it would take to make
their respective institutions adopt those rather-easy-to-specify patterns
of thought and action as a core competence. To establish the basic
necessary behaviors, I ask executive classes to consider the following
teaching case, which is a very straightforward hypothetical scenario
involving the reduction of highway fatalities. Here is the challenge
they are given:

Imagine that as of next October, you are appointed Commissioner of a State
Highway Patrol department. (I pick an American state in which none of the

participants work). Please accept the following basic facts of this (hypothetical) assignment:

- *Political commitment to harm-reduction:* shortly after your appointment as commissioner, the state elects a new Governor. The new Governor comes from the private sector, and is known to be committed to management by objectives (MBO). Given her track record, it is clear that anyone who fails to deliver important results will not last long in her administration.
- *Specific goal established:* At the end of December (i.e. only a few months into your tenure as commissioner), the Governor selects five strategic priorities, and intends to announce publicly the goals that her administration is embracing with respect to each one. One of the strategic priorities concerns what she describes as "an unacceptably high rate of highway fatalities in the state." On December 29 she asks you to indicate what reduction in the death rate you believe you can achieve the following year. Caught unawares, you pluck a number out of the air, and offer 15 percent. The Governor subsequently announces in a televised speech that you, the new commissioner, have committed to a 15 percent reduction.
- *Background statistics:* This year, 960 people died as the result of accidents on the state's roads. Per head of population, the state ranks 44th out of the 50 states.
- *Overlapping jurisdictions:* The state consists mainly of rural farm country, but a few major towns have their own municipal police departments. Issues such as highway design and maintenance, driver licensing, insurance regulation, and emergency health services all come under different departments at the state level.
- *Organizational resources & structure:* Your Highway Patrol department has an authorized staffing level of 500 officers, 90 percent of whom work shifts, on patrol. The remaining 50 officers staff a small number of specialist units including a detective bureau, media relations office, and schools liaison unit. Civilian personnel handle support functions such as finance, information technology, and human resource management.

The ensuing discussion revolves around the approach our newly appointed commissioner should take to this (hypothetical) challenge. Laying out this scenario only takes a few moments, and normally leads to some moaning and groaning in the classroom. Participants put forth all the normal reasons executives regard this form of accountability as fundamentally unreasonable: "It is an arbitrary goal." "We can't do this by ourselves." "We are not God." "We can't control the weather." "There will always be careless drivers." "We should not be held accountable for what the other departments do." "This might not be our problem at all; it could be the quality of paramedic services, not policing."

Others seek to dull the sharpness of the goal in some way: "Couldn't we set a goal over five years, rather than one?" "Shouldn't we use more sophisticated measures that adjust for changing demographics?" "Shouldn't we compare changes in our state with changes in other states, rather than using absolute numbers?"

But a few participants of the executive program point out to their colleagues that this type of accountability, however uncomfortable, is becoming more common these days. Some of them have already had to set "stretch goals" for their own organizations, and live up to them.[1] In the United States, the Government Performance and Results Act (GPRA, 1993) has produced considerable pressure for federal agencies to be more deliberate and outcome-oriented in setting goals, and more accountable for achieving them. At the state level, performance based budget statutes (PBB) have pushed in the same direction, even making budgets contingent on results. Under various versions of *CitiStat* programs in American and British cities, agency heads find themselves obliged to stand at a public podium in front of their political superiors and give their analysis of problems or patterns observed, and the cures they propose.[2] These management models, many of which trace their roots back to New York City police department's *Compstat* program, involve "a confrontational, accountability-holding process."[3] In other parts of the world aspects of the *New Public Management* philosophy, or equivalent reforms, have emphasized results-based management. Consequently, such pressures are quite familiar to the participants of executive education programs, whatever country they come from, even if they still regard these pressures as fundamentally unreasonable.

In the classroom setting we quickly move beyond these complaints. For the purposes of the exercise, they must accept the obligation to deliver on this goal, understanding that their (hypothetical) job depends on it, and that there will be no fudging the numbers. The reductions must be real, and the economic conditions in the state make any increase in budget or personnel out of the question. So the issue, therefore, is what to do with the resources they already have; not what they would *add* if they were afforded the luxury of additional appropriations. I ask the participants to imagine they have a weekend to think about it, plus one extra day, because January 1 is a public holiday. Sitting at the commissioner's desk early in the morning on January 2, even before their senior staff arrive for work, what is on their mind? What ideas do they have? How might they proceed? I also tell them seven people died already on the highways, on January 1, just to press home the urgency of the situation.

The specific harm selected for this exercise actually does not matter much. I could equally well have made them responsible for reducing deaths from accidents in commercial shipping, or asthma rates in New York City, or wetlands loss in Florida, or the extent of beach-closures (measured in beach-mile-days per year) due to contaminated coastal waters in California. Any of these would serve reasonably well to elicit the basic patterns of thought and action that go with this type of task.

The highway fatalities example has a number of properties that make it work relatively well in the classroom. First, it is clearly accessible to people from all walks of life, as they all drive or ride and therefore have plenty of ideas about what makes roads dangerous and what might make them safer. Second, the problem does not appear on its face to be the preserve of highly specialized technical experts (which is not true for the beach closures or asthma problems), so lack of expertise is not available to them as an excuse for ducking the challenge. Third, the outcome metric – the number of road accident fatalities – is rather stark and unambiguous. Allowing the use of more sophisticated measures (such as fatality rates per head of population, or per highway-mile-driven), or extending the metrics to include subjective classifications (e.g. "deaths and serious injuries"), might complicate or obfuscate the issue. Focusing on fatalities, where accident victims are either dead or alive, leaves no room for definitional ambiguity or data manipulation. Fourth, deaths on highways are a relatively quick-acting harm (contrasted, for example, with cancer risks or damage to ecosystems), making prospects for statistically significant improvements within one year quite feasible.

These properties virtually eliminate the possibility of manipulating the performance *account*, and that puts all the emphasis on the performance itself. It does not make the task (reducing the death rate by 15 percent any easier; it just makes it easier to *define* the task and to monitor success or failure. So this example leaves no wiggle room between the *performance* and the *performance account*. Never mind any subtleties of reporting practice . . . the new commissioner simply must *save lives*. The only question is how to do that.

There is never any shortage of ideas from a group of executives on how to proceed. One thing that has surprised me from using this hypothetical exercise in different countries and over several years, is how often someone in the group will declare immediately what the problem is, and what should be done about it. "Speeding is the problem. Reduce the speed limit." "Teenagers are the problem. Raise the driving age." One drawback of using such an accessible example is the possibility that some participants might hold entrenched beliefs about road safety in their own countries, and they naturally assume the same conditions must apply elsewhere. Any such declarations tend to be quickly made, and equally quickly regretted as the rest of the class impresses on them the fact that they have no idea what the problems might be until they have done some analysis.

The ideas that pour forth predictably fall into three main categories. One involves a search for relevant knowledge. Conduct focus groups among the patrol officers. If this state is ranked 44th, who is 1st, and how did they get there? Reach out to the states ranked 1 through 5 at the top of the league table. What issues have other rural states found that need to be addressed? Go to the literature, and find out what other countries have done. (A literature search on this would reveal some extraordinary successes elsewhere. For example, the territory of Victoria, Australia, has driven their highway fatality rate down from roughly 1000 per year in the early 1970s to just 276 in 2006.)[4]

A second category of suggestions concerns potential partners. If highway and junction design is an issue, then we'll need the highway engineering department. If the issues include driver competence, then we'll need to review driver training programs with the schools. If we find problems with paramedic services, emergency rooms or trauma units then we'll need to work with the department of public health. If accidents are clustered by weather conditions, then we'll need to work out advance warning systems with the meteorological office. Non-governmental bodies might have a role to play too, depending on the nature of the issues: the media, Mothers against Drunk Driving, insurance companies, vehicle manufacturers, parent-teacher associations, and so on.

But the biggest group of suggestions, regardless of the participants' professional backgrounds, reveals a sudden and powerful hunger for analysis. They cannot wait, even early in the (hypothetical) morning of January 2, to get their hands on the accident data and start pulling it apart. More than half the executives in the class, typically, point to this as the most urgent and pressing need, and the obvious first step. They want to use data to identify the principal causes or patterns of accidents. Some of them even point out that there is no point picking your partners until you have discovered through the analytic process what the problems are. Only then would you know which partnerships might count.

As this conversation progresses it becomes apparent to everyone that the status of analysis (and therefore of analysts) just shot through the roof. Apparently all it takes to produce that effect is an unambiguous focus on a risk-reduction imperative. Practitioners seem to know, instinctively, that any big broad problem, like "highway fatalities," has *parts*; and they need analysis right at the outset to help them discover what they are.[5] They will also need analysis later for other purposes, such as exploring the structure of any specific risk-concentrations that come to light, and for evaluating the effects of interventions. But the first role of analysis, right up front, involves decomposition of the overall task into its important and actionable pieces; in other words, to *find the knots*.

As a practical matter, the class discussion dwells for a while on what the participants hope analysis will do for them at this stage, and how the commissioner might best obtain the analytic insights he or she needs. Given the urgency of the project, the class understands that contracting with a local university to study the problem (which might take months or years) is not really an option. They need research for sure, but of an operational rather than an academic kind. They might not have time nor the capability within the department to produce sophisticated or definitive analyses. But they do need to use the data intelligently as the basis for operational decision making, and they need to start work on it *immediately*.

At this point in the discussion I offer the class – now thoroughly engaged in the challenge the new commissioner faces – some help. I tell them that the only analyst to be found at headquarters on the morning of January 2nd is a new recruit, 26 years old, named Nigel.[6] This is Nigel's first day on the job, and – because the head of the office of statistics is away on vacation – he finds himself summoned to the commissioner's office first thing in the morning. I tell the class that Nigel, despite his lack of knowledge or experience in highway safety issues, is nevertheless an analytic whiz-kid. He knows all about statistical inference and hypothesis testing, knows how to do regression analysis, how to manipulate and merge databases, and can operate a Geographic Information System if that were necessary. Nigel also knows how to use charts and graphs to present technical information to not-so-technical audiences. And he knows technology inside out – not just how to use computers, but how to take them apart and put them back together again. In other words, this really is the commissioner's lucky day: our (hypothetical) Nigel represents *analytic versatility* combined with *a complete absence of prior assumptions*. The best of all possible worlds!

According to the hypothetical, Nigel quickly locates the relevant data file covering all 960 fatalities. It takes the form of an Excel spreadsheet, with one row for each fatal accident, and seventy-six columns representing the seventy-six questions (or fields) on a standard fatal accident report. These fields are mostly multi-choice or numerical answers, and they cover the bulk of relevant variables: weather conditions, road condition, category of road, junction type, ages of drivers and passengers, seat-belts in use or not, airbags deployed or not, maneuver being undertaken, estimated speed of vehicles, indications of drunkenness or drug use, make/model/year/color of each vehicle involved, latitude and longitude, and so on. Once again, for teaching purposes, this is a rather plain and straightforward example. For the sake of getting quickly to the actual process of analysis, we bypass many of the normal difficulties associated with accessing relevant data. We are assuming (contrary to many of the participants' normal professional experience) that (a) the relevant data is readily available internally; (b) that the data is accurate and complete, with no substantial quality issues; (c) that the data is all in one place and in a common format (i.e. no data integration is needed), and (d) the data resides on a platform that makes it easy to manipulate.

Despite these simplifying and several luxuries, the question for the commissioner – "what exactly do you want Nigel to do for you?" – draws a wide range of answers. Anyone who had their own pet hypothesis about the causes of accidents wants that hypothesis tested. Instructions to Nigel, therefore, include an extensive list of specific hypotheses to test. Is it about drink? Is it about the youngsters driving at night? Is it speed that kills? Is the death rate correlated with distance from emergency rooms? Cell phones? Tiredness? Smaller vehicles being squashed by larger ones? Are there clusters of accidents at specific road junctions?

We might label this first category of requests the *testing of hunches*. The usefulness of this type of analysis depends a great deal on where the hunches came from, and therefore how likely they are to represent important truths. I ask the class to guess – assuming they could produce twenty-five different hunches for Nigel to test – what they would expect the analytic hit rate (in terms of actionable findings per analysis conducted) to be in practice. Understanding that the majority of the hypotheses tested, for sure, would turn out "not present," or perhaps "not a significant concentration," they guess the hit rate might be as high as 10 percent, but probably lower than that. In other words, this is very much a hit and miss business, and mostly *miss*. The analytic task at this stage does not feel at all like the routine application of familiar devices, with predictable operational consequences. It feels more like a search for some hidden nugget, demanding creativity and persistence. The commissioner should not be the least bit surprised, or discouraged, if the first fifteen analytic reports show absolutely nothing of interest. And if that should happen, the commissioner ought not to get upset with Nigel. Both of them need to know this is the nature of the business.

Even though the testing of hunches is the most obvious type of analytic request, it is not the only kind. There are two other modes for tasking the analyst, which reflect a broader appreciation of the analytic possibilities and a little less reliance on one's own prior assumptions. One of these involves specifying a type of analysis, or analytic approach, without specifying in advance which dimensions or variables might count. For example, participants will often want to know *which particular factor appears most often* within the fatal accident data. Or, slightly more complex, *what combination of two or three variables accounts for the bulk of fatalities*. Or, assuming the availability of data for non-fatal accidents, *which factors make the difference between fatal and non-fatal crashes?* If comparable data is available from other states, then *which factors distinguish our accident mix from others?*

The third mode for tasking the analyst reflects a higher degree of respect for the analyst, and an awareness of the commissioner's own lack of technical imagination. It is usually the older and wiser participants in class who say "just tell Nigel your problem. Let him figure out what to do. He's the analyst after all." Putting that kind of trust in a 26-year-old, first day on the job, when the commissioner's job depends on a successful outcome, seems a little perilous to others in the class. But modesty regarding one's own analytic imagination goes a long way. Any well-trained analyst, once they've understood the task at hand, ought to be able to generate a range of analytical approaches and ways of presenting the findings that non-technical managers and executives could never have imagined. A seasoned analyst, knowing what does and doesn't count in terms of operational consequences, will also do a lot of filtering of the results, presenting to operational managers only those findings that look in some way promising. Such filtering spares the boss from the tedium of the 90 percent or more anticipated null returns, which otherwise involve an endless string of "I don't see anything useful here. Sorry, boss."

To trust the analyst to do this filtering, or to do it oneself, requires clarity about one thing: what type of finding are we looking for at this point in the harm-reduction task? What properties make one analytic finding *promising* or *operationally significant*; and another completely useless? I start drawing various charts and graphs on the blackboard (yes, Harvard still has blackboards), and ask the class which ones they, as commissioner, would like. If one of the hunches tested was that lots of people die in the morning and evening rush hours . . . then we would have the analyst chop the day into half hour intervals and produce a bar-chart, showing what times of day mattered most. We expected to see two humps representing the morning and evening rush hours, but actually this chart comes back from the analyst mostly *flat*, and with an accompanying explanation that there are indeed lots of accidents in the rush hour, but they are relatively slow speed thanks to the congestion, and therefore not, on the whole, fatal. Yes, the participants in the exercise say, this one is somewhat useful, but only in dispelling an assumption and thereby showing how *not* to proceed. What about using other dimensions on the X axis . . . months of the year (to make any seasonal effects visible), age of the drivers, ratio of the weights of vehicles involved in a collision; or pie charts showing different maneuvers or road types?

The graphs the participants say they would like to see most of all are the ones with pronounced *humps* or *lumps*, not the flatter ones. The flat ones suggest, if anything, that we are dealing – at least by this dimension or method of analysis – with a uniform, bland, undifferentiated reality. The executive participants know instinctively that is not likely to be true, and therefore they reject *those dimensions* as *not promising*. The dimensions (or combinations of dimensions) that count are the ones that produce pronounced unevenness, where the lumps or humps represent tight concentrations of risk. The analytic search, at this early stage, involves a *search for maximum lumpiness*. The more pronounced the lumps, the stronger the significance of the finding, and the tighter the resulting operational focus. The lumps and bumps, and the choice of dimensions that produced them, provide a way to target resources and attention efficiently. And by revealing the dimensionality of a specific harm, they also provide clues about the underlying nature of the thing, and what might be done to unravel it. These are the analytic insights that count: those that identify specific knots, reveal their natural shape and size, and thereby provide some view to action.

Discovering the *parts*, of course, is not the same as dealing with them. Analysis helps reveal the parts. Now the organization must tackle them.

In order to shift the conversation from patterns of thought to patterns of action, the next stage of the exercise reveals what our hypothetical analyst, Nigel, discovers. During the first two weeks of January (during which time another seventy people die on the state's highways) Nigel conducts thirty different analyses, testing everyone's standard hunches and slicing and dicing the accident data in every conceivable way. Along the way, he informs his search through bibliographic searches and inquiries of other states. In the end twenty-six of the resulting analytic reports showed nothing at all of interest: "null returns." The remaining four, however, showed four specific concentrations, all defined in quite different dimensions, and none of which had been properly understood before.

The next stage of the exercise involves teasing out the managerial and organizational challenges involved in dealing with the problems identified through analytic decomposition. I describe for the participants four problems (entirely hypothetical) which have no obvious functional or geographic home within the existing organizational structure. Discovering problems that do not fit sharpens the dilemmas involved in delegating responsibility. I tell them that these four accounted for just over half of the prior year's 960 fatalities. The four problems, in brief, are as follows:

Problem (a): A summertime slippery road condition. A long hot dry spell allows dust, pollen and chaff to accumulate on the roads. A slight sprinkling of rain (not enough to wash the accumulated layer away) mixes with the dust to produce a slick oil-like surface, and motorists are mostly unaware of any danger. This condition (which New Zealanders call "summer ice") arises on no more than about five or six days per year on average, but frequently produces multi-vehicle pile-ups on fast interstate highways.

Problem (b): Non-compliance with stop signs at rural intersections. The state has many rural roads, out in farm country, which are long and straight. Traffic is sparse, and people drive fast. Crossroads are governed by STOP signs, which require drivers to slow down from 80mph to zero, and then speed up again. It has become fashionable among younger drivers to ignore the STOP signs altogether, and drive straight across at speed. Most of the time there is no conflicting traffic, and if there is one can usually see it from miles away across the fields. Collisions occur when hedge-rows or crops conceal contrary traffic, and when they do occur they often produce multiple fatalities due to the speeds involved and the fact that these accidents occur in remote areas far from help or medical care.

Problem (c): High-schoolers, driving parents' cars late at night. When a group of high-school students needs to get from one party to another the question arises "who has a car available?" Even kids who are normally responsible face severe peer pressure to borrow their parents' car. If the car is in the driveway, parents are asleep, and the keys accessible, "why not, they'll never know." The result is inexperienced drivers, driving big powerful cars packed with excited school friends, and plenty of distractions. They kill themselves, or others. Most of these accidents occur between 11pm and 3.00am.

Problem (d): Kids under 5, driven by their mothers, not strapped in correctly. Accidents in this category involve lack of proper child restraints: no car seats, wrong type of car seats, car seats placed the wrong way around or in the front seat, and seats not properly anchored. In some cases, the kids are riding in the back of the truck with the hay-bale and the dog, not strapped in at all.

Noting that all these hypothetical problems are defined in different terms, some students think I have been deliberately awkward in constructing them. But when one considers the vast range of dimensions in which road-safety problems *could* be clustered and described, then the chances that two or more, from any set of four, would be expressed in the same dimensions are actually fairly small. This awkwardness, though, is one predictable result of a genuine analytic versatility. If the organization were accustomed to performing only one type of analysis (e.g. spatial analysis), then it would only be able to spot spatial concentrations. All others would remain invisible under that particular lens, and hence all the problems the department confronted would be expressed in the same form, and might even get the same treatment. A broader analytic versatility increases the range of problems one can find, and improves the chances they will be properly understood and described; but it does create very considerable organizational awkwardness as a result, presenting a basket of completely dissimilar objects.

The notion that any one broad harm, when carefully analyzed, would yield four major components all of different dimensions has precedent in real life. In 1987 the Clean Water Act authorized the US Environmental Protection Agency to set up a new project to address water quality issues in the North American Great Lakes system. Jurisdictional complexities had hampered previous efforts, as the shores of the Great Lakes span eight different US states as well as the province of Ontario, Canada. Under the new project, the EPA was authorized to play a coordinating role and invite participation from several state, federal and international agencies. The first job, of course, was for scientists and analysts to figure out what were the important problems to address. That took several years of scientific research, enhanced monitoring and analysis. Ultimately they chose four major issues for operational attention, no two of which were expressed in the same dimensions.[7]

The first involved establishing Lake Superior as a *zero discharge area*, which meant that no persistent toxic chemicals could be discharged into the lake at all. Lake Superior presented particular vulnerability to persistent bio-accumulative compounds because of an extremely slow flush rate. Any one molecule of water would remain within the confines of the lake, on average, for about 200 years.

The second issue involved not one *lake*, but one *industry* – the automobile manufacturing industry. At the time, 61 percent of US car-manufacturing occurred within the eight states bordering the lakes, and project officials engaged the industry in collaborative pollution prevention programs aimed at reducing contaminants discharged from production facilities.

The third issue involved neither one lake, nor one industry, but one specific form of pollution: urban non-point-source storm-water runoff from cities and towns.

The fourth focused on aspects of public awareness and attitudes towards protection of the Great Lakes system. Project staff set up symposia to educate American and Canadian citizens about the relationship between pollution prevention and economic prosperity in the region.

A number of features make the Great Lakes project considerably more awkward than the highway fatality example. A great many more jurisdictions were involved, making the issues of inter-agency collaboration more complex. Also, the dimensions of the *consequences* of the harms were different, as well as the dimensions in which the four priority issues were defined. In the highway safety exercise, all the consequences of the four problems are measured in the same units (accidental deaths), even though the four problems are quite different. One feature of environmental problems is the diversity of the dimensionality of their consequences, and thus greater diversity in applicable outcome measures.

Despite its comparative simplicity, the highway example still serves perfectly well in illustrating the range of options for dividing and allocating the work. I normally present Nigel's analytical findings *before* asking the class to list possible approaches to delegation. That way, they at least have the option of fashioning their response according to the (already available) decomposition of the problem. But there are quite plausible ways of dividing the task and allocating responsibilities without any reference to the analysis whatsoever.

It is surprising to me just how seldom, even in a class of experienced and senior agency executives, anyone says at this point "oh, the way we do that kind of work in my agency is as follows...," and proceeds to describe a well established protocol or institutional framework. Most institutions do not seem to have established systems for managing such work, and hence the sense one gets during this classroom exercise is that participants are making it up. Making it up, given the chance, and freedom from existing organizational constraints, turns out to be not particularly difficult for them. They find it relatively easy to list a set of plausible options, and they quite readily agree (subject only to minor variations) which one they think would work best in practice.

Plausible approaches to the problem of delegation include the following:

Option 1: Delegate the task according to the agency's existing geographic divisions. If the commissioner needs a 15 percent reduction overall, then all they need is for each geographic division to reduce its own share by 15 percent. Different regions might even compete with each other to see which could achieve the greatest reduction.

Option 2: Delegate the task according to the agency's existing functional divisions. The commissioner could require the director of each functional unit (e.g. patrol division, detective bureau, juvenile liaison unit, etc.) to revise their own targeting plans to take account of the new focus. Each functional director might further be required to submit reports explaining what adjustments they propose, and how these will contribute to fatality reduction.

Option 3: Delegate the entire task to the apparently-most-relevant function. This puts responsibility for the entire project unambiguously in the hands of one manager – the one who directs the functional area deemed closest to the problem.

Option 4: Disseminate the analytic findings broadly throughout the agency, and throughout other government agencies, and ask each unit to focus their own efforts accordingly. This *informs* rather than *controls* lower level management, and leaves them free to apply their discretion and creativity in re-orienting their own plans to this common objective.

Option 5a: Establish a new task force, with representatives from all relevant functions, to focus on the fatality reduction task. This means creating a new organizational entity, on either a temporary or permanent basis, drawing a range of staff together around the task.

Option 5b: Establish four task forces, one for each of the four problems identified through analysis. This follows the same basic approach as option 5a above, but recognizes that the diversity of the component problems might make different forms of expertise relevant. Dissimilar problems require dissimilar task force composition. So this job needs four groups, not one.

Option 6: Contract the work out to consultants!

Choosing among the options: Option 6 seems most appealing to the executives who are most pessimistic about their own staff's capacity for this kind of work. Perhaps for an isolated project, this might be a serious option. But it cannot remain a serious option in the long term if the organization plans to make this kind of work routine, and to master the relevant patterns of behavior.

Options 1 through 4 all have the advantage of utilizing existing structures, rather than creating anything new, but the disadvantages of each are readily apparent.

Dividing the task geographically (Option 1) has several appeals. It releases the commissioner, and all headquarters staff, from the obligation to think very much about the problem. They simply chop the task up, and pass the responsibility down one level. This would result in the situation where each of the regional commanders now finds themselves in exactly the same position that the commissioner had been in. The problem is now theirs. Such delegation might not be so bad if the important subcomponents of the problem sat nicely within one region or another – for example, if the Stop-Sign violations all occurred within one region. Tackling such a case through the regional structure seems appropriate. But where the problems straddle regions, or span the entire state, no one regional commander would be in a position to tackle the problem as a coherent whole. They would only own a fragment. The most efficient way of tackling a problem is to address it *once*, at the level which matches the natural size and shape of the problem itself.

Nevertheless, appreciating the value of experimentation, and the potential motivating force of competition, one might still be drawn to dividing the task geographically. Why not encourage several different approaches to develop, and see which one works best? Rapid experimentation and the engagement of many minds might find effective solutions quicker. Maybe so. But this *divide and delegate* method has its own natural limits. These limits become more apparent if we push the delegation further and further down, *ad absurdum*. If it was appropriate for head office to delegate the task, regardless of the size or shape of the constituent problems that analysis has revealed, then why should the regional commanders not push the work down one more level, to the precincts? All the regional commanders need is for each precinct to achieve a 15 percent reduction. And why, then, might the precinct commanders not push it down to the beat officers? If every beat officer across the entire state achieved a 15 percent reduction for their beat, then the commissioner would have achieved the goal!

Pushed to this extreme, the fine-grained delegation begins to look ridiculous. The task has been pushed down to a level where it exceeds the capacity of the officers to address it. Furthermore, any semblance of *respect for the natural shape and size of the harm itself* has been lost.

The foolishness of delegating too far becomes even more apparent if we switch to a different type of harm. Suppose the job were to prevent nuclear terrorism in London. Following this particular style of delegation, the Metropolitan Police Commissioner could chop up the task and hand it down one level ... requiring divisional commanders to prevent any nuclear terrorist assaults within their divisions. And so on, all the way down to the beat level. All Londoners would need is for each beat officer to exercise vigilance sufficient to prevent such an event on their beat, and they would all be safe from this threat.

But something about the nature of terrorism prevention makes this obviously foolish. Vigilance and intelligence gathering by beat officers might indeed be a vital component of an anti-terrorist strategy; but none of us would expect anti-terrorist strategy to be *conceived and orchestrated* at the beat level. Given the nature of the problem, the *locus of control* belongs at a higher level. We would expect counter-terrorist operations to involve broadly connected national and international intelligence systems, capable of tracking and countering the activities of international terrorist organizations and movements. We would expect control strategies to be orchestrated at the same level at which terrorism itself is orchestrated.[8]

Similarly, in dealing with the environmental problems of the Great Lakes, we might well value experimentation, yet one would not expect local field offices within state environmental agencies to devise or administer a coherent plan for the system as a whole, even though they would certainly play their own roles within such a plan. Tackling the problems of the Great Lakes requires a coalition roughly resembling the shape and size of the Lakes system itself, embracing all relevant jurisdictions, and conceiving strategies based on this higher-level perspective.

Dividing the task functionally (Option 2) is also appealingly quick and easy. It pushes the cognitive work down from the top levels of the organization, and does not require creativity in shaping new organizational tasks and structures. In fact, the commissioner could use this delegation method either with or without the fruits of Nigel's analysis. Without the benefit of analysis, the commissioner could ask the functional directors to address the overall fatality problem, stressing the high priority now placed on it, and requiring them to adjust their scheduling and targeting to reflect that focus. If the functional directors had confidence in the existing *theory of operations*, and the importance of their traditional contributions, then one likely response would be "we know the answer to that problem: all you need is more of what we already do" – a response which leads to demands for more resources, or more overtime, or for staff to work harder; but which does not produce any new thinking.

Even *with* the benefits of the analysis, functional delegation has one serious pitfall. If the commissioner lays out the analysis for the functional directors, they may be able to see more clearly that their existing functional methods (i.e. carrying on business as usual) would be unlikely to fix one or more of these problems. But they will tend, then, to filter the list of specific problems according to a tool-centric relevance test, "is that problem relevant to me, and to my unit, given what we do?" If the answer is "no," then they will assume that particular problem is not their responsibility, and hope that other functions will deal with it. Where the answer is "yes," they will embrace the problem as confirming the value of their existing methods. As they engage in this selection process, they hold a familiar *tool* in their hands, watching a series of *tasks* pass by, picking out those that look right for the tool. This form of delegation does not produce the markedly different behavior that we need: where somebody holds the *task* in their hands, and watches a series of *tools* pass by, picking out those that look right for the task, and confronting the possibility that none of them do. Dividing the task functionally fails to make any unit unambiguously responsible, either for the overall task or for any of the specific pieces of it.[9] It permits the natural and familiar tool-orientation to persist. Only a task-orientation is likely to reveal those occasions when "we do not have a tool for this," and lead to the necessary invention.

Delegating the task to the most relevant tool (Option 3) fixes one of the problems of Option 2, but introduces others. It does indeed place responsibility for the task unambiguously with one official. But that official now has exactly the same responsibility that previously rested one level up, at the top of the organization; the disadvantage the functional manager faces is that they have less resources available. They may, by default, engage only the resources of their own unit.

They may feel justified to some degree in so doing, because the act of delegating the task to one function signals that senior management considers their methods most appropriate.

If that one functional manager does adopt a broader view, recognizing the limitations of their own unit and seeking to engage others, then in fact they begin to function as director of a task-force of sorts, which is more formally presented as Option 5. The difference is that the functional manager, given overall responsibility for the task, faces two handicaps that would not pertain to the appointed head of a more formally assembled task force. First, he or she lacks authority over other parts of the organization. Second, other parts of the organization, reading the signals, might assume they have been absolved from responsibility for the task and thus be less willing to engage.

Option 4, (disseminating the results of the analysis to all units, functional and geographic, and allowing each to interpret them as they see fit) similarly has the convenience of using existing structures. But it does not make any one person or team responsible either for the overall task or for any specific pieces of it. Some managers might approve of the enlightened managerial style this option suggests, preferring management through information over command-and-control. But this option carries all the drawbacks of Options 1 and 2, and adds further confusion by combining them. It makes everyone a little responsible, and no-one truly responsible. The executive levels of the organization skip over one of their most important duties in this business – figuring out the size and shape of the problems to be tackled, and marshalling an appropriate set of resources around them. The executive level is leaving the middle managers to work all that out amongst themselves, if they feel like doing that work.

Once the drawbacks of Options 1 through 4 have been discussed, most classes come to a general consensus that some version of Option 5 – the task force approach – represents the way to go. Some come to that decision reluctantly, having no great love for committee work and not wanting any recipe for organizational behavior that would create a lot more of it.

Given a problem with four distinct subcomponents identified, participants differ on some of the practical details. Some want one task force to cover the whole task. Others prefer four groups, recognizing that the four knots are each quite different. Each knot, they say, will require its own individual analysis and intervention plan. The set of

relevant players, therefore, will be different in each case. Some participants suggest a compromise – one task force with four subcommittees –
pointing out that the groups of relevant actors for the four problems
will at least overlap significantly.

Whichever version of *task force* they favor, or whatever name they
like to give it, the underlying principle for action is clear. *Respect the
natural shape and size of the harm itself. Fashion your response around
its structure, rather than forcing the harm into your structure. Use
a control structure which mirrors the structure of the harm itself.* If
the harm has four principal components, all different, then something
within the control apparatus should show four pieces, or four groups,
or four parallel series of meetings. That way each specific knot can
be studied, honored for its uniqueness, and unpicked. If one of the
four turns out not to be *one coherent whole*, but to consist of two
unlike objects; then the organizational response would consist of four
projects, with one of those projects divided into two subcomponents.
And so on.

In the language of Figure 2.2, this pattern of behavior means holding
one's attention *below the line*, for longer: discerning the structure of
the thing you seek to undo, and remaining faithful to that structure,
not yours, so you can address it piece by piece.

As long as this underlying principle is appreciated, different organizations can figure out the practical arrangements that work best for
them. Quite a few details need deciding: at what point to split a task
force, rather than expecting one group of staff to address multiple
objects at once; whether to allocate staff to this kind of work on a
full-time basis, or whether to let them retain their "real jobs" (and
the sense of security that goes with them) at the same time; whether
to use volunteers only; on what terms to engage outside partners, and
how to sustain the commitment of multiple groups through the life of
a project.

One important matter is drawing the right types of people into this
type of work. The analysis and planning stages favor creative, analytic
types; not champions of particular functions with entrenched views;
not necessarily senior staff or authority figures; rather those who work
well in lateral teams, far away from their normal supervisor, the only
one-of-their-kind in a diverse group; people not wed to any one particular set of tactics but willing to engage in brain-storming, working
and re-working strange new ideas until they eventually morph into

something feasible, legal, publicly acceptable, and (hopefully) brilliantly effective.

Such people are not necessarily nor usually those in positions of authority over resources. In which case, management will need to separate the responsibility for analysis and planning (the work of the creative analytic types) from the responsibility for approving the plan, allocating resources to it, and implementing it (for which one needs the authority structure of the organization, or of *several* organizations). Hence any team, or teams, established to tackle these four highway fatality problems will most likely be asked at the outset to study the problem and produce an action plan, but they will not actually be responsible for implementing the plan, nor solving the problem. The team or teams might retain a longer term role for monitoring the impact of the plan, and if necessary for revising plans later on. But their upfront inventive work has to be linked to the authority and resource-allocation structures of *each* contributing organizational unit, and of any other institutions enlisted as partners. Without that connection, no problem of any appreciable size (i.e. beyond the immediate capacity of a small team) could ever be tackled effectively.

Our highway commissioner must not only work out how to get the right kind of thinking done, by the right kind of people, in the right kind of mix; they must also devise the mechanisms through which that thinking will be translated into action. The team's task is to hold up the knot, turn it this way and that, and work out what it would take to unravel it. It is by no means a trivial task, thereafter, to make the rest of the organization play its role in the intervention. The tendency of the remainder, predictably, will be to write off such work as a cerebral luxury and a peripheral distraction from the *real* work – which is, of course, functional and process-based. As it always was!

Notes

1. Many of these, however, relate to productivity, timeliness, error-rates, and efficiency, and are thus more oriented towards process-based goals than harm-reduction goals.
2. Various versions of "CitiStat" (which is the name of the program in Baltimore City) have been implemented in cities including Somerville, Massachusetts; Atlanta, Georgia; Providence, Rhode Island; Syracuse, New York; St. Louis, Missouri; San Francisco, California. A similar approach

has been piloted and evaluated by Scottish local government agencies in Edinburgh, Aberdeen, and Tayside. The Scottish authorities adopted a less adversarial management style for their meetings than the prevailing US model. Robert D. Behn, "The Core Drivers of CitiStat: It's Not Just About the Meetings and the Maps," *International Public Management Journal,* 8 (December 2005), 295–319. (p. 296); Cathy Sharp, Jocelyn Jones & Alison M. Smith, "Research for Real" (Edinburgh, 2006). Available at: [www.scotland.gov.uk/Publications/2006/07/21102410/0].

3. Behn, "The Core Drivers of Citistat," p. 308.
4. Presentation of Christine Nixon, Commissioner of Victoria Police, to the Executive Program on Regulation and Enforcement, Australia and New Zealand School of Government. Brisbane, Australia, December 7, 2006. Commissioner Nixon has announced her intention to continue driving this rate down, with a goal of 200 fatalities or less per year.
5. The non-uniform distribution of environmental pollutants, and the consequent need to identify concentrations as a basis for operational interventions, is discussed in: William D. Ruckelshaus, "Risk, Science & Democracy," *Issues in Science and Technology,* 1 (Spring 1985), 13–38.
6. I picked the name "Nigel" because it seems to be familiar and easy to pronounce for virtually all overseas students; and, for some reason, there is seldom if ever a real "Nigel" in the class.
7. For a more detailed examination of the Great Lakes Project, and the novelty of the regulatory approaches involved, see Malcolm K. Sparrow, *Imposing Duties: Government's Changing Approach to Compliance* (Westport, Connecticut & London: Praeger Press, Greenwood Publishing, 1994), pp. 52–59.
8. The assumption of the 9/11 Commission report was that the failure to "connect the dots" was a central state failure resulting from the absence of unified intelligence analysis. The Commission therefore proposed better central coordination as part of the remedy. Judge Richard Posner later attacked this position, recommending broader mobilization of decentralized analytic entrepreneurship rather than enhanced centralized planning. For a discussion of the conflict between these perspectives, see: Sheila Jasanoff, "Restoring Reason: Causal Narratives and Political Culture," in Bridget Hutter and Michael Power (eds.), *Organizational Encounters with Risk* (Cambridge: Cambridge University Press, 2005), pp. 209–232 (particularly pp. 221–225). See also: Thomas H. Kean & Lee H. Hamilton, *The 9/11 Report: The Complete Investigation,* National Commission on Terrorist Attacks Upon the United States (New York: St. Martin's Press, 2004), Chapters 8 and 11; for Posner's critique, see: Richard Posner, "The 9/11 Report: A Dissent," *New York Times, Sunday Book Review,* August 29, 2004.

9. Failure to unambiguously allocate responsibility for controlling a risk is one of the modes of organizational failure described in: Max H. Bazerman & Michael D. Watkins, *Predictable Surprises: The Disasters You Should Have Seen Coming and How to Prevent Them* (Boston, Massachusetts: Harvard Business School Press, 2004), p. 96.

6 | *Puzzles of measurement*

C itizens should surely expect that government institutions whose core mission involves the reduction of harms should be able to give an account of their performance in terms of harms reduced, suppressed, mitigated or eliminated. All the more so if it is a regulatory agency, which imposes obligations, inconveniences, and costs on citizens and businesses. Those who are regulated have every right to know that regulatory impositions not only served worthwhile purposes, but were effective in achieving their aims. "If your business is harm-control, show me harms you have controlled."

If the bulk of the work done, however, is organized around *functions* (such as enforcement), *programs* (e.g. partnership programs) or *processes* – rather than around identified concentrations of harm – then a compelling account of *harms controlled* will remain frustratingly elusive. Functional and programmatic work generates a natural and straightforward performance story about levels of activity, or *outputs*. The police made this many arrests and obtained that many convictions. OSHA visited this many worksites and generated so many millions of dollars in fines. Customs officials searched this many shipping containers, and seized that much contraband. In general, reporting officials like these numbers to be large, and preferably increasing year by year. These numbers demonstrate to taxpayers that their public officials are working hard and keeping busy. Dividing these numbers by the number of employees, or the financial resources expended, allows the public also to gauge productivity and efficiency.

The operation of core, high-volume *processes* (e.g. handling calls, or complaints, or permit applications, or tax returns, etc.) also generates its own natural story. This process story has to do with workload volumes handled, timeliness and efficiency in handling transactions in bulk, accuracy and error rates, and potentially some measures of client satisfaction.

Even the combination of these two performance stories falls short with respect to demonstrating effective harm-control. It might show the agency worked hard to apply the functional tools it has, and that it operated its established processes with alacrity and precision. But it leaves open the question of whether tool selection is effective, and whether the processes established touch the pressing issues of the day. The audience can see agencies working *hard*, which they like. But they would like to be convinced they are also working *effectively* on the problems they choose to address, and that they are identifying and selecting the most important issues to address. Neither the function-based performance story (e.g. "we completed this many high-quality investigations") nor the process-based version ("we cleared our backlogs and streamlined our system") provide such assurance.

That failure explains the wave of demands, seen around the world during the last ten to fifteen years, for institutions to develop performance accounts that focus less on activities and efficiency, and more on *outcomes*, *impacts*, or *results* achieved. In the United States, pressure at the federal level is most obviously expressed through the Government Performance and Results Act (1993), which requires all federal agencies to develop a results-based account of their performance. At the state level, Performance-Based Budget statutes push in a very similar direction. Similar pressures have appeared in many other countries, and feature strongly as one aspect of the New Public Management (NPM) philosophy. The obligation to demonstrate effectiveness can come from law, or from political directives covering executive agencies; sometimes it is incorporated into budget approval processes, or end-of-year performance review and evaluation procedures.

The odd thing about these pressures, whatever form they take, is that they say a lot about the performance *account*, but nothing at all about the *performance* itself. They specify the nature of the *story* that overseers would like to see at the end of the year, but virtually nothing at all about what the agencies should *do* differently, if anything, throughout the year. At first sight this omission seems extraordinary. But when one remembers that harm-reduction work remains widely unrecognized and poorly understood, then it seems a little less surprising that legislatures were unable to detail the harm-reduction performance itself. So they just specified what story they would like to hear, and left it to the executive agencies to figure out how to produce it.

Unfortunately, many agencies tried at first to satisfy the pressures on their performance reporting without changing their operating practices. In other words, they too focused on changing the *account*, rather than on changing their *performance*. In practice what that meant – for the first eleven months of the year – was "carry on as usual." Then, in the twelfth month, panic! Somehow executives had to take the fruits of business-as-usual, and dress them up as a convincing account of harms-controlled. Too often this felt like a late-in-the-year salvage operation, an exercise in creative writing. The resulting accounts were not terribly convincing, because the connections between aggregate measures of efficiency and harm-reduction effectiveness remained tenuous.

Quite obviously, a *performance account* ought to be an *account* of one's *performance*. A performance account, to be persuasive, works best if it is a straightforward, natural, stress-free description of *what an organization did*. Surely it would be better to focus practitioners' intellectual energies on the transformation of operational *practice*, rather than on creative writing after-the-fact. After all, when operations were organized around functions and processes, the resulting report (consisting of aggregate outputs and efficiency measures) took the form of a natural, straightforward, stress-free description of that behavior. If we could properly establish the nature of a new performance itself, then it might be interesting to see how many of the pressures on the *account* would in fact be satisfied, simply by describing in perfectly straightforward terms that *new performance*.

We should note at this point certain features of the old account which the public and political overseers had always appreciated. They liked the fact that agency reports consisted of neat tables of aggregate, numerical data, and that these were easy to understand. They liked the tables always taking the same form, so that results were comparable across time periods. They liked the fact that the various activity counts were objective and numerical (e.g. cases opened, closed, convictions obtained) and therefore appeared more trustworthy than alternatives dependent on subjective judgments or interpretations. And they liked the fact that the contents of the tables unambiguously represented one agency's actions, not mixed with or confused with the contributions of others. So there was much to like.

Virtually the only thing they did not like was that the content reflected *outputs* rather than *outcomes*. If agencies successfully make the switch to reporting outcomes, their audiences would still prefer they retain all of these other desirable properties. In other words, they would hope to see performance reports consisting of neat statistical tables, comparable over time, comprising aggregated numerical *outcomes*. They would like the contents to remain independent of subjective judgment, and not subject to manipulation. And they would like the reports to show unambiguously what *this agency* accomplished in terms of harms reduced. The fact that the crime rate went down, or that fifty lakes were restored to *swimmable* or *fishable* status, or that there were no commercial airline crashes during the year: all of these constitute good news, but these successes are not particular enough. To justify expenditures on specific agencies – police departments, environmental agencies, or transportation-safety administrations – taxpayers and overseers want to know what these particular institutions contributed, and what difference their contributions made.

Pressures to develop more convincing performance accounts have been circulating in various forms for a decade or more. Nevertheless several thorny issues relating to these remain largely unresolved. Judging by the feedback from regulatory executives around the world, three core questions account for most of the remaining consternation. They are:

(a) *Is it possible to prove causality?* This issue is fundamental in justifying the value of any harm-control operation. The fact that overall levels of harm or risk increase or decrease over time might have little or nothing to do with specific interventions. The demands for outcome-reporting seem to require institutions to be able to isolate their own impact on the problems they address.

(b) *Is it possible to assign credit for harm-reduction to particular functions or programs?* As agencies broaden their toolkits, and potentially deploy several different approaches simultaneously, will they be able to parse the credit in sufficiently convincing a fashion to justify budgetary allocations?

(c) *Is it possible to measure prevention?* Can anyone measure accidents that didn't happen, or count the criminals averted from their purpose or deterred? If an agency incorporates preventive methods within its toolkit, does it lose the ability to measure its accomplishments? Bear in mind that reactive work, built around response to incidents or violations, was really very easy to count.

Without any change in organizational behavior and operating practices, the answers to these three questions – so everyone seems to agree – are three no's. If the agency persists with functional and process-based business as usual, then all three of these no's reflect the difficulty of establishing the connection between an organization's functional outputs and important changes in external conditions.

What's less clear is how much difference adopting a new harm-reduction *performance* might make. If we could devise and perfect the relevant organizational practices, would we end up with three yes's instead? That would be nice. But if not, how many would change to yes? And for the remaining no's, could we get any closer to a persuasive (if not definitive) account of *outcome*-based accomplishments?

The relevance of these questions is by no means limited to the public sector. Grant-making foundations in the not-for-profit sector are now demanding greater accountability from their grantees, expecting them to demonstrate what specific programs did and did not accomplish in terms of alleviating suffering and harm. This trend emerged at first in relation to public-health oriented grant-making, but has since become more widespread.[1]

In the private sector corporate risk officers, ethics officers, and compliance executives also have to master a mix of reactive and preventive methods, and to understand how their formulation of tasks and tool-selection will affect what story they can or cannot tell.[2] These executives are responsible for reducing corporate exposures to financial, reputational, litigation, or regulatory risks. They too need to know how to justify budgets for *preventing* bad things from happening to the company and its assets. Like their public sector counterparts, they too employ a wide range of contributing tools: staff hotlines, whistleblower protections, audit programs, data-mining and anomaly detection, ethics training, internal management consultancy, internal investigations, and so on. Moreover their work imposes costs, inconveniences and obligations on the rest of the corporation, denting to some extent the bottom line. So they must figure out how to relate the use of these techniques to specific risks reduced and disasters avoided. If they cannot do that, tolerance for their methods and costs will evaporate over time.

In order to see what difference a *new performance* might make, let me refer back to the patterns of thought and action explored in the previous chapter. Let us assume, for a moment, that our hypothetical commissioner of police, in his efforts to reduce the state-wide high-way fatality rate, acted in all the ways described there. The scenario described presents relatively simple measurement puzzles when compared with some other harm-reduction domains, since highway fatalities are relatively easy to count, and to categorize. Nevertheless all three of these core questions still pertain to that example. The commissioner needs to be able to connect the agency's actions to the outcome, place a value on contributing functions, and may well be asked to quantify accidents prevented. So, for these three questions, we can at least see what difference the new behaviors might make to what can and cannot be claimed after the fact.

In order to be able to use that example, we need to know (or invent) what might actually result from Nigel's systematic disaggregation of the fatality statistics, his discovery of the four specific problem areas, and the creation of task groups (or similar structure) to devise and propose remedies. Let us imagine the task force or task forces came up with the following interventions:

(a) For the summertime slippery road condition, the team focused on advance warnings, and driver awareness. The department brokered an agreement between the meteorological office and the media, so that on days when the condition was likely to occur, all the morning radio and TV shows would carry warnings for drivers. The department also sought a variety of other opportunities to educate the state's residents about the nature of this threat, and to take seriously the "slippery road" warning signs when displayed on the electronic highway notice boards during the summer months.

(b) Further analysis of the rural intersections problem rank ordered thirty-seven junctions at which such accidents most often occurred. The worst three were redesigned (turned into staggered crossroads) by the Highway department. The next most dangerous ten had cameras installed, linked to speed sensors, with automatic issuance of a penalty ticket and fine for non-compliers. A media blitz was planned for the moment when 1,000 tickets had been issued. The remaining twenty-four junctions had dummy boxes installed to look like cameras, and the department never publicly disclosed the fact that these did not contain real cameras.

(c) The solution to the teenagers driving their parents' cars late at night was a "take the keys to bed" campaign, aimed at the parents.

Table 6.1

	Last year, fatalities	This year, fatalities	Percentage change
(a) summertime slippery roads	135	47	−65.2%
(b) stop signs at rural intersections	85	56	−34.1%
(c) teenagers in parents' cars at night	214	104	−51.4%
(d) kids <5yrs not restrained correctly	74	92	+24.3%
Residual:	452	511	+13.1%
Total fatalities:	960	810	−15.6%

The campaign consisted of a series of TV commercials featuring bereaved parents, paid for by the insurance industry.

(d) For the child-restraint issue, the department sought to identify and exploit "teachable moments" for mothers (e.g. waiting time outside primary schools at pick-up time, amd parking lots adjacent to health clinics and supermarkets), offering free check-ups and providing relevant product information and advice, with an invitation to come back the next day to have any new equipment installation checked. These free check-ups would be provided by patrol officers, local partners, and some volunteers specially trained for the purpose.

Let us assume, further, that Table 6.1 shows the end of year outcomes, compared with the prior year's results. Note the good news: the goal of an overall 15 percent reduction has been achieved, due in large part to very significant reductions in three of the four identified problem areas. But note, also, that one project (children under 5 years old, not properly restrained) has not yet shown a decline. Notice also that the *residual* (i.e. fatalities not connected with any of the four identified problem areas) has increased substantially, which might indicate the emergence or growth of some other problem which analysis has not yet revealed.

Such a pattern is perfectly typical for this type of work. Creative, tailor-made solutions applied to carefully scrutinized problems produce quite substantial reductions or, in some cases, virtual elimination of problems altogether. In this example, to reach the overall goal the commissioner needs quite substantial reductions in the identified problem areas, because altogether they only covered 53 percent of the overall fatalities, and there is no particular reason to expect the four tailored interventions to produce any reduction in the residual. The purpose of this discussion is to find out what difference, if any, this kind of operational practice makes to the performance account available at the end of the year.

If the department had *not* followed this approach, (i.e. had performed no systematic disaggregation of the fatality data, and therefore conducted no special projects based on identified concentrations) then the only piece of Table 6.1 available at the end of the year would be the bottom line, showing the aggregate change in the fatality rate. Imagine that the department had carried on business as usual, but – given the ambitious goal – had simply worked harder: more patrol hours, more summonses, more drunk-driving arrests, a few hundred extra hours devoted to driver education in schools. Then, once the results were in, they might ask their audience to draw a connection between all that extra effort (functional outputs) and the resulting macro-level outcome (fewer fatalities overall). The connection between these would be difficult to argue one way or another, and cynics and critics might offer alternative explanations that had nothing to do with the department's actions. Better vehicle design, improved emergency services, or more expensive gasoline might appear equally plausible as explanations. In trying to prove what the department had accomplished, departmental leadership would be playing a familiar game, trying to connect their macro-level outputs to the macro-level outcomes, connecting them by reference to their prevailing *theory of operations*.

But in this scenario, they did *act* differently, and we need to see what difference that makes. Does a natural, straightforward, stress-free description of their new operational performance get them any closer to being able to prove causality, parse the credit for the outcomes among the contributing tools, or measure prevention?

Proving causality?

In order to prove a causal connection beyond doubt, the commissioner would either need to have available a *control sample* (i.e. another copy of the state, where all other factors could be held common, except for the intervention treatment), or run a randomized controlled experiment applying the intervention to parts of the state but not to others (which in this scenario would mean protecting parts of the state's population from media coverage). In public administration, opportunities to run such experiments are comparatively rare. Of course, the medical profession manages to run such experiments all the time, to test a new drug or treatment, even involving issues of life and death. But the medical profession has the advantage of *informed consent*, and restricts such experimentation to patients who choose to participate. Without informed consent, experiments in public administration present ethical challenges, and are conducted much less often. As a practical matter, our commissioner only has one state, and no chance of shielding part of its population from the media. So the chances of being able to draw definitive conclusions about causality remain slim.

Nevertheless, as a result of the operational strategy, the commissioner does have the rest of Table 6.1 available, and that does make a considerable difference when it comes to demonstrating effectiveness. In each of the four specific problem areas (three showing improvement, and one not), the department has *project level outcomes* to show. In three cases, the reductions are significant as a proportion of the starting level. Most important, in trying to explain the macro-level aggregate outcome, the department no longer depends solely on macro-level outputs for the explanation. Rather, they would point to the *project-level* or *micro-level outcomes* as important contributions. The logic by which the department claims influence on the overall outcome has changed. The explanation no longer rests on macro-level outputs (as it did before), but on the contributing micro-level outcomes: *the stories of the projects*.

At this point, the department's audience might be surprised at the nature of the performance account. No longer does it feel so much like a simple, objective, aggregate statistical table, even though (in this particular example) there is one overall macro-level score. The substance of the performance account now revolves around the project-based work, and therefore consists of a collection of short stories, one for each project. From the audience's point of view, the surprise would be simply that no-one asked for *stories*. They liked tables. They just wanted them to be about *outcomes*. But now the overall outcome is explained by reference to micro-level outcomes, each of which has a story attached.

Referring back to Figure 2.2 (page 56) for a moment, the claim to have made some impact on the bottom right hand cell (the generic category of harms) is now based on contributing successes in the bottom left hand cell (a set of specific harms reduced), rather than through the aggregate organizational outputs in the top right hand cell. In fact, to obtain the structure of the performance report, one merely has to reverse the arrows on that diagram. The arrows, with their original direction, showed how work was divided and defined, and laid out two quite different routes from the macro-level harm (bottom right) to the micro-level actions (top left). The two different routes reflected two quite different modes of organizational behavior. Whichever route one chooses as the basis for operations, the performance accounting process reverses the arrows, and adds things up again by reversing the way in which the work was divided and distributed. For the highway fatality problem, given the project-based approach we have assumed, the performance reporting path relies on the contents of the bottom left cell (which shows several specific harms suppressed) rather than relying on the aggregate output story (top right cell).

The style and structure of the stories that go with each of the projects is predictable, and common across them, even though the issues addressed differ markedly. For each project, the story has five parts:

1. The data and analysis which led the department to focus on this particular phenomenon. Others can check it for themselves if they wish. But the department concluded, on the basis of this data, that this particular problem needed addressing, and was worthy of special attention.
2. Metrics the department put in place, and benchmarked up front, so they could tell if they made any headway in reducing the problem. (In this example, the relevant metrics for the projects consist of fatality data simply filtered by category).
3. A description of the intervention implemented. And maybe the second one if the first failed to have the desired effect. And the third. And so on, until one was eventually found that worked.
4. The impact, measured in terms of changes in the designated project-specific metrics, which either show the problem was successfully brought under control, or not, as the case may be.

5. An account of any resulting decision regarding project closure, coupled with any longer term monitoring or maintenance plan put in place to prevent the problem, once suppressed, from re-emerging.

When the commissioner lays out the four stories, each with these five elements, is he any closer to proving a causal connection? Even at the project level, the results cannot be definitively proven to result from agency actions. And if the commissioner had only one such project-story to tell, or maybe even with three successes out of four projects launched, critics might still write the success off as a fluke or as the result of random fluctuations. But if the department makes this a sustainable pattern of operations, and over a period of two or three years accumulates a record of fifteen such projects, twelve of them finished and showing significant reductions, three more not yet satisfactorily concluded and still being worked upon, seven more lined up ready to go as soon as resources become available; what then? Does this now *prove* the connection? No, it does not. But the pattern of practice would surely convince all but the most skeptical observers of a few things: that the department was now data-driven and results-oriented; open-minded and analytical in trying to determine what the problems are; rigorous and honest about measuring progress; creative and open-minded about methods; persistent and adaptive in the face of initial failures and setbacks. And if, project after project, the public sees the department sticking with a problem, trying this plan and then another and another, *until* it unravels; surely then they would be persuaded that the department was not only working hard, but smart.

Perhaps the real cynics would still write off the project stories as anecdotes, claiming that they represented no substantial accomplishment. If there were merely one or two projects, and nothing like them had been seen before or would be seen thereafter, and if the problems addressed constituted an insignificant fraction of the overall harm, then indeed they could be written off as anecdotal, or insignificant. But the performance story here comprises the collection of the projects, and the sum of their accomplishments; not a generalization from them, nor an extrapolation. The commissioner is not asking people to believe that, just because he tells a good story or two, the department behaves like this more broadly. No, the story is precisely the sum of the project outcomes, and their contribution to important strategic goals. And if the problems addressed represent good sized bites out of important harms, they cannot be written off as anecdotes, or peripheral to normal operations. This now becomes *the principal method of operating.* The collection of project accomplishments will only count if together they comprise a significant change in the overall levels of harm. And in that case, the public should surely believe the agency is not only working hard, and smart, but *on the right things*.

It is surely possible for an institution to adopt this approach, to work hard, and smart, but not on the right things. We could easily imagine a different version of Table 6.1, where the projects generally worked well and produced encouraging results, and yet the aggregate fatality rate scarcely moved, or (worse) moved in quite the wrong direction. Any commissioner worth his or her salt would not wait until the end of the year to discover such a thing. All through the year, perhaps on a weekly or even daily basis, they would have staff tracking progress, monitoring cumulative distribution graphs, comparing progress-to-date with prior years' trajectories, to see if they remained on track to reach their end-of-year goals. Once the four projects had been established, they would probably monitor each subset separately, as well as watching the overall total (which includes the residual set). One would expect that if the project trajectories all looked good, and yet the macro-level aggregate failed to respond, then immediately the question would arise "what are we missing?" What other knots exist that, for some reason, we have not been able to discern? Who to call at this point? Nigel, of course! Re-run the analyses. Try twenty new forms of analysis. Use dimensions we have never used before. Check with neighboring states. What *new thing* is happening that we cannot see? What problem exists for which we have no suitable analytic lenses? Working hard and smart is not enough, unless the bites are big enough to add up to something. Anecdotes don't suffice. To count, the projects, taken as a collection or portfolio, ought to constitute significant progress towards important strategic objectives.

Even when they do, the commissioner cannot normally prove causality definitively. But describing the method of operation, even in a rather straightforward way, provides a much more compelling account of effectiveness than was available before.

Assigning credit to functions

Even given the new organizational behavior, the opportunities for specific functions to claim credit for particular outcomes will remain quite rare. It could happen, in cases where one function or one program-matic area takes on a particular concentration of harm, and achieves demonstrable reductions without any help from any other group. In that case, they are entitled to the credit for that particular (micro-level) outcome.

The more normal situation, though, is that the identified knots fail to align neatly with existing organizational divisions. Resources from several relevant functions and outside agencies are organized around the task. And the tailor-made solutions so typical of this problem-oriented approach usually end up comprising a cocktail of treatments from several contributing units.

So has the situation changed at all when it comes to parsing credit for outcomes? In fact it has. In the fatality reduction example, the media unit (for instance) would be able to list the specific projects in which they played a part; and each of those projects has micro-level outcomes associated with it. Therefore the media department – or the juvenile liaison department, or the patrol division – can lay claim to a share in a specific set of micro-level outcomes: those in which they were involved. That *is* different. Without the new method of operation, there would not have been any micro-level project-based outcomes, because there would have been no problem-specific projects. There would only be macro-level outputs, and macro-level outcomes, and anybody's guess as to the relationship between them.

The story changes once the organization orients itself around the identification and treatment of specific subcomponents of the harm. Now the assessment of functional contributions resembles the manner in which the medical field assesses the value of specific medical proce-dures or devices. Surgery might be part of the treatment for a range of conditions, but few conditions are cured or alleviated by surgery alone. Depending on the condition, the treatment might also include dietary modification, or antibiotics, or physical therapy. It might require the use of durable medical equipment, or involve a range of other thera-pies. In the medical world it is clear that we do not ask how many lives are saved by surgery, or by penicillin, or by home-health care. Such tool-based questions would only have meaningful answers in relation to conditions that had a one-tool fix. Most illnesses require treatments involving combinations of therapies. Conditions with a one-tool fix are as rare in medicine as in any other harm-control domain.

The evaluation of clinical medicine starts with the story of specific conditions or diseases; not with the tools. For each condition, the medical community develops a treatment protocol with multiple components, and measures the impact of that combined treatment across the set of patients with that condition. So, in relation to late-stage diabetes, or in relation to colon cancer, we evaluate the number of quality-adjusted-life-years added (or other suitable outcome metric) resulting from any one specified treatment protocol. Then, if we want to know how important is one drug, or one device, or one type of surgical procedure, we list the multiple conditions for which that one component appears as part of a treatment plan. For each disease, we can point to measurable outcomes, all of which involve the use of that one component.

I could have used cooking for an analogy here, rather than medicine, but somehow it seemed less grand. In the kitchen, how valuable is sugar? Or yeast? Odd questions, these, because we rarely use such ingredients alone. If the cook had to evaluate the importance of any specific spice, surely any meaningful answer would begin with the list of tasty food items that involved the use of that ingredient.

Likewise, once an organization adopts and implements a problem-oriented approach, the following rules emerge in relation to assigning credit to specific functions. First, one function can claim credit for a specific *outcome* only in the rare cases of a *one-tool fix*. Second, in general, if a function wants to hog credit, then it will be for functional *outputs*. Third, functions *can* now take credit for specific (i.e. micro-level) project-based outcomes, but only if they are willing to share that credit with other contributors to those project-based interventions.

Measuring prevention

One of the appeals of reactive or responsive strategies is that things were relatively easy to count. Numbers of incidents, accidents, violations, or reports provide unambiguous and objective measures of workload. Related process measures – timeliness in response, accuracy in disposition, and customer satisfaction – show how well an agency handles that workload. Taking into account the levels of resources consumed in running the processes provided measures of productivity and efficiency as well.

But as institutions shift their attention from the lowest unit of work (individual incidents) to higher levels (patterns, issues, problems) then one would prefer they held no ideological preference for reactive

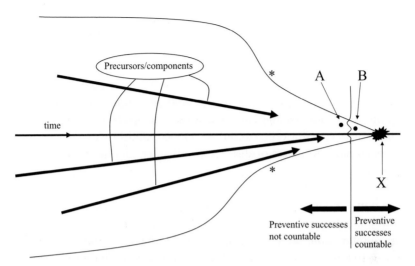

Fig. 6.1 Unfolding chronology of a harm

strategies over preventive strategies; or vice versa. In fact, one would like practitioners to consider carefully the whole sequence that constitutes the chronological unfolding of any particular harm, so they could find the *best* time to intervene. Figure 6.1 presents a simple schematic which represents this. The point X marks the materialization of the harm society seeks to control or reduce. X could represent a road accident, a nuclear power plant meltdown, a terrorist attack, or an oil-spill. The funnel leading to point X contains all the various factors and actors which have to come together for X to occur. If X is a crime, then the field of *situational crime prevention* teaches that X requires a perpetrator, a victim, and a circumstance or situation in which the crime can occur. Stop any one of these ingredients from arriving at point X, and the crime is prevented. Any intervention after the fact we term *reactive*, and virtually anything before it is broadly labeled *preventive*. Use of this binary distinction sometimes tends to mask the range of choices available within the preventive category. For crime, we might choose to focus on "designing out crime" through attention to architectural and environmental factors that make attacks more or less likely.[3] Or we could focus on reducing the vulnerability of potential victims. Or we could focus attention on constraining, excluding or deterring potential offenders.

Not only can we choose which pre-cursor of X to focus upon; we can also choose to intervene at many different moments in the unfolding chronology. Way off to the left, abortion policy might affect the rate at which potential offenders are being born. A little less far to the left lie a host of early childhood interventions that might lessen the chances of delinquency later in life. Still *preventive* but much later in the chronology would come video-surveillance or warning systems that might reveal a crime about to happen, and provide last minute opportunities to divert or distract an offender, and alert or protect a potential victim.

If the particular disaster represented by X was "death of a nursing home resident due to fire," rather than a crime, then the unfolding chronology in advance of X similarly presents many potential moments for intervention. Years before, one might change construction standards to require better fire-proofing or electrical installation. Closer to the event, one might choose to exclude smokers, or ban smoking on the premises. Moving even closer to X in time (and considering interventions that kick in after a fire has begun but before deaths occur), one might focus on smoke detection systems, fire-drills, and evacuation skills and technologies.

As the unfolding chronology of any one harm provides so many potential moments for intervention and so many contributing pre-cursors upon which one might focus, how should practitioners go about choosing when and where to intervene? Assuming they want to produce the maximum risk mitigation for the minimum price, then they will seek to identify the following combination:

- a *moment* within the unfolding chronology;
- an *object* upon which to focus (one of the pre-cursors or factors which lead to the harm);
- a *method* for intervention (tools, technologies, or approach), where this combination of moment, object, and method
  - falls within their jurisdiction, or within the jurisdiction of available partners;
  - is both resource-efficient and effective in mitigating the harm; and
  - produces minimal (harmful) side-effects.

Picking the *moment* in the chronology at which to intervene involves fundamental trade-offs. Earlier interventions provide more distance from the harm itself, and therefore seem safer in the sense that whatever slips past early controls might be caught later. But earlier interventions also have to reach more broadly, as it is less clear at this distance which objects of attention are actually on a path for point X. Waiting longer (i.e. intervening at a later point) narrows the chronological funnel, and facilitates a more careful focus on groups at higher risk. The longer one waits, the greater the precision in targeting.

Disease management provides many examples of such trades. Childhood vaccination campaigns provide broad preventive protection for some diseases, but their wide-reaching nature makes them expensive and may elevate the importance of low-probability side-effects. For many diseases, current practice waits for early warning signs or signs of increased susceptibility, and focuses interventions more narrowly on people deemed to be at higher risk. In seeking resource-efficient intervention points, practitioners naturally value those phases or stages in the chronology where the funnel suddenly narrows significantly, where one gains significantly tighter focus for the price of relatively little delay (for instance, at the stage indicated by an asterisk on Figure 6.1).

Preventive work involves sliding up and down the chronology of any particular harm, examining the full range of pre-cursors, and the pre-cursors to the pre-cursors, searching for opportunities to remove, restrain, or divert some essential ingredient or ingredients of the harm, and thus reduce the frequency or likelihood of the disaster X happening. It helps, too, if the interventions specified by such combinations of *time*, *object* and *method* are themselves legal, ethical, politically acceptable, and publicly supportable – which makes the choice of such strategies as much artful as it is scientific.

Given the complexity of this choice it would be a shame if the issue of measurability biased the selection of intervention opportunities in an unhelpful way. Just because reactive competence is, on the whole, easier to monitor than preventive success, one would not want to wait longer, and therefore see more harm done, simply because an agency could not demonstrate the value of its preventive options.

Hence the very practical concern which practitioners express: "how can I show what did not happen?" "If my agency is supposed to use preventive measures as well as reactive ones, how will we ever get credit for disasters that do not occur?" Indeed, who can count oil-spills that did not take place, workplace accidents that did not happen, or the number of instances where terrorists decided not to attack?

The majority of preventive interventions do not, in fact, produce countable results. A peculiar subset of them, however, do. The newspaper headline "terrorist plot foiled" tells the story of an attack, due to happen rather soon, prevented by the actions of law-enforcement or intelligence agencies. When a bomber is caught with explosives in the car, en route to a target, we can readily surmise what would have happened but for the intervention. However, if terrorism control operations intervened much earlier (e.g. at a terrorist organization's formation stage, and if counter-terrorist operatives successfully undermined the group's internal trust through the use of disinformation) then nobody would have been able to predict with any degree of assurance how many attacks that group, had they matured, might have launched. Counting *attacks prevented* becomes harder and harder the earlier the intervention falls within the chronology.

Similarly, we can in fact count the number of times nursing home residents are successfully evacuated from burning buildings, and thereby avoid fiery deaths. But we cannot count the number of fires that did not even begin because of a ban on smoking in the bedrooms. We can count the number of people involved in head-on collisions over 40mph, whom we predict would have died but for the last second intervention of seat belts or airbags. But we cannot actually name the people who did not have accidents at all because of better driver training. We might be able to name individuals or families who are "lifted out of poverty;" but we could probably not name nor even count those that did not fall into poverty in the first place because of an intervention orchestrated earlier in the chronology.

The boundary between countable and non-countable preventive interventions can be both sharp, and decidedly quirky. Consider, for example, an occupational safety inspection at a construction company, as a result of which construction workers begin complying (for the first time) with rules governing the use of fall-protection harnesses when working at heights above 8 feet. The very next day one worker slips off a roof at 36 feet, and is lowered to the ground at 4 mph by a restraint harness and walks away uninjured. Imagine this was the first time the worker ever wore a harness. The inspecting agency might claim with some degree of assurance that the worker's death, or at least very serious injury, had surely been prevented by their intervention the day before. But consider the possibility that the intervention had instead focused on the wearing of non-slip shoes rather than fall-restraints, and as a result the worker had not even slipped. In that case, who would know how likely the person was to slip, and – even if they did – how likely they were to fall as a result? No longer could the agency or the company tell that wonderful story of preventive success which begins "I'd like you to meet (so and so): this person is alive today because...." On Figure 6.1, the adoption of non-slip shoes is represented by point A, and the operation of a fall restraint harness by point B. In the unfolding chronology of this particular harm (i.e. death or injury resulting from falls in the construction industry) these two interventions operate at times separated only by a very few seconds. Nevertheless one falls squarely in the identifiable and countable domain, and the other falls outside it.

So, can we count preventive successes? The answer, regrettably, is usually not, except for a rather arbitrary and quirky sliver of interventions that come late in the unfolding chronology, and in many cases worryingly close to the disaster itself.

If *not countable* turned out to mean *not measurable*, then demands for performance accounting in the harm-reduction businesses might have some dangerous consequences. Pressure for countable results might bias the choice of interventions towards the set that lies to the right of this strange dividing boundary (shown on Figure 6.1, running between points A and B), even if better options were available. More resource-efficient and effective intervention opportunities might exist, earlier on, but they would not produce countable results.

Where preventive successes are not countable, it seems to be perfectly common practice to use *aggregate reductions* as a proxy for preventive accomplishments. It is important, however, not to confuse reductions in levels with instances of prevention. They are not at all the same thing.

Consider, for example, the "take the keys to bed" campaign. This produced a significant reduction in the (hypothetical) problem of high-schoolers driving their parents' cars late at night, and without permission. Table 6.1 showed a reduction in the number of related fatalities from 214 to 104 in one year, which is a 51 percent reduction. If the commissioner makes the mistake of declaring in public that this campaign "saved the lives of 110 kids," some cynical journalist is surely going to ask the commissioner to name one of them. The commissioner cannot name any, because the intervention (making the keys unavailable) is targeted quite early in the unfolding of this particular harm:

after the accumulation of peer pressure to go find a car, but before the journey begins. Even if the commissioner can find some teenagers willing to declare that they *tried* to find the keys, but couldn't, and therefore didn't drive, nobody would know which of them might have been involved in accidents.

Table 6.1 shows the total fatality rate dropping from 960 to 810, for a reduction of 150. It would be tempting to claim that this means 150 deaths were prevented. Indeed, there may be some countable examples of deaths averted, but only if some of the interventions came late enough in the unfolding chronology of a highway fatality to be countable. Mostly, the preventive effects will not be countable. The best clue to their effect might lie in the overall reduction in levels, but there are all kinds of reasons why these are not the same thing. For one thing, a great many *other* accidents might have been prevented during this last year (potentially thousands) by ordinary police presence, or even by public assumptions about police presence. So the actual number of deaths prevented would most likely far exceed any visible reductions.

It is also conceivable that aggregate levels might rise, even in the presence of countable preventive interventions. If *reductions* are equated with *preventive results*, this would be a contradiction. We can easily imagine a year in which the number of terrorist bombs detonated *increased*, even though the number of *countable terrorist plots foiled* (at the last minute) was positive. The number of successful nursing home evacuations might increase, even as the overall level of fire-related deaths also increased.

In general, the visible reductions represent only a small subset of the real preventive accomplishments, as the starting level is already affected by prior levels of preventive success. Changes in levels might also result from factors not related to any specific preventive interventions implemented.

Perhaps the most compelling reason for agency executives to avoid confusing *reductions* with *prevention*, is that significant reductions may only be available in the short term. Inherit a problem out of control, and one might perfectly well be able to produce a 20 percent reduction in overall levels in one year through systematic decomposition of the problem, identification of its important components, and suppression of them one by one. Maybe the second year it would be possible to bring the overall level down again by another 20 percent. Maybe a smaller reduction the third year, and so on. At some point, and for many types of harm, the curve will inevitably flatten out, and probably not at *zero*. The aggregate levels will asymptotically approach some non-zero level, where driving it down further would be inordinately expensive, burdensome or intrusive. At this stage, aggregate levels remain roughly flat, and the overall category of harm remains largely suppressed. It takes a lot of effort, however, to *keep* it suppressed; and that means justifying a budget (and other forms of support) in order to maintain the control operation. If the budget justification previously rested on aggregate reductions, and they are no longer available, then at this point in time something else must take their place.

Long-term success

This particular puzzle begs the long-term version of the performance measurement question: if the harm-reduction story rested in the short term on reductions in levels, then on what will it rest in the long term, once all the major harms have been suppressed and no more significant reductions are available? At that point, the work of harm-control becomes less newsworthy, even less apparent, and therefore in danger of losing necessary support. Mark Butterworth observes this in the context of corporate risk-management:

It is an axiom of risk management that the more effective their performance, the less noticeable risk managers become – losses, control failures and similar occurrences are avoided and their absence is taken for granted. In order to win and maintain the board's support for their work, risk managers need to demonstrate clearly its value to the company.[4]

The good news here is that the method of demonstration – that is, the relevant performance account – flows somewhat naturally once the mechanisms and protocols for the performance itself have been understood. The work of *continued suppression*, just like the work of harm reduction described in the last chapter, does not consist of broad approaches to generalities: rather it consists of specific remedies for specific problems. The difference, in the long-term continued-suppression mode, is that the problems tackled are nascent or emerging, rather than well established and out of control.

What long term control success means, I would suggest, is *spotting emerging problems early and suppressing them before they do much damage.*[5] Even when aggregate levels remain roughly flat, the substance of the control story still lies beneath, at a more textured level, just as it did before. It still consists of a collection of short stories. But now the stories are not about established harms reduced; rather, they relate to emerging threats choked off and prevented from flourishing. How to justify the budget, when the aggregate levels did not move? Answer: look at *this problem*, which we spotted and suppressed; and *that one*, and another. The collection of stories provides the compelling account, demonstrating continuing attention to data, open-mindedness and versatility in monitoring for emerging patterns, and organizational flexibility in organizing around any new threat and nipping it in the bud. This account becomes all the more compelling if neighboring jurisdictions or peer organizations were not so quick to spot new threats, and suffered significant losses by failing to control them so quickly.

In the long term, the art of harm suppression is analogous to the game of *whack-a-mole*, which one finds children playing in fairgrounds and amusement arcades. The equipment consists of a flat board, with a number of moles (in American versions of the game) or mushrooms (the traditional British version) embedded in the surface. These pop up at random, and the object of the game is to whack them back down again immediately. The quicker and more accurate the player's response, the higher the score. To be good at whack-a-mole takes three things: First, a deliberate and energetic vigilance. If you watch children playing this game you see them intensely engaged, hovering over the board, scanning constantly for any sign of new movement, ready to pounce. Second, a speedy response. Not casual. Not sluggish. Not waiting until there is large accumulation. Third, the player needs an effective implement in hand, sufficient to set the mole or mushroom back down below the surface once again, preferably with one swift blow.

In conversation with regulatory executives over the years, I have often discussed what it would take to make government agencies, responsible for the suppression of various harms, better at *whack-a-mole*. These agencies too need an energetic and deliberate vigilance if they are to spot emerging threats earlier rather than later.[6] They too should put a premium on timely response, in order to minimize the amount of harm done.[7] And they too need effective implements in hand – which often means inventing new methods when existing ones do not suffice, or enlisting partners to bring additional capabilities to the table. Certainly these agencies should beware relying too heavily on the passage of new legislation to cover every new threat, because that path may take too long and much harm might occur meanwhile. Operational inventiveness might make a difference much quicker, even if legislation eventually follows.

I often ask executives which of these three *whack-a-mole* capabilities their agency staff think about most. Without hesitation, executives admit the focus falls too much on the third: having effective implements in hand. Agencies always want more resources, more laws, more powers. Less attention is paid to vigilance, and to timeliness of response. Perhaps if agencies could adjust the balance among these three, so that they became more watchful and nimble, then perhaps they wouldn't need to be so large, or powerful, or expensive. Nipping harms in the bud might only take secateurs; wait much later, and you may need a chain-saw.

The *whack-a-mole* analogy provides an opportunity for people to distinguish two different types of "rapid response." In this context, as we try to understand what it means in the long run to be successful in harm suppression, we are not talking about response to *incidents*, or *accidents*, or *violations*. For many of those, rapid response is of course important. But that kind of timeliness belongs in the domain of incident-response, and is taken care of through organizational processes. If an agency needs better incident-response, then it should examine the relevant response processes and seek to improve them.

In this context, the objects to be spotted early and suppressed are emerging *problems* or *patterns*, which lie above the level of individual incidents. This kind of timeliness is about analytic monitoring across a mass of data, rather than the ability to detect and respond to individual incidents. Seeing emerging patterns more quickly means doing analysis more often. Recognizing patterns that are novel and unfamiliar means trying a variety of creative analyses that have never revealed anything significant before, and which stand some chance of revealing anomalous and emergent patterns even before one can know for certain what they might mean. In this vein, epidemiological monitoring for outbreaks of diseases scans novel forms of data and analysis, seeking unusual patterns emergent within them. Examples of such data sources include aggregated purchase records for health care products, drug prescriptions, laboratory test orders, clinical indications as recorded in ambulance logs, and changes in levels of absences from work or school.[8] Using novel data sources and analytic methods serves to supplement formal public health reporting mechanisms, which cannot always be trusted to work reliably, comprehensively, or quickly enough.[9]

Appetite for early detection of emerging problems means that Nigel (here representing our newly elevated focus on analysis) should be busy all year long, periodically monitoring for any new movement, whether of familiar or unfamiliar types, and without waiting for harms to grow to the levels at which they stand out as self-evident control failures.

Enough said, for now, about the puzzles of measurement. The nature of the *performance account* and the nature of the *performance* itself are inextricably linked. After all, to be convincing, one should be a natural and straightforward description of the other. The right way to produce a compelling account of harms-reduced is to learn the patterns of thought and action that underpin operational harm-reduction; and then, at the end-of-the-day, an organization can describe what it did in a natural and rather straightforward fashion.

Special classes of harm

There are several remaining measurement puzzles, but these are connected directly to certain categories of harm, and so discussion of them fits more naturally in Part II of this book, which examines these categories one by one.

- Some harms are *invisible* by nature (Chapter 8), which means that the underlying scope and nature of the problems to be addressed is not readily apparent, and changes in process volumes (which constitute the most readily available indicator of change) are difficult to interpret reliably.
- Some harms involve conscious opponents (Chapter 9), who adapt to control interventions. In this area, practitioners might easily overcount or overestimate the effects of their interventions if they do not properly anticipate adaptive responses by the opposition, which may shift the harm outside the zone being monitored.
- Some harms are catastrophic in nature (Chapter 10), having enormous potential impact, but which have never or scarcely ever happened. In this setting the aggregate number of instances, year after

year, will be zero, zero, zero. These settings present distinct challenges when it comes to justifying expenditures, dividing work, defining responsibilities, and measuring progress. For these risks, all the
operational nitty-gritty of control operations sits among the precursors to the disaster itself, and the precursors to the precursors, way
back in the unfolding chronology of the harm.

• Some harms are slow-acting, especially those that involve natural or
biological systems. For these, outcome metrics might take many years
to show discernible improvement. (For example, lung-cancer rates
tend to lag changes in smoking behavior by roughly twenty years.)
Monitoring of outcomes in such cases will normally include a range
of intermediate or interim measures which can reveal small steps in
the right direction, long before the overall desired effect becomes
apparent. In the meantime, decision making and budget justification must often depend on the behavior of such interim measures,
even while their validity and relevance rests (tenuously sometimes)
on plausible scientific theories.

For these specific categories of harms it is largely the related performance measurement issues that make operational control of them especially challenging. These are all areas where it is particularly difficult to
tell, in any systematic way, what has and has not been accomplished.
And, when it is not clear what has been accomplished (in terms of
changes in external conditions), then it is very difficult to see clearly
what to do next. These are especially difficult areas, which Part II of
this book examines in greater detail.

Notes

1. The *United Way*, the *W.K. Kellogg Foundation* and the *American Cancer Society* were among the early adopters of grant policies requiring
recipients to demonstrate outcomes. See: Robert L. Milstein & Scott F.
Wetterhall, *Frameworks for Program Evaluation in Public Health, Morbidity and Mortality Weekly Report*, Department of Health and Human
Services, Centers for Disease Control and Prevention, Atlanta, Georgia,
48 (September 17, 1999), pp. 33–34.
2. For a discussion of the emerging role of *Chief Risk Officers* as internal regulators, facing many of the same quandaries as traditional (external) regulators, see: Michael Power, "Organizational Responses to Risk: the Rise
of the Chief Risk Officer," in Bridget Hutter and Michael Power (eds.),

Organizational Encounters with Risk (Cambridge: Cambridge University Press, 2005), pp. 132–148.

3. Attention to the *situation*, rather than to the victim or the offender, has been the major focus of *situational crime prevention*, within the field of criminology.

4. Mark Butterworth, "The Emerging Role of the Risk Manager," in special series, "*Mastering Risk,*" No. 1, *Financial Times* (April 25, 2000), p. 12.

5. The importance of identifying emerging threats earlier is described in: Max H. Bazerman & Michael D. Watkins, *Predictable Surprises: The Disasters You Should Have Seen Coming and How to Prevent Them* (Boston, Massachusetts: Harvard Business School Press, 2004), Chapter 7, pp. 157–177.

6. Stephen Hill & Geoff Dinsdale, *A Foundation for Developing Risk Management Learning Strategies in the Public Sector* (Ottawa, Canada: Canadian Centre for Management Development, 2001), p. 8.

7. The ability to "enhance our ability to detect problems, as well as to anticipate problems before they become widespread" is the stated goal of the US Securities and Exchange Commission's risk assessment initiative. See: Testimony of Lori A. Richards, Director, Office of Compliance Inspections and Examinations, US SEC, before the Senate Committee on Banking, Housing and Urban Affairs, March 10, 2004. Richards also describes in her testimony a range of new surveillance and monitoring techniques the SEC proposes to use to provide early detection capabilities. Testimony available on the web at: [www.sec.gov/news/testimony/ts031004lar.htm].

8. James W. Buehler, Richard S. Hopkins, J. Marc Overhage, Daniel M. Sosin, & Van Tong, "Framework for Evaluating Public Health Surveillance Systems for Early Detection of Outbreaks: Recommendations from the CDC Working Group," *Morbidity and Mortality Weekly Report,* Vol. 53, No. RR-5, Department of Health and Human Services (Atlanta, Georgia: Centers for Disease Control and Prevention, May 7, 2004), pp. 2–6.

9. Defining patterns that might be found in alternate data sources is somewhat analogous to the search in early cancer screening for *markers* – biological compounds that show elevated levels or are only present when a malignant cancer occurs. See, for example: Henri T. Pham, Norman L. Block, & Vinata B. Lokeshwar, "Tumor-derived Hyaluronidase: A Diagnostic Urine Marker for High-grade Bladder Cancer," *Cancer Research,* 57 (February 15, 1997), 778–783.

7 | *Structures, protocols, and interactions*

T
he idea of focusing on carefully identified concentrations of harm and unpicking them one by one sounds simple and straightforward enough: pick important problems, and fix them. The fact, however, that initiatives and organizational behaviors pointing in this direction are seen as departures from the norm and celebrated as *innovations* suggests there is something not entirely obvious about the practical implementation of this idea. The associated operational practices remain awkward, unfamiliar, and (for many institutions) elusive. If the relevant organizational behaviors were well established, and the mechanisms needed to support them well understood, then there would be nothing innovative about this type of conduct.

I find that practitioners often take offense, at first, when we discuss what it would mean for their organization to *pick important problems, and fix them.* "You are insulting us," they say. "Everything we do is about that." They assume their existing operations cover this, even though most of their work is still organized around functions and processes. Sometimes they can point to specific problems spotted and solved (like the US Customs Service, with their port-running problem), even though the patterns of thought and action they used in those cases have not been generalized nor institutionalized.

A series of straightforward mechanical questions about problem-solving operations quickly exposes the extent to which this type of work has or has not been recognized and incorporated into an agency's business model: If picking important problems and fixing them is a routine part of the business, then whose job is it to *pick?* Is it a person, or a committee? When did they last do the *picking?* Who is allowed to nominate problems for attention? Who keeps the list of problems nominated, from which to pick? What do you tell people about the problems that are *not* picked? What criteria do you consider in deciding which ones are *important?* How many important problems have been selected, with projects now underway to fix them? What progress are these projects making? Who keeps the records for each project? Does everyone understand which managers check up on progress, and how often? How many projects have been successfully concluded? On what basis do you decide when to close a project? How are these project-based accomplishments incorporated into the agency's performance account? What is the organizational interface between this type of work and other, more familiar, types of work? And so on.

It normally does not take much questioning along these lines to establish whether or not this type of work has really been embraced, understood, and built in. For many agencies, this line of questioning reveals a complete absence of systems and machinery to drive such work. And as executives begin to grasp the extraordinary range of judgments and decisions that would need to be made in the course of such work, they rather soon drop their protest – "we do that already" – and express quite a different conviction: "oh, we could never do that here."

Five phases of learning

The process of learning this operational practice, judging by observations across a broad range of regulatory agencies, follows a rather predictable sequence of five phases. Laying these phases out provides an opportunity for practitioners to consider what their institutions have already learned, and what might be next. Very few practitioners, given time for reflection, claim that their organizations have finished this particular journey.

Phase 1: "Shaking loose"

In this first phase the agency realizes that it has traditionally relied on a rather narrow set of tools. Sometimes this happens when new and unfamiliar problems emerge, for which existing techniques are clearly inappropriate. Sometimes agencies observe peer organizations in other jurisdictions enjoying success with alternate methods, and explore adoption of similar ideas themselves. Some agencies face political pressure to adopt a different style or stance with respect to the regulated community, or to take more or less notice of some other stakeholder group, and the shift in allegiances or alliances begs a change of operating methods. Sometimes this realization is spawned from accumulating frustration, when existing methods fail to deliver the kinds of results expected. For any of these reasons, institutions broaden the range of tools they are prepared to try.

Phase 2: Make significant shift in investments

This phase follows a period of experimentation with an expanded toolkit, and involves a deliberate shift in the mix of tools used. A specific direction for reinvestment is set at the political or executive level. New organizational units or programs may appear, acting as incubators and drivers of preferred new methods. Usually, something else has to decline. In recent US experience, the general direction of this shift has been away from enforcement tools and towards voluntary compliance, education, outreach, partnership, technical assistance, and a range of other innovative regulatory methods which mostly have a gentler and more cooperative flavor.

Phase 3: Determine preferences among methods, and set a new balance

Once the reinvestment process has proceeded some distance, executives will eventually have to confront the question "how far should this go?" They know it would be foolish to abandon enforcement altogether (or whichever tool was set in decline), but until this point nobody has needed to specify at what point the reinvestment process should stop. The job now is to establish some new balance point, or *optimal mix* of tools which will yield maximum compliance at least cost. Given limited overall resources, setting the right balance feels to the executives like a constrained optimization problem: the task is to optimize the overall compliance rates (or some other aggregate outcome measure) by setting the best combination of *levels* for each tool in the toolkit – just like setting the sliders on a sound-mixer to get the best overall sound quality.

Observers might find it strange that government agencies would attempt to establish the mix of tools even before they know what type of problems might arise during the year. What craftsman would pick the tools before understanding the task? But a variety of practical considerations can push executives in this direction. First, budget processes might require them to determine up front what level of resources to allocate to each functional unit. The less versatile these resources, the more constraining such advance choices will turn out to be. Second, the mixture of tools corresponds in some sense to the character, or regulatory style, of an agency. An agency that relies most heavily on enforcement is a quite different animal from one that mostly offers technical consulting services. From time to time, political or legislative pressures might demand a change in character: perhaps towards a sterner or tougher stance as a result of elevated public concerns, or towards a softer touch as a result of industry's complaints or accumulating regulatory burden. To bring about such a change, legislatures might use budget structures or even new mandates to adjust the mix, and hence guarantee the new character.

The search for the *optimal mix* provides an opportunity for agencies to deploy sophisticated analytical tools – typically regression analyses – to help them solve their constrained optimization problem. However sophisticated the analytic tools employed in this process, the value of the results remains limited by the circumstances of the inquiry: namely, the predominant and careful focus on *tools*, with only a broad and generic view of the *tasks*. Such analyses seek a single, overall allocation of resources among a finite set of familiar functional approaches, and scarcely consider the evolving nature of the task environment over time. Nor does such analysis consider the particularities of lower level objects within that environment, each of which might require quite different treatments. Moreover, conducting such analysis and redeploying resources accordingly offers nothing in terms of opportunity to develop integrated cocktails of treatments, or novel approaches tailored to specific problems.[1] Rather, it presumes that each tool will act in isolation, at some specified level of effort, seeking out its own targets and without any coordinating managerial framework.

The targeting of each tool might be analytically sophisticated, and might even incorporate some formal risk-assessment process applied across the universe of potential targets. Thus a financial regulator might rank-order the companies or banks it regulates, prioritizing them for an existing audit program. A customs agency might develop risk-based models for selection of passengers, or freight, for search and examination. Environmental agencies might rank-order industrial facilities for inspection using a compilation of risk-factors and other considerations. Applying "risk-based" targeting in this manner provides the opportunity for an agency not only to have an optimal mix of tools (according to some macro-level calculation), but also to prioritize the targets for each of its tools on some sensible basis.[2]

But this type of analysis, by failing to pick up and examine *any* specific problem or pattern, could never produce the critical realization that "we don't have a tool for this," nor motivate the search for methods never before considered and therefore not present in the optimization equation.

In reaching phase 3, an institution has come a long way. It is surely better to be open-minded to a broader range of tools than bound to a narrow tradition, and surely better to base resource allocation decisions on some form of analysis than on subjective preferences or ideology. But at this point, institutions still fall substantially short of their potential. The patterns of thought and analysis associated with this phase might bless a newly adopted tool with some substantial budget allocation, and they might point each tool in the existing arsenal towards higher-priority targets; but they will never produce a new tailor-made solution for any specific problem.

Phase 4: Shift to a task focus

Phase 4 brings a completely different orientation, as attention shifts from the contents of the tool-shed to the nature of specific problems in the field. Rather than picking the important tools, and sending them off into the field one by one, the organization starts picking the important problems, and examining each of them in their own right, and without regard for any tool-based traditions or preferences. This is the moment where institutions discover the essence of craftsmanship, deploying combinations of tools around carefully defined tasks, and recognizing more quickly when they need new tools. In this mode, agencies consider first the intricacies of what needs to be accomplished, and only then consider what tools or methods might work. Prior to this stage, they considered first which tools they preferred, and derived from that what targets to go after.

At this fourth stage, in terms of the structure of Figure 2.2 on page 56 (which contrasted the two modes of organizational behavior, attention finally switches from the top right cell to the bottom left cell. And in terms of Figure 3.1 on page 80 (which showed the five different levels at which *harms* or *problems* could be defined and addressed), the scale of the objects now under consideration has now shifted downwards from level 5. The specific risk-concentrations being tackled now belong at levels 2, 3, and 4; no longer at level 5 (which considers only generalities), nor at level 1 (which considers individual incidents or violations).

At this stage agencies enjoy their first problem-solving successes, like the US Customs service with their port-running project. Specific knots are identified, tackled, and undone. If the work involves new, tailor-made solutions, then these successes might indeed be labeled "innovative." Typically these early successes arise (in terms of Figure 3.1) either at levels 2 or 4. Either they involve harms sufficiently visible and pressing that they constitute an inescapable crisis; or they involve problems small enough to be tackled by a small group of highly motivated individuals, and without much in the way of formal organizational support. These are the two levels which typically supply the early learning opportunities.

Even when agencies successfully engage and resolve such problems, they frequently do not grasp the broader promise of the methods they just employed. In the absence of further crises, or continued pressure from entrepreneurial staff, everything relaxes back into more familiar work habits. Or worse: executives take the heralded invention and transform it into another blanket prescription for the whole organization, to be applied elsewhere as energetically as possible, regardless of its suitability.

The very fact that these early successes tend to remain isolated, and are viewed as departures from business-as-usual, coupled with the danger of confusing one innovation with a more general *innovativeness*, emphasizes the fact that one more important step remains.

Phase 5: Institutionalize the harm-mitigation approach

This last stage involves taking this mode of operation and making it a core competence for the organization, and constructing all the systems and structures necessary to support and manage it. When an organization reaches this stage, one would expect it to construct and maintain a portfolio of harm-mitigation projects, each one aimed at a carefully identified and delineated concentration. There would no longer be any ambiguity about which problems had been selected, and which ones not; nor who was responsible for designing relevant interventions. Task-focused projects would have resources allocated, schedules imposed, and periodic managerial review. Managers would be familiar with the types of decision-making required by this form of work, and would be ready to explain and defend the choices they made. The terms of engagement for external parties and partners involved in the process would be clear. Analytic resources would be sufficient, and sufficiently versatile, to support this work. And any agency with a mature harm-reduction operation would have a growing list of projects successfully concluded, representing harms successfully reduced. The related project accounts would figure prominently in agency performance reports.

Many executives appear uncertain about the need to construct *any* formal systems for this. "Is it not enough," they ask, "that my staff understand that this type of work is different, and important, and that we are committed to doing it? Do we really need to weigh it all down with systems and structures?"

A very similar question arises with respect to risk-management within a corporation. Here, the risks are *to the company itself*, as opposed to societal risks. In seeking to control or mitigate various classes of risk (e.g. market risk, reputational risk, litigation risk, regulatory risk, etc.) does a corporation need any new apparatus; or could the task of risk-control be handled sufficiently well by existing line management, provided they were all suitably informed and aware?

The private sector answer to this question, based on plenty of unexpected calamities, comes down emphatically on the side of creating a dedicated structure.[3] Why? Because if a company relies on existing line-management for this purpose, the risk-control function fails miserably at the very first step: the step of risk *identification*. If you ask managers to identify all the relevant risks for which they might count themselves responsible, the chances are they will identify those risks: (a) which neatly align with their areas of responsibility, (b) of which they are aware, and (c) which they are prepared to disclose. Invariably, these risks represent a small subset of the overall risk portfolio; and, because these are the ones spotted most naturally and confronted most readily, they tend to be the ones best controlled already.[4]

The dangerous risks, for most institutions, are those that awkwardly straddle departmental lines, so it is not at all clear who is responsible for them; those that are invisible or uncertain; those that are not represented or captured by existing process flows; and the ones that nobody in the organization is prepared to acknowledge or discuss. In view of these considerations, prevailing private sector wisdom recommends the creation of dedicated structures, and we see the emergence within the private sector of compliance departments, ethics officers, corporate risk managers, and enterprise-wide risk management systems. These, separate from core operational units, focus deliberately on the identification, calibration, and mitigation of a wide range of risk exposures.[5] Dedicated structures provide a means for taking particular care over those risks most likely to be neglected or overlooked by line management.[6]

Reliance on existing structures seems to work equally poorly for public sector agencies, even for those with harm-reduction at the core of their missions. Teaching people to recognize this as a different type of work, and to appreciate its potential value, just does not seem to be enough. I have witnessed several major agencies train staff in the relevant techniques, fail to construct any supporting apparatus, and then wonder why on earth nothing new is happening. In many instances, the staff heard the message, understood its value, and then became more and more frustrated when they saw no support forthcoming. "Why ask us to do this," they complain, "and then make it impossible?"

What is it, exactly, that makes this work seem impossible in such circumstances? A host of reasons, apparently, according to the reports coming back from practitioners:[7]

- Process-based work takes all day and everyday, plus overtime and weekends, just to keep up; so there is no time left for this.
- Processes and programs all have schedules and deadlines, and specific mandates; therefore they all take precedence over this work, which has none of those things.
- Managers do not know their responsibilities with respect to this type of work.
- Real world problems come in awkward shapes and sizes, which do not align with our structures, and therefore nobody knows where responsibility rests.
- The problem-solving approach brings unfamiliar forms and degrees of discretion, and nobody really knows what kinds of choices they are actually authorized to make.
- Analytic support is in desperately short supply.
- The agency is held hostage by its own reporting traditions, so everyone is busy "keeping the numbers up."

- And the oddest one of all, which might be humorous if it were not so sad: "we don't have *forms* for this type of work." (All the forms available relate to incidents or cases; not to problems or patterns.)

Such expressions of frustration are sufficiently commonplace to make it clear, I believe, that this new form of work – if we really expect practitioners to do it – must be supported and managed at least as formally as functional and process-based work. Perhaps even more so, given the relative unfamiliarity of the new type of work, and the powerful tendency of the other forms to gobble up all available resources and attention. There are plenty of reasons why this type of work will not flourish and blossom simply on the basis of its potential value. *Not doing it,* if that remains an option, is just so much simpler and more comfortable.

To drive this work, an organization needs to develop and establish three rather different structures:

(a) *a protocol for problem-solving*, comprising a sequence of distinct stages through which any one harm-reduction project might proceed;

(b) *a managerial infrastructure*, by virtue of which an institution can construct, direct, support, and monitor its overall portfolio of harm-reduction projects;

(c) *an organizational interface* between this type of work and others, so that all the proper interactions between them can be understood and facilitated.

The problem-solving protocol

Many different professions offer some type of risk-management or problem-solving template, usually consisting of a few discrete steps. The most common elements are the most obvious ones, namely: identifying or diagnosing a problem, planning and implementing an intervention, and monitoring the effect of that intervention. Police departments variously use the four-step SARA model (Scanning, Analysis, Response, Assessment), or Professor Herman Goldstein's eight-step process, or something in between. Other professions similarly tend to specify some outline with more than three but less than ten distinct steps. The more detailed the template, the more bureaucratic and ɪrdensome it appears. The less detailed the template, the greater the danger of some essential piece of work being glossed over or short-changed.

Having seen a variety of such templates in use, I propose the following six-stage outline as providing the absolute minimal level of granularity necessary to avoid the most common traps.[8] Of course, an organization might choose to make available much more detailed guidance about each of these steps;[9] and some have, producing comprehensive manuals for the benefit of harm-mitigation project teams.[10]

Problem-solving protocol:

Stage 1:   Nominate & Select Potential Problem for Attention
Stage 2:   Define the Problem Precisely
Stage 3:   Determine How to Measure Impact
Stage 4:   Develop Solutions/Interventions
Stage 5(a):   Implement the Plan
Stage 5(b):   Periodic Monitoring/Review/Adjustment
Stage 6:   Project Closure, and Long Term Monitoring/
                    Maintenance

The simplest three-step versions might specify *diagnosis, treatment,* and *monitoring.* This six-stage version looks a little more complex but, for the price of just a little extra detail, incorporates a number of important lessons learned from practical experience.

First, it recognizes stage 1 as administratively separate from everything that follows. Nomination of a problem for attention might occur long before a project is launched, and the nominator is not necessarily a part of the project team, nor even a part of the organization that undertakes or manages the project. Separating stage 1 from the rest therefore recognizes the possibility that the nomination of the problem, and decisions about whether or not to select it for priority treatment, may occur elsewhere and at a different time, and involve actors separate from the project team.

Second, designating the work of defining a problem precisely as a distinct stage (stage 2) emphasizes the significant amount of analytical work involved in developing an accurate problem-specification. It recognizes that the problem-nominator might not actually fully understand the nature and scope of the problem. It recognizes that knots, even once found, still need to be studied. It acknowledges the complexity of the choices involved in setting the scale, and picking the right dimensions by which to characterize a harm. It acknowledges the need to consider multiple and competing perspectives on what the problem is, and negotiations over how it should be framed.[11] And it helps to control the *leap-to-action* syndrome, slowing down those who would otherwise assume at the very first mention of a problem that they already knew the solution well enough to launch into action without further thought.[12]

Third, this slightly more detailed template helps to guarantee the single most critical piece of methodological rigor in the problem-solving process: it obliges a project team to consider relevant metrics carefully (stage 3), and to do so *before* they consider or select any intervention plans (stage 4). Making the selection of metrics a distinct step signals the fact that this also represents a substantial piece of work, often demanding as much creativity and ingenuity as design of an action plan. The order is important also, because if project teams choose their metrics *after* selecting a plan, they will face the inevitable temptation to measure the organization's implementation of, or compliance with, *the plan* rather than measuring the plan's impact on *the problem*.

In agencies (such as in law-enforcement) where the leap-to-action syndrome seems particularly powerful, I urge managers to press on their project staff an even more draconian version of this discipline and to establish the rule: "*no new action*, until the relevant metrics have been selected, and benchmarked, and you have a clear understanding of how you would expect each to move if you succeeded." Sometimes staff protest, and get impatient, eager to try out a new strategy. But if they do not determine ahead of time which indicators count, and how they expect them to behave, then there is simply no way for them to evaluate whether any plan is actually working or not.

Fourth, by splitting stage 5 into parts (a) and (b), highlighting the need for *periodic review*, this outline makes it clear that picking an action plan is not necessarily a one-time-thing. Many brilliant and effective solutions (like the Customs eventual answer to the port-running problem) were not the first ones tried. In order to get to the second or third action plan, an organization has to be ready, both culturally and analytically, to recognize when a plan is not working and be prepared to abandon it so they can try the next idea. Any presumption that the first plan chosen must necessarily succeed drives out the possibility of honest and timely evaluation, and leaves organizations doing what public agencies seem to do so often – running a program for ever, without serious regard for its effects, just because once-upon-a-time it seemed like a good idea.

Fifth, this template formally recognizes the need for project *closure*. In the harm-reduction business it is much easier to open projects than close them, not least because closing a project usually involves accepting some residual level of harm.[13] In the absence of a decision framework for closing projects, an agency will tend to keep opening new ones until it drowns under a mass of unfinished projects. For this type of work to be sustainable in the long term as an operational strategy, agencies need to observe the *law of conservation of projects,* which states, simply, that projects need to be closed at roughly the same rate, on average, as they are opened. Otherwise projects proliferate, energy becomes too broadly dissipated, the whole machinery grinds to a halt, nothing ever gets finished, and the whole approach ends up discredited.

As a practical matter, projects might be closed for one of two general reasons: either the project *succeeded*, with the concentration of harm sufficiently mitigated (even if the resulting level is non-zero) that this particular concentration no longer represents a special priority.[14] At this point, the project may enter a longer term monitoring or maintenance mode (to prevent the problem recurring), but it should not continue to consume the same level of resources or attention as required during the intervention stage.

The other basis for closing a harm-mitigation project would be the realization that, for some reason or another, there was no real prospect of success. The problem is utterly intractable, or the necessary partners refuse to cooperate, or the problem lies too far beyond the agency's jurisdiction or competence, or resources available are inadequate, or the project faces insurmountable legal or political obstacles. At this point executives need to be able to face (and probably to defend) the decision to re-invest resources and attention in more promising areas.

A third possibility involves temporary suspension of a project during some time of crisis, but in a way that guarantees an orderly resumption once the crisis has passed.

The managerial infrastructure

Running one project is quite different from establishing and managing a portfolio of them. Designated project teams run specific projects, and follow the relevant protocol. But handling the overall portfolio of projects, making sure the collection of them amounts to something significant and produces important strategic outcomes, is a task for the management structure and requires a different set of systems.[15] At a minimum, such systems would necessarily include the following basic components:[16]

- **A nomination system**: for inviting and generating nominations, and then funneling them to some centralized selection point.
- **A selection system**: for comparative assessment of nominated issues, prioritization, and selection of projects to proceed.
- **Assignment of responsibility and resource allocation system**: for committing personnel and resources to projects, where necessary relieving staff of other duties.
- **Project records**: project files (paper or electronic), which track discussions, decisions, actions, and progress.
- **Managerial oversight and periodic review**: for monitoring and adjusting (where necessary) the course of a project; for approval of action plans; evaluation of results; and decisions about closure.
- **Reporting system**: for channeling an account of project-based accomplishments into the agency's routine performance accounts.
- **Support system for teams, team leaders, and managers involved in an oversight capacity**: to provide guidance in the harm-reduction art for staff and managers less familiar with it, analytic support, access to consultants, knowledge bases, and other relevant resources.

The following components, if not absolutely necessary, would certainly be desirable:

- **A reward system**: to provide recognition for project teams that achieve important harm-mitigation results.
- **A system for learning**: to pool knowledge the organization acquires with respect to what works, what doesn't, what resources are available within and outside the agency, and who to call for advice with respect to particular types of problem.

Although these systems are distinct from the problem-solving protocol, they are not entirely disconnected from it. These are the systems that will determine whether and when to launch specific projects, allocate staff, periodically review progress, evaluate proposed intervention plans, provide resources and authority necessary to implement approved plans, and decide when to change course and at what point to bring each project to a close. These systems will impinge on *all* projects, at various points in their life-cycles; by contrast, a specific project team sticks with just one, but deals with it in all its detail, from start to finish.

Organizations may differ substantially in the arrangements they choose for carrying out these portfolio-management functions. Some might take an existing unit, such as a research and planning department, and make it the central coordination point. Others create entirely new units for the purpose. Some agencies designate their own internal specialists in the problem-solving art, giving them extra training in the associated methodologies and analytic skills, and then deploy them as internal consultants to assist project teams and managers.

This is not the place to run through an extensive or exhaustive list of the possible arrangements. Suffice it to say, here, that it is hard to imagine this type of work flourishing, or even surviving, if any one of these essential systems were missing. Recognizing the need for them is a very important step in itself. When executives ask "why isn't this type of work happening?" the answer, invariably, is that one or more of these systems does not exist at all, and no amount of goodwill or energy from individual staff members can compensate for that structural and managerial deficiency.

The organizational interface with other forms of work

As the harm-reduction operation matures over time, executives will discover many important ways in which this type of work interacts with functional and process-based operations.

There are some obviously destructive forms of interaction which might occur. Champions of one type of work might decry the importance of the others. Staff buried under high-volume processes may well resent any staff who are relieved and removed from that grinding pressure, especially if they look to them as if they are sitting around, thinking and talking a lot (which is a normal precursor to effective action!) Conversely, staff assigned to harm-mitigation projects, and experiencing the formidable intellectual challenges associated therewith, might find themselves jealous of the comparative predictability and lack of ambiguity that goes with functional and process work, where *what to do* is perfectly well established, and nothing much needs to be invented.

And of course different units, methods, theories of operation, and even modes of organizational behavior can easily end up competing (through their human representatives and champions) for resources, attention, and credit.

Fortunately there are also several healthy, constructive, and symbiotic ways in which these different types of work can interact. Here are a few of them:

- An intervention plan might include adjustments to existing processes, or adjustments to the treatment of a specific category of incident as they pass through incident-response or other routine processes (e.g. a tax agency, aware of an emerging form of taxpayer non-compliance, might add a new line of inquiry to its standard audit protocol).
- Where harms are successfully reduced, the load on related response processes should diminish over time (e.g. safer highway conditions should eventually result in fewer accidents).
- In the long term, organizations will hope to be able, therefore, to re-invest resources from process and incident response into harm-mitigation projects. The reinvestment process should never proceed so far that it undermines the response capability, nor should it run too far ahead of the relief produced by successful harm-reduction efforts. On the other hand, re-investment needs to be deliberate and aggressive enough so that the organization does not wait passively for "spare time" or extra resources before new projects can be launched. After all, the related decline in response loads will normally lag the project-based interventions to some extent.
- Analysis of process loads – in particular monitoring for the emergence of any new clusters or patterns of incidents – is one of the more readily accessible methods for spotting emerging risk-concentrations worthy of special attention.
- Experimental treatments might be administered through adjustments to routine processes. Novel treatments can be allocated randomly within a target category of incidents, to help test the effect of different treatments (e.g. an experimental treatment for domestic violence might require that reports of domestic disputes be handled by police in specific ways).
- Different types of work may involve the same people. Problem-solving projects may engage staff who continue to hold process-based

responsibilities, and who are therefore obliged to split their time and attention between the two different types of work. (In which case, they are likely to discover that the process work takes more time, whereas the project work takes a lot more thought.)

• The detailed analysis of a problem might require collection of data not normally kept in case files, nor obtained through routine operations. Additional data-gathering requirements might therefore be temporarily superimposed on normal response operations ("please ask the following additional questions ... ").

• Staff engaged in routine processes can often provide insight into the existence and nature of underlying patterns, even though traditional responsibilities have focused on processing the incidents rather than spotting or dealing with the patterns. Front line staff represent one very important source for insightful problem nominations, and they are normally quite pleased and relieved when they discover someone is actually interested in patterns they have noticed. Often these are things they might have known or suspected for years, but had nobody to tell.

Given all these various ways in which the different types of work interact, it might be tempting to conclude that these forms of work are therefore not so different after all. That would be a huge mistake. They are still very different; they are just not entirely *separate*.

In figuring out how to integrate harm-reduction work into the body of an agency, one option is to segregate staff entirely, keeping project teams apart from the remainder of the organization. Some organizations have found value, for a while at least, in establishing dedicated units to handle the problem-solving work. Segregation protects the project teams from the pressures of the process load, so they can actually find the time and mental focus necessary to get to grips with their analysis and design worthwhile plans. Dedicated units also serve as incubators for the relevant methodological skills and work practices.

The downside of segregation, however, is that it can disconnect the project-based work from front-line operational realities. After all, the harm-reduction approach is supposed to be an operational method, not a research method. It will surely get sidelined if it is allowed to morph into a primarily academic or intellectual research endeavor.

If possible, managers need to recognize the value in these connections, and prevent the project-based work from becoming detached from the remainder of operations. At the same time, they must never lose sight of the distinctive nature of this work, and the very specific supports and systems required to drive it. If they do, experience suggests the whole business of spotting important concentrations of harm, and unpicking them one by one, will dissipate in a flash. It is a very fragile business.

Notes

1. Some, familiar with the concepts of *enterprise-wide* or *integrated* risk-management philosophies might be puzzled by use of the word "integrated" in this context. Here the question is whether, in addressing any one risk, an artful combination of tools can be combined to produce an integrated solution for that specific risk. The alternate use (as in *integrated risk management*) indicates the bringing together of all classes of risk under one common monitoring and management system, providing greater clarity with respect to assessing organization-wide risk appetites, managing portfolios of risks, and understanding interactions between risks of differing types. See: Lisa Meulbroek, "The Promise and Challenge of Integrated Risk Management," *Risk Management and Insurance Review,* 5 (2002), pp. 55–66. This usage of "integrated" is also clearly stated in: Zack Mansdorf, "Integrated Risk Management," *Occupational Hazards,* 60 (1998), 29–30.
2. The Financial Services Authority in London, in the early stages of developing their "risk-based" approach to financial regulation, first developed some quite sophisticated models for prioritizing companies and other financial institutions for audit. Likewise, the US Food and Drug Administration has experimented with similarly sophisticated risk-based methods for prioritizing its inspections of pharmaceutical manufacturing sites.
3. For a concise history of the development of *risk-management* systems within the corporate world, see: Ben Hunt, "Survey – Mastering Risk: The Rise and Rise of Risk Management," *The Financial Times,* London (June 27, 2000), 4.
4. Avoiding the narrow focus that results from concentrating on familiar and quantifiable risks is one principal driver for the emergence of the Enterprise Risk Management philosophy. See: *Overview of Enterprise Risk Management,* Casualty Actuarial Society, Enterprise Risk

Management Committee (May 2003), 3. Available on the web at: [www.casact.org/research/erm/overview.pdf].

5. Steven Briers, *A New Language of Risk – A Foundation for Enterprise Wide Risk Management* (South Africa: Unisa Press Publications, 2002); *Framework for Enterprise Risk Management* (Jersey City, New Jersey: Committee of Sponsoring Organizations of the Treadway Commission, 2004); Anthony C. Valsamakis, Robert W. Vivian, & G.S. Du Toit, *Risk Management – Managing Enterprise Risks* (Sandton: Heinemann, 2005). The Turnbull Report specified the need for formal risk identification, analysis and management systems for all companies listed on the London Stock Exchange. See: Mike Page & Laura F. Spira, *The Turnbull Report, Internal Control and Risk Management: The Developing Role of Internal Audit* (Edinburgh, Institute of Chartered Accountants of Scotland, 2004). This document specified greater formality and the creation of managerial infrastructure necessary to deliver the type of integrated risk assessment and control recommended in an earlier report: Nigel Turnbull (Chair), "*Internal Control: Guidance for Directors on the Combined Code,*" Internal Control Working Party, Institute of Chartered Accountants in England & Wales (London: Institute of Chartered Accountants, 1999).

6. For a discussion of the differences between a *dispersed* approach (where each functional unit defines and controls its own risks) and an *integrated* approach sufficient to deal with cross-cutting issues, see: "*Enhancing Shareholder Wealth by Better Managing Business Risk,*" Financial and Managing Accounting Committee, Study no. 9 (New York, International Federation of Accountants (IFAC), June 1999), 25–27.

7. The following list of reasons draws from feedback from British police (engaged in problem-oriented policing) and from Florida's Department of Environmental Protection during the early days of their Environmental Problem-Solving program. A fuller discussion of these obstacles as confronted by regulators, and consideration of how they might be overcome, can be found in: Malcolm K. Sparrow, *The Regulatory Craft: Controlling Risks, Solving Problems & Managing Compliance* (Washington DC: Brookings Institution Press, 2000), pp. 208–211.

8. The simplest templates for problem-solving generally have four steps, covering *risk identification, risk assessment* (or *measurement), risk control* (i.e. actions/interventions), and *risk monitoring* (to measure the effects of interventions). For example: Benton A. Brown, "Step-by-Step Enterprise Risk Management," *Risk Management*, 48 (September 2001), 43–50.

9. Chapter 10 of Sparrow, *The Regulatory Craft*, provides a much more detailed account of the problem-solving process as exercised by regulatory agencies, and considers the range of obstacles and dilemmas that can arise at each stage.

10. For example, see "*Guide to Environmental Problem-Solving*," Revised edition (Tallahassee: Florida Department of Environmental Protection, 2000).

11. Paul C. Stern & Harvey V. Fineberg (eds.), *Understanding Risk: Informing Decisions in a Democratic Society*, National Research Council (Washington DC: National Academy Press, 1996), pp. 157–161.

12. Clear separation of the analysis of a problem from the determination of action accords with the distinction between *risk-analysis* and *risk-management*. Such careful separation is advocated in: William D. Ruckelshaus, "Risk, Science & Democracy," *Issues in Science and Technology*, 1 (Spring 1985), 13–38; also, in *Risk Assessment in the Federal Government: Managing the Process*, Report of the Committee on Institutional Means for Assessment of Risks to Public Health, Commission of Life Sciences, National Research Council (Washington DC: National Academy Press, 1983), pp. 6–7. The possibility of neatly separating these in the policy development process, however, has been questioned by others on a variety of grounds. Some point to the imperfections and impurity of scientific risk assessments. For example: Dale Hattis and David Kennedy, "Assessing Risks from Health Hazards: An Imperfect Science," *Technology Review*, 89 (May/June 1986), 60–71. Also, William Leiss & Christine Chociolko, *Risk and Responsibility* (Montreal: McGill-Queen's University Press, 1994), p. 21. Others argue that the early stage of *framing* a risk issue, which is part of *defining* it, ought to be an interactive and democratic process and thus not left to scientists alone. For a discussion of the recent re-emergence within Europe of pressures to separate risk assessment from risk management, see: Ragnar E. Löfstedt, "Risk Communication and Management in the Twenty-First Century," *International Public Management Journal*, 7 (2004), 335–346.

13. The imperative to establish "acceptable levels" for specific risks, given practical budget constraints, is well established in the context of macro-level economic analysis. W. Kip Viscusi, *Fatal Tradeoffs: Public & Private Responsibilities for Risk* (Oxford: Oxford University Press, 1992), pp. 4–5.

14. The use of problem-solving as an operational methodology, involving a continuous cycle of opening and closing risk-specific projects, results in middle and upper level managers bearing the responsibility for prioritizing amongst unlike risks and for formulating acceptable residual

levels of risks in specific focus areas. Operational managers thus engage in the "portfolio management" of risk-reduction projects.

15. Stephen Hill & Geoff Dinsdale, *A Foundation for Developing Risk Management Learning Strategies in the Public Sector* (Ottawa, Canada: Canadian Centre for Management Development, 2001), p. 10.

16. A more detailed analysis of these components can be found in Sparrow, *The Regulatory Craft*, pp. 155–170.

Harms can be grouped together in several ways, and for rather different purposes.

The most familiar groupings bring harms together if they belong to the same general field, which might be highway safety, tax compliance, environmental protection, or infectious disease control. Grouped this way, harms are likely to fall within the same area of professional responsibility, and the task of controlling them draws upon the same body of technical or scientific knowledge. On this basis it makes sense to group together *crime problems* (the domain of criminologists and law enforcement; *infectious diseases* (the domain of public health experts, and medicine), *occupational safety hazards* (structural engineering, industrial hygiene, and toxicology). Similarly with tax non-compliance problems, transportation hazards, threats to financial markets, and so on. In each area we would expect to find experts who have mastered the relevant underlying disciplines, and who keep themselves current with respect to emerging and evolving threats within their field. Specialization along these lines bolsters the knowledge bases and scientific disciplines upon which effective control depends. It is also efficient in the sense that an expert in one domain does not need to know much about all the other domains, assuming that the groupings by professional area align reasonably well with relevant underlying disciplines.

The interdisciplinary study of risks (including risk-analysis, risk-communication, and risk-management) has introduced a different set of categorizations. Some of the novelty in the general science of risk lies in its willingness to scan broadly across traditional categories, paying more attention to the properties of certain risks, and a little less attention to the field in which they belong. Presumably there are thousands of *properties* that might be worth considering, for one reason or another. Some properties might make a risk particularly dangerous, or disproportionately expensive to control, or especially difficult to agree about, or awkward to measure. For practical purposes, it is also useful to know which risks can actually be reduced or mitigated, and which ones society must learn to live with because they are systemic.[1]

Among all of the possible properties on which scholars and practitioners might focus, one set of properties has turned out to be of special interest, attracting a lot of attention from behavioral economists and experimental psychologists: namely, *the properties of a risk which affect the perceptions of potential victims.* Attention to these properties has spawned a number of rather interesting and quite central research questions within the risk-management field. For example, which properties or qualities of a risk affect people's emotional response to the threat? Which properties affect people's estimation of their own likelihood of exposure to the risk? Which properties cause such estimations to be substantially wrong, or persistently biased (either up or down)? What types of context-setting, mood manipulation, or psychological conditioning can change an individual's estimation of their own exposures? And what properties substantially affect an individual's willingness to expose themselves or their loved ones to a particular risk, or to engage in hazardous activities?

Part II of this book, in considering properties of risks, does not seek to advance, nor even to summarize, these already well established lines of inquiry. Much important work is already being done by others in that regard. Rather, the task here is to take a different tack, and consider the *properties of risks that complicate the task of controlling them.* So the following chapters are less about human psychology, and more about *operational challenges.* They attend less to the mindset of potential victims, and more to the challenges confronting officials. In fact the audience for this part is not so much academics and psychologists, but regulators, public officials who have harm-reduction responsibilities, international organizations which take on international problems, not-for-profit organizations contributing to the control of social harms, and foundations and others who would fund or otherwise support such tasks.

Officials in all of these organizations, if they are not to suffer interminable frustration, might like to know what it is about certain harms that makes controlling them particularly awkward or troublesome. Some properties guarantee a certain intractability. Other properties render all the readily available metrics ambiguous, and therefore make the effectiveness of any interventions particularly difficult to assess. Certain properties elevate the importance of intelligence gathering, or introduce circularity traps in focus and attention. Other properties make budget-justification on a short term basis problematic. And some settings in which harm reduction has to be performed turn out to be naturally hostile to the control task. All of these phenomena stem from identifiable properties of the harm, or of the harm-control context, and do so somewhat independently of the technical or professional domain in which the harm belongs.

I hope that focusing on these properties will provide useful insights for practitioners. I do not imagine for one moment that these insights will in any way displace, or render less important, domain-specific technical and scientific expertise. In fact, my motivation for pursuing this line of inquiry stems largely from the rewarding experience of watching groups of regulators, drawn from quite different professions and each quite expert in their own area, discover the importance of these properties as they compare notes *across* fields.

So, for instance, a senior police executive embarks on a major program to address the problem of domestic violence. They have to explain to their political overseers that if their campaign succeeds, the number of complaints received about domestic assault incidents should at first rise sharply (as reporting and detection rates rise), then flatten out and eventually decline to lower levels (as the underlying problem abates). An official from the Equal Employment Opportunity Commission, responsible for reducing discrimination in the workplace, points out that a successful campaign launched against a pattern of discrimination produces the same type of behavior in complaint levels, which should rise at first and then eventually fall to lower levels. The executives from both agencies have a hard time persuading political overseers to interpret the behaviors of these metrics appropriately. A Customs official points out that seizure rates relating to a newly identified drug-smuggling method behave in exactly the same way, producing a flurry of arrests and seizures when a smuggling tactic is precisely targeted, followed by an eventual decline when the smugglers abandon the smuggling tactic. In all three settings, the behavior of these metrics is utterly predictable because the underlying problems all share the same property: they are *invisible by their nature, or by design.*

On one occasion I worked with a group of environmental scientists when the subject of toxic-waste dumping came up. This problem, they complained, did not behave like most of the other environmental problems they dealt with. Their normal inspection regimes failed to control it, and their normal approaches to measurement seemed not to fit. Why was that? For anyone who has a background in law-enforcement, the answer is fairly clear: because, with toxic waste-dumping, there is a *brain behind the harm.* In tackling this problem the environmental regulators faced conscious opponents, including organized crime groups, who rapidly adapted to thwart any attempt to control their illegal businesses, moving their methods and places for dumping out of the authorities' line-of-sight. Most environmental problems did not have this property, and the scientists' background training in biology, chemistry, and toxicology had not provided much insight into the practical consequences of dealing with opponents. Such insight might come quickly from conversation with other professionals whose harm-reduction tasks routinely involved taking on opponents. Professionals who deal daily with smugglers, traffickers, computer hackers, terrorists, or thieves could quickly shed some light on the consequences of criminal entrepreneurship and adaptation, the role of intelligence, and the importance of preserving mystery and unpredictability in compliance management strategies.

When practitioners discover analogous challenges across very different fields, their first reaction is normally surprise. Then quickly follows a sense of relief, because each had assumed they faced these oddities alone, and had to figure out all the operational consequences by themselves.

I have chosen in the chapters that follow to focus on a small number of the most commonly observed and most troublesome characteristics. I shall mention three categories rather briefly, and then deal with five others more fully. The three classes, which I regard as "runners-up" in terms of the frequency with which they manage to surprise and confound those engaged in the control task, are:

- *High-level harms:* these are risks or harms which exist at a level which transcends the scope of existing control systems.

- *Slow-acting harms:* most of these involve natural, biological or physiological systems, and the distinctive operational challenges these harms bring results from the fact that the time intervals between causes, interventions, and outcomes may run to several decades.
- *Where the risk-control function finds itself in a hostile context:* harm-reduction functions frequently conflict, to some degree, with the core purposes or culture of an organization. Those with risk or harm-control responsibilities may therefore find themselves alienated or unwelcome and their methods unappreciated within the organization.

The five most common categories, at least judging by the collective experience of professional regulators, are these:

- *Invisible harms:* where low rates of reporting or detection make the bulk of the problem invisible, the underlying scope of it uncertain, and the effects of any intervention difficult to discern.
- *Harms involving conscious opponents:* where those responsible for control find themselves engaged in a dynamic game played against adaptive opposition, each side seeking to outsmart the other.
- *Catastrophic harms:* these involve calamities of enormous consequence but of very low probability, and which may never have happened before, even once.
- *Harms in equilibrium:* some systems rest in harmful equilibrium states, wherein any small perturbation produces forces acting to restore and maintain the status quo. Freeing systems from such stable equilibrium positions requires an initial "big shove" sufficient to overcome the gravitational pull of the starting position, followed by skillful navigation towards some other (preferred) equilibrium position.
- *Performance-enhancing risks:* sometimes improper or unlawful risk-taking enhances core aspects of an organization's performance. Performance imperatives may therefore produce powerful pressures in opposition to the control of such risks, as the organization overtly or covertly seeks to protect the performance advantages it derives from such risk-taking behaviors.

These five properties crop up so often, and across so many different professional domains, that I have devoted one chapter to each of them. My intent is to illustrate each of these classes with a broad enough range of examples that practitioners will immediately recognize harms within their own domains that are analogous. These chapters also tease out the essence of the challenges that each class presents, and says a little of what different fields have discovered in terms of how best to deal with them.

It might be wise to declare at this point, and for the sake of minimizing disappointment, three things which readers of this analysis really ought *not* to expect.

First, this is not a *taxonomy*. The chapters that follow each describe one property, and its operational consequences. Some harms exhibit more than one of these properties, and thus appear in more than one category. Political corruption, for example, belongs in the *invisible* category, and in the *conscious opponents* category, and – if it reaches high enough to subvert the justice system – might also belong in the category of *high-level* harms (those that exist above the level of the available control apparatus). The categories corresponding to these properties overlap, and therefore this schema clearly does not present a complete and disjoint partition of the universe of harms in the manner of any satisfying taxonomy. Where a harm displays two or more of these properties, then the control operation has to deal with each of the sets of related consequences, simultaneously. Controlling such harms is therefore doubly difficult, or worse!

Second, readers should not expect the properties selected for attention here to be entirely novel. Some of them are perfectly well understood in some fields. I'd like them to be well understood in *all* fields. In particular I'd like what's been learned about them in some fields to be available to practitioners in all fields. Also, some of these properties (or at least some of their *labels*) already appear within risk categorizations designed for other purposes. For instance, we know that *invisibility* of a risk affects psychological assessments and emotional reactions. An invisible poison gas induces greater fear than a visible one.[2] Likewise a contagious disease is more "dreadful" if no symptoms are visible during the infectious period. So the property of *invisibility* counts when the purpose is to work out what affects risk-perception and psychological reaction. But *invisibility* in a slightly different sense (where the underlying scope of a problem is essentially unknown) has broad operational consequences too. And many problems to be controlled (such as white collar crime, fraud, consensual drug-dealing) fit in this category even though they would not normally be regarded as objects of dread. The two purposes seem quite different, even though the same label appears under each purpose.

Third, no-one should imagine that the listing that follows is in any way comprehensive. Without doubt, a great many other properties count also, and may have substantial implications for the operational task of control. The ones I have picked here are simply the ones that show up most often. These are, if you like, the basic ones, and hopefully a useful starting point for such analysis. If this way of categorizing them turns out to be useful, then extended lists might follow later.

In deliberately limiting this list I am mindful not to make harm-reduction seem utterly impossible by dwelling exhaustively on endless difficulties. My goal is simply to help as many practitioners as possible, across many fields, with a relatively short and carefully selected set of ideas. So I make no pretence of completeness here. The awkward properties addressed in these next few chapters are probably sufficient to test the usefulness of categorizing harms this way. And enough, hopefully, to help significant numbers of practitioners understand more clearly why one or another problem has frustrated them so much.

Even with these caveats, some readers might quibble with my selection. Over the last two decades I have had the privilege to work with thousands of professional regulators, and their concerns and collective experience have largely driven my choices here. There is obviously a longer list of candidate *types* of harm, and a broader constituency of practitioners interested in the challenges of harm-reduction. Many contributions to important harm-mitigation goals come from non-regulatory bodies. Perhaps the interests of the broader audience will turn out to be different from the concerns of regulators. I suspect that my three runners-up might be of special interest to civil society, not-for-profit and other non-governmental organizations, and to institutions that operate at levels other than national or regional governments.

Let me at least describe these three "runner-up" categories briefly here, even though I shall leave detailed analysis of the operational consequences for another occasion, or to others better qualified to address them:

(1) High-level harms

International non-governmental organizations and coalitions organized around global or regional problems might well be concerned with *high-level* harms. By this I mean those problems or threats whose natural shape and size transcends any one legislature, source of authority, or coherent control apparatus. In addressing these, the injunction to *respect the natural shape and size of the risk itself* becomes especially problematic. There is no one body, or agency, or nation that has the authority to orchestrate interventions at the level of the harm itself.

This category of problems includes global warming, management of ocean fish-stocks, international trafficking in drugs or human beings or nuclear materials, worldwide monitoring and control of infectious diseases, control of international terrorism, and efforts of international communities to reduce regional conflicts and prevent genocide.

In the absence of centralized control structures, effective and efficient control of high-level harms depends upon cooperative and voluntary agreements among multiple parties, with no over-arching authority.[3] Differing perspectives on the nature of the risk and cultural differences in approach confound planning, execution, and measurement. Growth in international trade and mobility increases the proportion of modern-day risks that present these issues. So too does our ability and apparent willingness as a race to mess with our planet's natural systems, which display higher degrees of connectedness than our collective governance. As issues that transcend national and jurisdictional boundaries proliferate, regulatory activity responds by becoming increasingly supra-national, acting through a range of agreements, treaties, international standards, mutual recognition schemes, as well as through jointly staffed and collectively authorized international bodies.[4]

(2) Slow-acting harms

Environmental, medical and public-health professionals also confront the special difficulties associated with *slow-acting* harms. Cancer risks may lag contributory causes by as much as fifty years. Ecological and biological systems might take decades or even centuries to repair. All of the relevant strategies and interventions, nevertheless, need to be funded through annual budget cycles and gain commitments from a political environment that operates with comparatively short-term attention spans.

For these problems, progress in mitigating harms is especially difficult to measure. The desired outcomes might not be at all achievable within budget cycles, political terms, or other short-term time frames. Proxy or interim measures, such as changes in contributory behaviors, may be used to demonstrate progress. But all such measures depend for their credibility on the existence of a compelling scientific theory that establishes them as stepping-stones on the way to the desired outcome. These scientific bases for operations may be disputed, evolving, or beyond the technical understanding of policy makers and the public. These vulnerabilities subject control operations to political whims and interference, making any long-term strategy difficult to justify and sustain.

I take a modicum of comfort from the observation that harms of this type tend to lie within professional areas densely populated with scientists, and that many other scholars have provided detailed analysis of the appropriate interaction between science and high-level policy-making processes, and the ways in which these interactions might be designed to accommodate these difficulties.[5]

(3) Risk-control in a hostile environment

This category involves risk-control or harm-reduction activities located within an organization set up for some quite different purpose. The harm-reduction function is therefore peripheral to the enterprise, and may be unwelcome or at least unappreciated given the core purpose and culture of the organization. The distinctive property for this class, therefore, is not so much a property of the harms themselves; it is more a property of the *setting* for the harm-control task.

Examples include the task of fraud control within health care systems, security operations in an academic environment, or the control of corruption or child abuse within a religious community. In these settings the core enterprise and its culture determines the tone, presumes high levels of trustworthiness, and establishes distinctive norms with respect to the nature of supervisory relationships and forms of accountability.

A health program, for instance, depends on its network of physicians in order to deliver health services, and the program may have to compete with other health plans to persuade providers to work for them. The social status normally accorded medical providers, together with the imperatives of the business model, lead program administrators to treat doctors very well indeed; to trust them, respect them, and always give them the benefit of the doubt when something goes awry. Administrators absolutely do not *want* to think of their physician partners as potential miscreants, or to imagine that the financial incentives and systems, based on trust, might actually attract criminal attention and invite assault. Within this environment, a unit responsible for risk-control or fraud-reduction, and which therefore specializes in *suspicion*, most likely finds itself in quite a hostile setting. Nobody wants to hear from them. Nobody likes their methods. Some distrust their values. And some may obstruct or sabotage their work, honestly believing they do so in the best interests of the organization. After all, senior management would rather not contemplate the possibility that the actions of such a unit might damage their provider-network, or embarrass the organization, or alarm their business partners, or – for that matter – unsettle the shareholders.

Security guards and campus police, likewise, find themselves largely unappreciated given the prevailing politics of academic communities. So too would anyone attempting to expose and deal with child-abuse among clergy, or embezzlement inside a charity. Such organizations like to ascribe positive motivations, believe in trusting people as a deliberate and constructive way of managing their behavior, and prefer to correct them should it become necessary through the provision of support and guidance. The control of serious harms in such environments requires hasher methods, less generous assumptions, and suspension of these prevailing norms. Executives may question whether the control of the harm is actually worth such intense discomfort and potential damage to the organization's norms, reputation, or capacity to operate.

I have outlined these three additional categories here, simply because they were close runners-up to the other five in terms of the frequency with which practitioners raise them, and because they might be of particular interest to professionals who work in non-regulatory settings.

These three ended up "runners-up" partly because these types of harms are somewhat less horizontally distributed across professions, and a little more vertically concentrated. Slow-acting natural systems belong mostly in the domain of health and the environment; and if a practitioner faces *some* problems like this, then they probably face quite a lot like this. That should make the property and its associated operational challenges more familiar, and the profession more accustomed to grappling with them. These properties and their consequences, therefore, should less often come as a surprise.

Similarly, organizations that deal with global or international problems are generally aware of the special challenges these present. And risk-control practitioners who work in fundamentally unsympathetic environments live with that reality *all the time*. This latter group do seem to experience enormous relief when, away from their workplace, they discover they are not alone. The chance to discuss the attitudes and actions of their organizations with others similarly situated, but in different professions, revives their spirits as well as giving them the chance to develop explicit strategies for dealing with the hostile context.

The remaining chapters in this book deal with the five classes of harm that seem to cause the most consternation for the broadest range of practitioners. These types of harm seem sufficiently commonplace, and appear across enough domains, that understanding them might legitimately be regarded as fundamental to the art of harm-reduction.

Notes

1. The Royal Bank Financial Group categorizes risks according to the degree to which they might actually be affected by risk-management operations, see: "*Enhancing Shareholder Wealth by Better Managing Business Risk*," Financial and Managing Accounting Committee, Study no. 9 (New York: International Federation of Accountants (IFAC), June 1999), p. 16.
2. For a discussion of the effects of disgust and horror in relation to exposure to poisons, both chemical and biological, gaseous and otherwise, see: Jessica Stern, *The Ultimate Terrorists* (Cambridge, Massachusetts & London, England: Harvard University Press, 1999), pp. 31–44.
3. For a discussion of the extent to which the connection between the fields of International Relations and Risk Theory has *not* been made, and the importance of filling this gap for effective control of risks spanning international borders, see: Darryl S. L. Jarvis & Martin Griffiths, "Risk and International Relations: A New Research Agenda?" Editorial, *Global Society,* 21 (January 2007), 1–3.
4. Business regulation since the 1970s has become an increasingly cooperative and international endeavour, utilizing a variety of mechanisms and institutions created to handle regulatory issues that span national boundaries: John Braithwaite & Peter Drahos, *Global Business Regulation* (Cambridge: Cambridge University Press, 2000).

5. See, for example: Sheila Jasanoff, *The Fifth Branch: Science Advisers as Policymakers* (Cambridge, Massachusetts: Harvard University Press, 1990); Nico Stehr, *Knowledge Societies* (London & Thousand Oaks, California: Sage Publications, 1994); Silvio O. Funtowicz & Jerry R. Ravetz, "Uncertainty, Complexity and Post-normal Science," *Environmental Toxicology and Chemistry*, 13 (1994), 1881–1885; *Science and Judgment in Risk Assessment*, Report of the Committee on Risk Assessment of Hazardous Air Pollutants, Board on Environmental Studies and Toxicology, Commission on Life Sciences, National Research Council (Washington DC: National Academy Press, 1994).

8 | *Invisible harms*

S ome risks do not fully reveal themselves. What I mean is that while the harm may be visible in some instances and invisible in others, the bulk of the problem is hidden and therefore the underlying scope of the problem may not be fully understood.

Harms are invisible for several different reasons. Some are invisible *by design*, as is often the case with sophisticated white-collar crimes such as fraud, embezzlement, and corruption. Perpetrators take steps to understand and then deliberately circumnavigate detection systems. From the perpetrator's point of view, the best schemes of this type are those that are not only invisible to authorities at the time of commission, but remain invisible in perpetuity.

Some harms – such as within-the-family crimes like sexual abuse, incest, and domestic violence – are invisible because victims and witnesses are reluctant, unable, or otherwise unlikely to report what they know. Similarly with rape, and date-rape in particular, which tend to have very low reporting rates. Blackmail is often not reported because victims fear the consequences for their own reputations. Crimes involving intimidation, such as extortion, go largely unreported. Another set of crimes, termed *consensual* crimes, are generally not reported because all the participants take part by choice, at least to some extent. These include drug-dealing, conspiracies, gambling, prostitution, and some forms of cooperative corruption such as bribery and nepotism.[1]

Of course, some incidents for all of these harms do come to light, despite the lack of reporting by people directly involved. Drug-dealing may be observed by others. Domestic violence victims turn up in hospital emergency rooms. Some instances of fraud or embezzlement may be uncovered through routine audits, or show up as anomalies in data-mining. These problems nevertheless remain firmly in the *invisible* category by virtue of the fact that what becomes visible depends heavily on the effectiveness of detection and exposure mechanisms. For these problems, *what you see is what you detect*, and what gets detected or reported might represent a thin sliver of the total underlying volume.

Those responsible for controlling these problems clearly should treat properly those cases that come to light. But the real challenge here is grappling with the invisible mass. That task requires systems and methods for determining the true nature and extent of the problem, and careful attention to overcoming or correcting the existing biases in detection methods.[2] Without some deliberate effort to gauge the prevalence of such problems, everyone can remain blissfully unaware of the overall extent of harm done, and control operations can miss important concentrations altogether.

Some problems are invisible because of defects in the design or limitations in the breadth of processes assumed to handle them. Perhaps the processes were designed with other variants of the problem in mind, and are out of date. Perhaps the methods by which incidents are fed into the process favor some types of incident but miss others, with the result that process-loads constitute a skewed sampling of the underlying problems. This possibility arises whenever something inhibits the reporting or detection mechanism. For example, whatever the overall reporting rate is for discrimination in the workplace, it is likely to be significantly affected by factors such as language ability and immigration status. Similarly, whatever the overall reporting rate for occupational injuries, it is likely to be considerably lower in industries or jurisdictions where employers pay experience-rated premiums for worker injury compensation insurance, and thus have an incentive to inhibit reporting by their employees.

Agencies that operate core high-volume operational processes as the principal engine for controlling harms do well to stand back from their machine, from time to time, and think carefully what it might be missing. The senior management of the IRS did exactly that during their executive retreat in 1991. When Commissioner Fred Goldberg asked his management team to list the top tax non-compliance problems in the US tax system, they quickly identified the problem of *non-filers* as number one on the list. The IRS used the term *non-filers* to describe the (estimated) eleven million individuals or businesses who had never filed a tax return, despite an obligation to do so (as discussed earlier in Chapter 2). Having agreed that the *non-filer* problem was the number one non-compliance issue, the executive team went on to discuss what they should do about it, and what tools they had available to address it. In the early 1990s the managerial methods being imported into government were all about process management. Yet the executive team quickly realized that these *non-filers* were not represented at all in the workloads for any of the IRS core processes. They did not file tax returns, nor write letters, nor call asking for help. This problem was therefore completely unrepresented in everything the IRS did on a daily basis. It took an executive retreat to provide the team with an opportunity to consider the *problem itself*.

When they did so, they quickly realized that for this problem – the most serious of all their non-compliance issues – they had no relevant processes, no person or department designated as responsible, no organizational approach, no measurement system, and no data about any of the non-compliers. The IRS did have massive operational databases, of course, but they were full of information about those who had filed, at least once. So if anyone who normally filed suddenly skipped a year, then the IRS would notice. But the persistent non-filers appeared nowhere within these datasets. Information about the non-filer problem was available *outside* the agency, in the realm of economic research on the black economy and cash-based businesses. Moreover, if the IRS had been so minded, they could have begun identifying non-filers using outside data sources. For example, by cross matching business listings in the yellow pages of the telephone directory against businesses that had filed, the agency could have generated a "remainder list" of businesses which were currently advertising but had not filed. But routine processing of *what came in* through the agency's core processes, however perfect, would not touch this problem at all.

This particular example provides an unusually stark reminder that agencies should never assume that process loads adequately reflect all the problems they need to address. The IRS non-filer example reveals an almost complete disconnection between processes and problems – the largest tax problem in the nation completely unrepresented in their operational processes. Professionals in other domains might take comfort from the fact that the separation is not often so stark, and that most substantial problems are represented at least to some degree within what is ordinarily visible. Still, I would prefer officials did not take much comfort on this point, as each one should consider quite carefully, and periodically, *which* problems within their portfolio of responsibilities might be insufficiently reflected in existing processes and therefore inadequately addressed. Invariably there are some.

Two years later, in 1993, the IRS confronted a new problem which was at least partially visible to them. A new type of financial support for the working poor, in the form of the *earned income tax credit* (EITC), was to be administered as a tax credit by the IRS, even though the payment had more the character of a welfare entitlement. Low income families that qualified for the EITC did not need to have paid any tax throughout the year to be entitled to a tax "refund," consisting of the credit. The EITC payment could exceed $2,000 per year. For the IRS, administering the credit presented some unfamiliar problems. They were not normally in the business of validating welfare payments, because any refunds to be paid out were usually offsets against taxes already received. Moreover, the EITC quickly became a target for fraud perpetrators, because they could send in fake tax returns, if necessary inventing children and the requisite level of earned income, and – without any face to face interview with any official – collect their payments through the mail. To make matters worse, the advent of electronic filing coupled with *refund anticipation loans* from commercial lenders meant that they could submit fraudulent tax returns and have the EITC amount in their hands within twenty-four hours. This was not only easy money; this was easy money *fast*, and with very little risk of an audit.[3] So the IRS had a serious fraud problem on their hands; they just didn't know how serious.

In April 1993 IRS executives were embarrassed when a TV documentary, NBC's *Dateline*, showed how easy it was to cheat this system. The documentary crew had filmed scam artists touring public housing estates, paying $400 cash to families (who would not normally file tax returns at all) for the use of their names and social security numbers. The fraudsters would then submit hundreds of fake returns, inventing the requisite incomes and dependents and, by setting themselves up as electronic filing agents under the electronic refund program, collecting the money themselves as financial intermediaries.

The EITC program was a perfect target for fraud. Perpetrators used hundreds or thousands of other people's identities, or invented fictitious ones. The IRS criminal investigation division detected some fraud schemes, with $7.5 million of fraudulent claims detected in 1989. By 1992 that figure had jumped to $67 million, and it more than doubled the following year, to $136 million. As is normally the case with invisible crimes, nobody really knew whether the rapid escalation in cases *detected* was due to better targeting of the problem, or an underlying escalation in the scope of the problem. In 1993 the IRS had no idea what their detection rate was, and therefore no idea what proportion of the whole problem the visible piece ($136 million) represented.

Without any reliable estimates of the size of such problems, different parties choose estimates that suit their purposes. Supporters of the EITC downplayed the problem, pointing out that a hundred million dollars or so, within a $15 billion program, might properly be regarded as an acceptable business risk. The criminal investigators at the IRS thought the problem was much larger, because they could see how the traditional IRS audit structures focused on under-reported incomes, and did not deal with over-reported, inflated, or invented incomes (upon which EITC fraud depended). IRS executives were alarmed by the *Dateline* episode, but faced the natural temptation in such circumstances to play down the problem, reassuring taxpayers and congressional overseers that this was just a case of a few bad apples, and that the EITC system was basically sound.

In fact the EITC-fraud detection rate turned out to be no greater than 5 percent. So for every fraud case the IRS detected, there were at least nineteen they missed. They only discovered this fact early in 1994, by instituting a statistically valid measurement program designed to determine the underlying scope of the problem. In the first few months of the 1994 filing season, the IRS selected 1,000 incoming EITC-based refund requests, at random, and subjected them to an unusually rigorous type of audit. The agency dispatched a criminal investigator to the taxpayer's doorstep, unannounced.

The investigator's job was not to make arrests or initiate cases, but to obtain information sufficient to determine whether the EITC claim submitted was valid. So they asked the taxpayers for supporting evidence for the employment income claimed, and wanted if possible to check the existence of the dependent children (at least seeing their bedrooms and toys, even if the kids were not at home at the time of their visit). In many cases, investigators sent out to validate EITC claims found themselves on the doorsteps of abandoned buildings, sandwich shops, vacant lots, and McDonald's restaurants. Using their best professional judgment, the investigators made a determination in each case as to the validity of the EITC claim, and these judgments were then checked by a supervisor. The results were compiled across the sample of 1,000 claims, and the resulting point-estimates extrapolated across the EITC population.

The results were staggering, indicating that 38.8% of EITC claims were either inflated or unmerited, with 26.1% of the money going to payments made "in error." Of the sample claims, 19% were deemed to be outright fraud, which suggested the aggregate fraud loss rate was over $3 billion per year. All of a sudden, the IRS could understand the sliver of the problem that their detection systems revealed ($160 million in 1994) in its proper context.

Even at that point, having designed and conducted their measurement study with a high degree of methodological rigor, it was tough for the IRS executive team to accept the results. It would have been a relief for them to find fault with their own study and dismiss the results; then the situation would not look so bad. Fortunately, they *had* designed and executed the study well, with a valid statistical sample, and defensible judgments applied in each case. Even more fortunately, Commissioner Richardson and her team resolved to deal with the problem, having fathomed its depth.[4] They did not actually declare the results publicly until a year later, giving themselves the opportunity to institute better controls in the meantime. But they did take the results to their congressional overseers in order to gain support for tighter controls. As a result, the IRS was granted supplemental appropriations and deployed 1,700 additional staff on prevention and detection of EITC fraud. They also tightened the eligibility requirements for electronic filing agents (the position from which many of the bigger schemes were being orchestrated). The IRS implemented an entirely new *pre-payment* audit program for EITC-based refund requests, knowing it would be almost impossible, practically and politically, to chase after funds purportedly paid out to the "working poor."

During the 1995 filing season the IRS repeated the measurement study to assess the effects of the additional controls. The error rate had been cut in half in just one year, and the EITC program came in under budget (for the first time ever), $2 billion lower than projections.

Such successes are quite rare when dealing with invisible problems. It takes considerable courage to commit to measurement, and to deal with the painful truths it may reveal. There are normally plenty of people opposed to any kind of systematic measurement, preferring the true scope *not* be known. These include not only perpetrators of crimes, but a range of others who might be inconvenienced or adversely affected by increased controls. Those opposed to measurement have a number of well-worn arguments available to them, why measurement ought not to be done. They may object to the use of random or representative samples for audit or inspection (which most measurement methodologies require), claiming that a high degree of attention to randomly selected individuals is basically unfair. They might also point out that it is more resource-efficient to focus on known trouble spots than on random samples. (Auditing randomly selected tax-returns produces less additional revenue, on average, than auditing suspicious ones. Random searches of passengers by Customs agents leads to fewer seizures than targeted searches.) Those opposed to measurement may also claim that accurate measurement is not technically possible, and therefore not worth attempting.

In fact, a great deal can be learned from a reasonably rigorous examination of moderately sized, but properly representative, samples. It was the rigorous examination of 1,000 randomly selected claims that completely transformed the IRS perspective on the EITC problem. Without measurement, they would have continued to focus on the visible sliver of the fraud problem, catching the relatively unsophisticated and careless perpetrators whose phony claims were easier to detect. They would not have known the scope of the underlying problem, nor would they have understood the biases in their own detection methods. In terms of the efficiency question, the purpose of the sampling was never to generate cases, nor maximize revenues; it was to obtain reliable information about the broader picture, and thus to better inform high-level policy-making and strategy-development.

Without deliberate measurement, the debate about invisible problems swirls around the underlying ambiguity: How big is it really? Are we worrying too much, or too little? Measuring invisible problems for the first time usually reveals results worse than anyone had imagined, and requires skillful political management. However painful or inconvenient the truths revealed, putting the facts on the table finally moves the debate past the arguments about the scope of the problem. Measurement provides a sound basis for adjusting the level of resources devoted to control, and advances the discussion to the next stage: how best to bring the problem, now visible, under control.

Deliberate measurement not only reveals the underlying scope of invisible problems, it also helps to correct biases in detection systems, and thus helps those responsible for control avoid or escape the *circularity trap*. Circularity is particularly troublesome for intelligence agencies. It arises when officials focus on parts of the problem already revealed. By targeting these, they learn yet more about them, and so those targets appear yet more central, hence more deserving of continued attention, and so on. Fishing in the same part of the river day after day, where one has caught fish before, might be the best way of guaranteeing a fish for supper. But wise fishermen cast about deliberately in other parts of the river, at least once in a while. Otherwise they could remain oblivious of changes happening around them, and might never find better spots nor bigger fish.

It becomes particularly important to understand the potential for circularity to exacerbate or fortify biases when one part of a harm is much more visible than a different, but closely-related, part. Attention will naturally drift to the more visible piece, and that may consume all available control attention, leaving the invisible variant untouched. In fact, the busier the visible pieces keep everybody, the less likely anyone is to notice the invisible pieces.

An interesting example of this phenomenon involves different types of credit-card fraud: some of which are naturally visible, others invisible. The most common types of credit-card scams involve a perpetrator making unauthorized use of somebody else's credit card account. Schemes of this type may vary with respect to the types of cards or cardholders targeted, the methods of obtaining card information, and the commodities that the perpetrators finally purchase for the "conversion to cash" stage of their scheme. Across all such variants, these scams have one important property in common: the unauthorized activity eventually shows up on a legitimate cardholder's billing statement. Provided the cardholders are paying attention to their statements, such scams will all become *visible*, and they will do so (subject to the particularities of billing cycles) within a few weeks of the commission of the offense. So at least the cardholder and the banks will discover that it happened, even if that discovery is too late to catch the perpetrator this time around. As a practical matter, *visible* problems tend to get controlled, (at least, much more so than their invisible cousins) and the credit card industry has been quite successful in suppressing this type of credit-card fraud. The rate of confirmed-fraud-losses typically hovers around one tenth of 1 percent of total transaction volume, which the credit card industry considers an acceptable business risk. The financial institutions involved are making, after all, 3 percent or more on each transaction through a variety of fees, commissions, and finance charges.

Meanwhile, some other types of credit card frauds remain invisible in perpetuity, and might grow to significant levels without the banks becoming aware of them. So called "bust-out" schemes provide a good example. A group of perpetrators invent or buy on the street several hundred fake identities, and obtain credit cards for themselves in these false names. They also set themselves up with *merchant* accounts, as businesses, possibly using rented store fronts for the purpose and procuring card-swiping machines so they can take credit card payments from "customers." With control over several hundred cards, and five to ten merchant accounts, the crime ring then sets up a pattern of incestuous trading, using their own cards at their own merchant sites. By doing this they essentially procure interest free loans from the credit card banks, because merchants are reimbursed by their bank within twenty-four hours of a transaction, but the cardholders have a few weeks before the corresponding payments become due. For the first few months, the whole group pays all their monthly cardholder bills in full, and on time, and may have their credit limits raised as a result. Over time, they ratchet up the volume of this incestuous trading pattern, doing so at a controlled pace to avoid tripping *acceleration-rate-monitors* (which they know the banks operate to monitor cardholder accounts, as well as merchant activity). After a year or so, the aggregate float – the total interest-free loan the group has accumulated – may exceed a million dollars or more; at which point the group disappears completely with the money (hence the term "bust-out"), and all of the related cardholder accounts go into default. The banks will eventually deem these accounts "uncollectible," because they cannot trace the cardholders.

The credit card industry knows these ring-level frauds do happen, because some scams of this type have been detected and prosecuted. But the underlying extent of such scams remains unknown, simply because they are not *generally* detected. It is perfectly plausible that nobody would know these schemes had happened at all, even after the fact. Of course, all the cardholder accounts going bad (becoming "uncollectible") does get noticed, but these delinquent accounts are lost within a much larger pool of *credit losses*, which might be generally attributed to a combination of poor economic times and the industry's own aggressive credit-granting policies. If the banks took the trouble to construct monitoring programs aimed at the *relationships among accounts*, rather than monitoring behavior of accounts one by one, then they might be able to detect the tightly-knit trading pattern and see a scheme developing over time. Then they could intervene even before the bust-out happened. But, in the absence of this degree of monitoring sophistication, these fraud losses are misclassified, lumped into the miscellaneous pool of credit losses, and the extent of this particular type of fraud remains unknown.

The problem of domestic violence provides another interesting example of the challenges involved in dealing with invisible problems. The most serious incidents of domestic violence, domestic *homicides*, cannot generally be hidden. So this slice of the domestic-violence problem is visible, assuming authorities are reasonably competent in investigating and establishing causes of death. Nonfatal cases nevertheless involving serious injury stand a good chance of being exposed or detected by hospital emergency room staff, neighbors, or schoolteachers. But the vast majority of domestic violence incidents do not result in hospitalizations, nor necessarily produce observable injuries. For these, the detection rate (which includes the reporting-by-victim rate), is substantially lower. The resulting bias, if authorities do not deliberately compensate for it, will result in attention being focused on the relatively few and serious cases which come to light, and with too little attention paid to the higher-frequency but invisible mass of incidents, with all of their pernicious effects and potential for escalation.

Different parts of this problem have different properties in terms of visibility, and this creates interesting implications for performance measurement. In 2004, the Victoria Police in Australia launched a concerted program to combat domestic violence across their state. Victoria's Commissioner of Police, Christine Nixon, explained to her political overseers, in advance, what *ought* to happen to the available metrics if the campaign were successful. She told them the domestic-homicide rate would unambiguously decline (because that part of the problem was naturally *visible*). Meanwhile, she said, the total number of domestic violence reports received by police and other agencies would rise at first, and then hopefully peak before beginning a gradual decline to lower levels. She anticipated the metrics would behave this way because the overall volume of reports relating to non-fatal assaults would be most affected, initially, by changes in reporting behavior. A police campaign and heightened community awareness of the problem would facilitate and encourage reporting, as the campaign promised

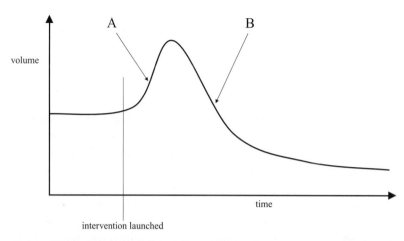

Fig. 8.1 Intervention-related activity measures

help and protection where necessary, along with services to victims who came forward. If the campaign were to succeed in the longer term, in which case the underlying levels of domestic violence would decrease, then the volume of reported incidents should eventually decline accordingly.

According to Commissioner Nixon, it was not obvious to her various stakeholders and partners why the two different metrics (the homicide rate and the incident-reporting rate) would exhibit such markedly different behaviors. It took some work on her part to help them understand this point. It is certainly important for all senior policymakers to grasp these nuances with respect to invisible problems, lest they make serious errors in interpreting metrics or in evaluating programs.

The anticipated behavior of the second metric – the domestic violence reporting rate – is so common, and common across so many domains, that metrics like these ought to have a name! As far as I am aware, these metrics do not have a specific name, even though they have the same characteristic behavior. I think of them as "intervention-related-activity metrics" and will hereafter refer to them, therefore, as IRAMs. If someone else proposes a nicer name for them I'll be happy to switch.

Figure 8.1 shows what happens to an IRAM when a control operation successfully identifies a risk-concentration that was previously invisible. The curve in Figure 8.1 could well represent reporting rates under a successful domestic-violence campaign. It could equally well represent arrest or seizure rates when customs agencies successfully hone in on a particular smuggling group or smuggling method. It might represent the rate of indictments or convictions generated by a new anti-corruption initiative. In each case, exposure leads to better visibility, which makes the IRAM rise. In time, continued attention dents the underlying problem, and then the IRAM should decline.

Changes in IRAMs generate two different kinds of discussion; the first as they move up, and another as they later decline. At point A, on the way up, everyone gets excited by the obvious success. Calls from headquarters to project leaders are naturally congratulatory. "Terrific program." "Good work. Keep it up." "Great numbers." At point B, however, the discussion is a little more ambiguous, and the calls somewhat less congratulatory. "What happened to that program?" "Why are your numbers declining?" At point B there are two plausible explanations for the IRAM's behavior: one positive, one negative. The positive explanation assumes successful reduction of the underlying problem. The negative explanation assumes effort is declining, staff are resting on their laurels or have been distracted from the task, or the offenders have adapted around the initiative and thereby reduced the detection rates once again. The ambiguity at point B can easily lead to acrimony. Project leaders want to assume the positive interpretation, and get mightily offended if others propose the opposite.

As any practitioner who has been involved in such discussions knows, one cannot resolve the ambiguity at point B without referring to some other, more reliable measures of the underlying prevalence of the problem. IRAMs are not actually measures of the underlying level of the problem. They are composite measures – the product of the *underlying scope* of the target problem together with the *proportion* of incidents which are exposed or revealed. So, when an IRAM moves in one direction or another, no-one can tell for sure which of the two components has changed. Was it the seriousness of the problem that changed, or the ability to see it?

The same ambiguity arises with respect to comparisons across jurisdictions as well as with respect to changes over time. Estimates of the level of public sector corruption across the fifty states within the US rely heavily on the number of indictments and convictions of state officials as reported to Congress by the Public Integrity Section of the Department of Justice. These numbers, divided by the number of public officials in each state, are assumed to provide an indication of comparative levels of corruption. But they could equally well reveal state-by-state variations in detection methods, willingness to report, or zealousness in enforcement.[5]

Interpreting IRAMs properly requires deliberate reference to other metrics, less related to the specific intervention, and more reflective of the underlying conditions.[6] The US Customs project to combat *port-running*, (described earlier in Chapter 2) illustrates this very nicely. Before launching any of their action plans to counter this drug-smuggling method, the Customs' team constructed a set of metrics by which they would be able to tell if they succeeded in reducing the problem. They selected a portfolio of three metrics, and established benchmarks (starting positions) for each one so they could watch to see if they changed. The most obvious metric for inclusion was the *number of observed port-running incidents*, where port-runners crashed through the inspection points and sped away. Even though some port-runners were waved through by intimidated officials (and thus these incidents were not counted) the majority of incidents were visible. Hence this metric was expected to decline unambiguously once any successful action plan began to take effect.

The second metric had the characteristics of an IRAM. Customs officials could count the number of instances where truck-drivers pulled out of the queue of traffic waiting for inspection, made a U-turn and drove back to Mexico, effectively abandoning their attempt to cross the border at that time. Termed "Returns to Mexico," these instances were highly visible, captured on video tape, and readily counted. Many of the Returns-to-Mexico involved port-runners who, for whatever reason, did not like what they saw ahead of them (either the physical arrangements or the selection of personnel on duty) and decided against proceeding. If the intervention team was successful in "hardening the ports" (i.e. making them less attractive for port-runners), then they expected the number of Returns-to-Mexico to rise at first, but then decline as drug-smuggling organizations abandoned this smuggling method.

To be certain whether or not they had succeeded, the team included a third measure which more faithfully reflected the underlying level of the problem. It involved data which they did not normally keep, and which they had to commission their intelligence agents to obtain. They wanted to know the *price paid to the drivers* by the drug-running organizations for running a load. After some inquiries, the intelligence agents reported back that the going rate was $5,000 per load, which may seem a high price, but is actually miniscule compared to the value of the drug loads carried through by this method.

Later, having tried several different intervention plans, the team finally discovered the deterrent effect of Jersey barriers placed in chicane formation behind the inspection point. This tactic effectively removed the port-runners' *rapid escape*, which was vital for them. Customs officials watched what happened to their three metrics. The *number of observed instances* dropped precipitously. The *Returns-to-Mexico* rose, peaked, and then began to decline, like any IRAM should. Most encouraging of all, when the intelligence agents repeated their inquiries about price, they found it had risen to $7,500 in just a few months. At that point, the team and their supervisors were satisfied they had found a suitable and effective approach.

Terrorism: an odd case

In the context of a discussion about invisible problems, it may be worth mentioning terrorism. The threat of terrorism is, by design of its perpetrators, invisible throughout the conspiratorial and preparatory stages, but then highly and deliberately visible at the very last moment – the moment of a terrorist attack. In order to optimize the impact of their attacks, terrorists seek targets and methods of attack that make their actions not only visible, but spectacularly so.

As one considers the chronological unfolding of a terrorist action, this particular harm switches at the very last minute from one that displays all the behavioral characteristics of an invisible risk to one that is highly and deliberately visible. This switch has peculiar consequences for performance monitoring and accountability, which – if not properly understood – can undermine support for prevention and affect the morale of counter-terrorism agents.

During the invisible phase, counter-terrorism operations consist primarily of intelligence and surveillance operations, largely covert, which cannot be discussed publicly and which are not normally visible to the public. Preventive successes, therefore, may need to be concealed for security reasons; and even if they are announced publicly, then authorities may feel highly constrained in what they can reveal, which makes their claims of preventive successes generally less persuasive for the public.

By contrast, the failures of the preventive operations – i.e. the attacks that materialize – are all highly visible and have profound and widespread psychological impacts. The net result is that ordinary members of the public, not privy to classified information about intelligence operations, are cognizant only of the failures. And when they observe these failures, the government operations they then witness and which fill the news are all about the *response* to the attack. Responsibility for dealing with the aftermath of an attack rests with a different set of agencies, such as emergency services and public health, and these are strangely decoupled from the preventive intelligence operations.

These simple properties of the terrorist risk, therefore, quite naturally produce a situation where the most important piece of the control operation – namely the preventive intelligence work – suffers. Few of its successes are visible to the public. All of its failures are spectacularly visible. And when an attack does occur, intelligence operations are presumed to have failed at exactly the moment when other government functions such as emergency response acquire highly visible opportunities to perform well.

Consequences for control operations

By way of summary, let me present a list of the ordinary operational implications to be considered when dealing with *invisible* harms:

- The underlying extent and seriousness of the harm is unknown.
- Perceptions of the scope of the problem, and consequently the level of investments in control, are based on the visible sliver of the problem – i.e. on the segment of the problem that detection and exposure mechanisms reveal.
- Significant under-investment in control is the norm for such harms.
- *What you see is not the problem.* The heart of the control challenge is to expose and deal with the invisible mass.
- Beware the circularity-trap. Circularity traps are more severe when the underlying problems are serious, because the *visible* part of the problem will be enough to keep everyone quite busy. When officials are busy with what they find, they are less likely to contemplate what they might be missing.

- Most readily available performance metrics are ambiguous. Many of them behave like IRAMs, and are easily misinterpreted, especially when in decline.
- Measurement is imperative. Measure the problem. Measure it. Measure it! Job number one, always, is to reveal the scope of the problem.
- Many parties will oppose measurement, and on a variety of grounds.
- Measurement takes some creativity, and a lot of courage; but it is possible.
- Measurement methodologies depend on comparatively rigorous audits of comparatively small samples. Samples must be random or representative. Measurement studies often require only "best professional judgments," made with respect to each element of a valid sample, from which point estimates of the underlying prevalence of the problem can be calculated. Analysis of such samples also provides more reliable information about the problem's distribution and concentrations.
- Once measurement has been instituted, the level of investments in control ought to be based in some rational way on the estimates produced; not on the trickle of cases coming from existing detection systems.
- Detecting changes in the underlying scope of the problem requires a commitment to measurement on a periodic or continuing basis.
- Policymakers will need to justify the systematic use of random audits or inspections. Rigorous review of randomly selected transactions shows authorities what they otherwise might never know. The value of such audits lies in the *information obtained,* not in the cases generated. Reliable information protects society from gross errors of underinvestment or overinvestment in controls, and helps to undo the biases built into existing detection and reporting systems. It enables control operations to re-adjust their sights.
- Proactive and intelligence work is vitally important for exposing the nature of the problem and identifying its principal concentrations. Law-enforcement field-craft, undercover operations, and other proactive methods can be deployed towards this end. The emphasis in such work should not be on making cases, but on gathering *strategic* intelligence which reveals the broader landscape and thus enables re-alignment of agency operations.
- Systematic debriefing of visible incidents, in order to shed light on others still invisible, becomes a priority. Often the information that

can be gleaned from a case, and then fed back into controls, is more important than the disposition of the case itself.
- Two fundamental questions should be asked about every instance that comes to light:
  (a) why was this one detected; and what would need to have been different for this one to have remained invisible in perpetuity?
  (b) how many other instances like this, or subtly different, might there be and us not know? How might we discover them?

The most important of all of these is *measurement*. For invisible problems, measurement is always job number one – the starting point for effective control.

Notes

1. It is possible for a corruption problem to be quite widely known within the ranks of an organization and yet remain essentially invisible to the relevant control authorities. So a problem can remain "invisible" to those with operational responsibility for controlling it, even while visible to many others. For a discussion of the distance between *knowing* and *reporting*, and the vital role played by social attitudes towards various corrupt behaviors in determining willingness to report, see: Angela Gorta & Suzie Forell, "Layers of Decision: Linking Social Definitions of Corruption and Willingness to Take Action," *Crime, Law & Social Change*, 23 (1995), 315–343.
2. The problem of illicit human trafficking – a generally clandestine activity – provides an excellent demonstration of all these difficulties. For a discussion of the various reasons the underlying scope of the problem remains unknown, and for a set of practical recommendations regarding methods for obtaining more reliable estimates, see: Frank Laczko & Marco A. Gramegna, "Developing Better Indicators of Human Trafficking," *Brown Journal of World Affairs*, 10 (Summer/Fall 2003), 179–194. For a synopsis of what is known about patterns of trafficking worldwide, see: Frank Laczko & Elzbieta M. Gozdziak, *Data and Research on Human Trafficking: A Global Survey* (Geneva: International Organization for Migration, 2005).
3. For a full account of the EITC fraud problem, and its subsequent resolution, see: Malcolm K. Sparrow, *License To Steal: How Fraud Plagues America's Health Care System*, 2nd edition (Denver, Colorado & Oxford, England: Westview Press, 2000), pp. 149–153, 208, 211–212, 228.

During the period described, the author acted as a consultant to the IRS on compliance-management and fraud control.

4. Commissioner Margaret Milner Richardson.

5. Luke Peterson, "Policing Public Integrity in the States: Do Ethics Enforcement Agencies Prevent Corruption?" Unpublished manuscript, John F. Kennedy School of Government, Harvard University, Cambridge, Massachusetts (April, 2007), p. 3.

6. For an examination of the range of creative systems that might be employed to measure the underlying scope of corruption within police agencies – a problem that belongs firmly in the category of invisible problems – see: Sanja Kutnjak Ivkovic, "To Serve and Collect: Measuring Police Corruption," *Journal of Criminal Law & Criminology,* 93 (Winter/Spring 2003), 593–649.

9 | *Conscious opponents*

M uch attention has been given to risks that emanate from natural or biological systems (as with diseases) or from complex technical systems (as with accidents and "man-made" disasters). The risk literature pays less attention to risks or harms emanating from the actions of enemies, criminals, or other classes of opponents, perhaps because these are to some degree less predictable or calculable based on prior experience and history.

This chapter examines harms that involve conscious opponents: that is, where a *brain* lies behind the harm. For these harms, the control task acquires the nature of a continuous, dynamic duel between those responsible for control and those opposed to it. The existence of a brain behind the harm introduces the possibility of deliberate adaptations designed to defeat or reduce the effectiveness of control interventions. It also transforms the analytic aspects of control operations into a game of intelligence and counter-intelligence.

The *opponents* might be drug smugglers, fraud perpetrators, thieves, terrorists, corrupt officials, poachers, illegal loggers, computer hackers, assassins, software pirates, or even students intent on cheating in examinations. All of these routinely assess the nature of controls in place, and develop novel methods to circumnavigate them. The more sophisticated criminal organizations alter their organizational forms as well as their operating methods in order to thwart the efforts of controlling authorities.[1] Whether these opponents thrive or fail in their enterprise depends on the degree of creativity they bring to the task of thwarting authorities, and the adroitness of authorities in not being thwarted.

Not all harms involve opponents, and some regulatory domains contain relatively few such risks. Occupational hazards, if correctly identified and suppressed, do not go searching for a new way to kill workers. Transportation safety hazards (with the exception of those that involve deliberate acts of sabotage or terrorism) have no consciousness and therefore no agenda. Control one hazard in either of these two fields, and there is no reason to believe another will emerge or increase as a result.

The majority of environmental problems also have no brain, and therefore exhibit no adaptive behavior. Saving one endangered species, barring the effects of predatory relationships, does not normally change the degree to which other species are endangered. And restoring one lake to a swimmable or fishable condition ought not to degrade any other water body.

However, environmental and conservation agencies do confront conscious and adaptive opponents whenever they deal with illegal logging, poaching, hunting of protected species, or illegal dumping of toxic waste. So *some* environmental problems do involve conscious opponents, even though most do not.

Similarly, some threats to transportation safety – those involving deliberate attacks or acts of sabotage – involve opponents. But the vast majority of safety issues depend more on complex systems engineering and on the control of human error; not deliberate acts.

Tax administrations also face a mixture. Many non-compliance problems stem from ignorance of the rules, misunderstandings, and genuine errors. Fixing these, through whatever means, ought not to generate new types of ignorance, misunderstanding, or error. By contrast, willful tax evasion, involving deliberate deceit and sophisticated methods of obfuscation, quite clearly fit this category. Closing down one tax haven or tax-shelter scheme is virtually guaranteed to produce a flurry of adaptive creativity. So tax authorities, like their counterparts in environmental protection and transportation, deal with a mixture of risks – some with, and some without, this property.

Coastguard operations have a pretty even split too. Their opponents, all eager to outsmart patrol operations and avoid surveillance, include illegal fishing operations, waterborne drug-running, illegal immigration, and illegal dumping of waste at sea. At the same time, coastguard agencies have maritime safety and rescue operations at the core of their mission, and in this area there is generally no deliberate intent and no brain behind the hazards. Coastguard operations also help to prevent and mitigate the effects of oil spills on marine and shoreline environments, virtually all of which are accidental, even when they involve a degree of recklessness.

In terms of this particular mix, law enforcement agencies sit close to one end of the spectrum. Law enforcement agencies tend to be much more familiar with the operational consequences of having opponents, for the simple reason that a greater proportion of the harms they are supposed to control exhibit this property. (Not all of them, of course. Police also deal with a host of safety issues, most obviously road accidents, behind which there is generally no malicious intent.) Security specialists and customs agencies also spend much of their time studying the behavior of opponents, and devising strategies to warn them off or catch them out.

Nearly every regulatory domain includes some problems involving, and some problems not involving, conscious opponents. This class of problems therefore does not line up nicely with particular regulatory domains, even though the balance in the mix varies quite considerably from one area to another. The agencies most likely to be surprised or confounded when they confront adaptive opposition are those which do so least often: that is, those organizations whose portfolio consists predominantly of harms with no brain behind them.

The presence or absence of adaptive opposition does not simply depend on the *involvement of human beings* in the harm to be reduced. Authorities seek to control, constrain or otherwise influence harmful human behaviors of many kinds. We ask people to drive carefully, give up smoking, exercise frequently, and wear their seatbelts or crash helmets. Harm-reduction operations, therefore, frequently engage in identifying specific patterns of human behavior which are non-compliant, or dangerous, or both. When such efforts are successful, we would not normally anticipate a deliberate adaptive response. A reaction such as "you persuaded me to give up smoking, therefore I must find another way of endangering my health," would be unusual.[2] Implementing certain safeguards (such as childproof caps on bottles of pills) might indeed make people more careless with respect to other controls (e.g. keeping the bottles out of reach of children), in what Kip Viscusi terms a "lulling effect."[3] Procuring compliance or any other kind of behavioral change from humans absolutely involves their *brains*. Hence the importance of compliance-*psychology*. However, changing behavior in one area does not necessarily produce adaptive responses designed to counter or defeat the control intervention; nor does it necessarily produce displacement effects. So the *involvement of the human brain* is not a sufficient condition, alone, to produce adaptive responses designed to defeat control efforts.

Nor does the presence of *conscious opposition* accurately capture the phenomenon. Consider the case of compliance with seat-belt or crash-helmet laws. Non-compliers might deliberately and actively oppose the legislation, preferring a less paternalistic state or placing greater weight on personal liberty. So they might indeed "consciously oppose" these specific laws. Conceivably they might hold a broader anti-authoritarian ideology, and oppose *many* laws. Nevertheless, if an enforcement campaign successfully changes their behavior with respect to one set of self-protective rules, it seems unlikely that many of the newly and grudgingly compliant would deliberately search out other rules to break, or try to invent compensating methods for making their road trips dangerous.

Of course, motorcyclists who like to ride without helmets might (and do) search for other *places* to ride, seeking out remote locations or alternate jurisdictions with higher tolerance or less enforcement. This might leave authorities puzzling over the dimensions in which they choose to define the problem they want to address: is the job to protect *these people* wherever they go; or is the job to reduce the death rate *within one particular jurisdiction*, regardless of where the victims might live? These two definitions of the problem (involving the use of different dimensions) would lead to quite different strategies.

In the absence of any broader anti-authoritarian streak, successfully changing behavior with respect to seat-belt laws, even if accomplished through coercion or enforcement, ought not to produce or increase any other harm. In which case, even the presence of *conscious opposition* does not necessarily produce displacement effects or adaptations of the harm.

What really counts, here, is *opponents with an intent to outwit the control operation*. That helps distinguish, for example, between problems of willful tax-evasion and problems of taxpayer ignorance or error. Both classes of tax non-compliance involve human brains. Both groups of non-compliers might oppose aspects of the tax code, or generally resent being taxed. But only one group is involved in deliberate attempts to outwit authorities, and that would be the one area where tax agencies need to consider intelligence and counter-intelligence operations, and all of the associated game-playing strategies.

The presence of a brain, therefore, does not necessarily produce this adaptive property. Nor does *absence* of a brain necessarily mean it cannot appear. Natural systems sometimes produce quasi-adaptive behaviors, even without a brain behind them to design the adaptations.

The most obvious example involves mutation of viruses and bacteria. These pathogens exhibit a range of adaptive responses, some designed to defeat their hosts' immune response systems, and others produced as a reaction against drug therapies. As these pathogens invade host organisms, their constant foe, even before any medical treatments are administered, is the host's immune response system. Pathogens develop with remarkable alacrity an amazing array of strategies for fooling or defeating that immune response. These strategies, according to Frances Brodsky, include *stealth* (using a mechanism of infection that avoids or delays immune response activation), *sabotage* (disabling or impairing the immune response system, as in HIV infection), and *exploitation* (finding ways to take advantage of the immune response, or turn it against the host).[4] Such adaptations are not the work of a brain, but they nevertheless appear artful and crafty, even imaginative. Brodsky states that "The multiplicity of pathogen strategies for evasion of the host immune response.... reflect evolution in action,"[5] and points out that the pathogens have much shorter reproductive cycles than the hosts, and can therefore evolve more quickly. The evolutionary response for the *hosts* therefore – who live longer and adapt more slowly – is to develop multiple redundant immune responses in the hope that at least one of them, when a pathogen attacks, will still operate effectively despite the pathogen's attempts to subvert them.[6]

The practice of medicine must deal with another evolutionary adaptation of pathogens – the development of drug-resistance. *Tuberculosis,* for example, now shows resistance to a range of drug therapies. And the sexually-transmitted bacterial infection *gonorrhea* has recently added one new adaptation to an impressive history of adaptive behavior. During the 1980s *gonorrhea,* already resistant to *sulfa,* developed resistance to penicillin and then to tetracyclines. Treatment shifted to a class of antibiotics known as *fluoroquinolones.* Strains of gonorrhea resistant to *fluoroquinolones* are now common in Hawaii, the Pacific islands, and in Asia.[7] Britain recommended against continuing use of fluoroquinolones in 2005, because of elevated levels of resistance there, and the Centers for Disease Control in the US has now followed suit, changing its treatment recommendations for US physicians as of April 2007.[8] The last line of defense against this particular disease, in terms of treatments currently available, lies with the *cephalosporin* class of antibiotics. Given the microbe's demonstrated capacity to adapt, the public health community will be watching very closely for any signs of developing resistance to that class of antibiotics too.

Given the adaptive behaviors of these diseases, medical and public health practitioners adopt some of the strategies and methods one more routinely associates with game-playing or military strategy. They anticipate and plan for adaptations.[9] They scan carefully and broadly for the appearance of any adaptation.[10] They limit the use of a drug once a certain level of resistance is observed, to prevent the drug-resistant form becoming ubiquitous. They hold some treatments (drugs) in reserve, deliberately denying the opposition (the virus) the opportunity to learn about or adapt to them, and maintaining the element of novelty (surprise) for some occasion, such as a major outbreak, when they might really need it.

Consequences for control operations

The presence of a brain behind a harm, seeking to outwit control operations (or a quasi-brain, as in the case of evolutionary adaptations), has several important consequences for operations:

It confounds our normal reliance on probabilities

Probabilistic assessments form the basis for allocation of resources and attention in harm control operations.

Using historical data, one can observe the incidence of lung cancer for life-long smokers, or the fatality rate for teenage motorcyclists. Assuming no major changes in the environment to affect these risks, scientists and policy makers can then use those historical incidence rates as probabilities, looking forward. Armed with these calculated probabilities, we compare and contrast different risks, rank order them, and develop some sense of threshold probabilities which separate acceptable risks from unacceptable ones. Examining the probabilities associated with different risks helps establish when, and at what point, governments or other actors should intervene to reduce exposures. Social policies depend heavily on such probabilistic assessments, and scholars have naturally paid much attention to the scientific methods used to generate them, and to the ways in which such assessments are used in the policymaking process.

In the absence of conscious opponents, the shorthand of probability to capture historical experience makes sense. Throw an evenly weighted die and you have a one in six chance of throwing a six. Pick a playing card from a deck at random and you have a one in thirteen chance of picking an ace. Smoke continuously from your teenage years, and you have a certain chance of developing lung cancer before you reach the age of 60.

The die, the cards, and the smoker all face their fate within systems which (putting aside the possibility of divine intervention, and the implications of Heisenberg's uncertainty principle) are determined physically and biologically. If we could observe carefully enough the trajectory and angular momentum of the die, the elasticity of the surface on which it will land, we could in theory (given enough computing power and patience) predict each bounce and the outcome with certainty. *But we use the concept of probabilities to cover the myriad details we either have not gathered, cannot observe, or cannot control.*[11] If we throw dice sufficiently carelessly, and enough times, then we know all six outcomes will occur with roughly equal frequency. There is nothing to favor one outcome over another, assuming even weighting.[12]

Similarly, cancers are physiological phenomena, not random ones. If we could observe all the contributing factors, grasp all the relevant science, and monitor precisely all the contributing circumstances, we could in theory predict the outcomes with certainty. Then we could divide smokers unambiguously into those who will contract lung-cancer and those who will not. Because we do not know enough about the causal paths, and cannot observe enough physiological detail, we lump all the smokers together and assign to the whole class one aggregate probability, which predicts how many of them are expected to contract cancer. The probability is no more than a summary of the past experience of people indistinguishable from this group.

What difference does the presence of conscious opposition make to our use or understanding of probabilities? Probabilities play a different role in roulette than in chess.[13] Roulette is a physical system, with the odds tilted against the player by a small margin, but the odds nonetheless are quite knowable. Roulette players know the odds of a black number, or an odd number, or a *bust*. But what would it mean, half way through a chess game, to say "I estimate my opponent is 50 percent likely to castle"? Such a statement seems oddly out of place.[14] It is a *person* about to decide; not a physical system. More particularly, this is an *opponent*, not just a person.

Despite this, such a statement could mean a number of things: conceivably, one might be viewing the opponent's brain as a deterministic physical and chemical system, and trying to assess the functioning of the neural synapses in the same way that you might assess and classify the outcomes of throwing a die. But that is not what most people would mean.

Much more likely, this statement could mean "having observed this opponent historically and on numerous occasions, I know she castles in about half of her games." Or it could mean "of all the plausible strategies *I can now see for her*, half of them involve castling; and I have no basis to weight the different strategies unevenly, so I am considering them all equally likely at this point, having no other information to go on."

In assessing what she might or might not do, add to the mix a few factors directly related to the fact that she is a person using her brain, and to the fact that she is also an opponent. She might like to *surprise* her opponents, by doing things she has never done before. She might deliberately do wild and whacky things once in a while in order to disorient her opponent. She might never have been in precisely *this* situation, in any prior game; in which case studying her past strategy could only yield general observations about playing style, but nothing about tailor-made tactics she might invent for this position. And if she suspected her opponent was making plans or allocating thinking time on the basis of probabilistic assessments of her next moves, then she might change tack just to mess all of that up. A roulette wheel never behaves that way. It does not react at all to the bets placed. Gamblers can rely on the fact that a roulette wheel does not notice what they are doing, nor does it care how they would like things to come out.

When facing opponents, probabilistic assessments based on historical observations lose much of their predictive value. The opponent can alter them at will, by changing tack. Therefore whatever probabilities one might derive from observations of past experience inevitably carry much higher levels of variance, and may be wrong by orders of magnitude, simply because of an opponent's decision.

Perhaps this greater and unpredictable variance helps to explain what some scholars have regarded as irrational behavior by Americans after the attacks of September 11, 2001. They point out that Americans avoided flying in jets for months afterwards, driving enormously long distances along highways instead. The extra highway miles resulted in an estimated 1,000 additional road deaths.[15] Why do some consider this choice irrational? Because, so the argument goes, the per-passenger-mile death rate in commercial aviation is much lower than the per-passenger-mile death rate on the roads. Moreover, the events of 9/11 did not kill enough people to significantly alter that underlying balance. So even after 9/11, the right choice, given a choice, was to fly. So then, how might we explain such irrational behavior? The psychology of risk assessment provides some plausible explanations: perhaps Americans were too much influenced by the novelty or spectacularly vivid nature of what they had just witnessed, or the need to feel in control of their own destiny. We know that all of these factors count, and some suggest that these factors explain why many Americans made the *wrong* choice.

But there is another explanation. Perhaps the American public, choosing to drive, instinctively knew the consequences of having opponents. Road accidents have no brain behind them; terrorist attacks emphatically do. So, with regard to terrorism, past experience provides no sound guide to future exposure. Moreover, the public had just seen one attack which was, in numerous ways, unprecedented. Presumably the next one would be similarly unprecedented. The events of 9/11 revealed the vulnerability of jets in flight, and the vulnerability of dense populations on the ground or in the air. So avoiding flights, crowds, cities, tall buildings, sporting events, and any other potentially attractive terrorist target seems quite rational under the circumstances, and not necessarily a distorted perception of risk. Given the nature of the opponents, keeping oneself out of the way of *unknowable* harms seems more rational, in fact, than relying on probabilistic extrapolations from historical experience. History, in this context, would be particularly misleading given the almost complete prior absence of terrorist incidents on American soil. Perhaps the American public recognized the threat of terrorism as a different type of risk – one where probabilities just don't behave nicely. Had they been confronted with the comparative death rates for flying and driving, they might have noted that it doesn't make much sense to compare probabilities between risks when somebody else's decision, taken far away and without our knowledge, might render those assessments obsolete or irrelevant in an instant.

The presence of conscious opposition affects the tools and methods that are relevant to the control task

The fact that the probabilities do not behave nicely means that control operations must find some alternate and more reliable basis for focusing attention and setting priorities. The key to this is getting inside your opponent's head, finding out what they are thinking. A poker player is not satisfied with knowing the odds; they also study their opponents' faces intently, looking for the slightest clue to what they are thinking. The chess player follows the eyes of his opponent as they roam over the board, trying to understand the plan being hatched.

The business of getting inside one's opponent's head elevates the importance of a range of intelligence gathering and analysis techniques not much used outside this particular category of harms. Some of these methods help in figuring out what the opponents *might* be thinking; and others more directly help determine what they are *actually* thinking. The first group, which does not require direct contact with opponents, and which is therefore viewed as less intrusive, include the following:

- *Establishing networks of contacts* among peer organizations to facilitate and accelerate exchange of information about newly emerging patterns of behavior, new methods, and new players that appear on the scene.
- *Establishing focus groups*, creating opportunities to pick the brains of staff, customers, and business partners about vulnerabilities and exposures, both observed and potential.
- *Proactive data mining*, employing a range of pattern recognition and anomaly detection methods on large databases, with careful examination of any unusual patterns that emerge.
- *Setting up tiger teams* within the organization to test the adequacy of existing controls. The task for such teams is to put themselves in the shoes of the opponents, and devise novel strategies against which existing controls can be evaluated.

- Monitoring market conditions, trends in advertising, and other publicly available information, in order to identify new opportunities that might attract the attention of one's opponents.

The second group of tools, which more directly addresses what the opponents are *actually* thinking, include the following:

- Systematic debriefing of *perpetrators caught*, who might reveal important information about the behavior and strategies of others in exchange for more lenient treatment.
- Undercover operations.
- Development of *informants*, and paying for information.
- Surveillance (visual or electronic) of opponents' organizations and operations.

The use of these kinds of methods, while utterly routine for law enforcement and intelligence agencies, tends to be quite unfamiliar for agencies that deal with environmental problems, occupational hazards, transportation safety, or the control of mishaps of other types. Having little or no experience with such tools and frequently feeling some aversion to them, these are the agencies most often bemused when they confront a risk of this type.

It affects the range of possibilities one should consider

Opponents seek novelty, and they also deliberately circumnavigate controls and detection systems once they know about them. For both these reasons, *what you have seen* in the past provides no reliable indication of *what you might see* in the future. Opponents will develop new tactics, and they will also deliberately select methods that defeat existing detection and reporting systems. The worst thing a control operation could do, therefore, is rely on well established and familiar detection methods to monitor well established and familiar threats. If the opposition is even moderately adaptive, such monitoring will typically show declines across the board, suggesting a broad improvement in conditions and providing a pleasant – but completely false – sense of security and accomplishment.

Using familiar methods on familiar threats is analogous to monitoring the incidence of familiar diseases, using familiar diagnostic and public health surveillance methods. For diseases that don't change over time, such monitoring provides a clear picture. Dealing with adaptive opponents, however, is more akin to monitoring for emerging infectious diseases, understanding that the most important patterns to spot will be those patterns which have never been seen before.

It affects the way problems are defined, and success is measured

Chapter 3 examined the *scale* at which problems to be addressed, or *knots to be undone*, should be defined. That chapter emphasized the importance of respecting the natural size and shape of the harm itself, and dealing with each harm, preferably just once, at the right level and as an integral whole. The presence of opponents, and the resulting likelihood of adaptive responses to control interventions, affects this calculus in one special way. Problems should be defined at a sufficiently high level to capture all the foreseeable costless adaptations that an opponent may make. If costless adaptations are not captured or covered by a problem definition, there is a real danger that subsequent elimination or unraveling of the particular problem selected is not, in fact, worth so much. If a particular drug smuggling method is curtailed at one border crossing point, but there is another border crossing point half a mile away where the smugglers can continue with impunity, then nothing much has been achieved. If one potential target is effectively protected against attack, but there is another equally attractive target close by which remains unprotected, then the value of protecting the first target seems substantially diminished. Problems need to be defined at a sufficiently high level that suppression of them, even given the possibility of adaptation, represents a meaningful and important accomplishment.

It is important, though, not to push this argument too far. Some might say that eliminating any one terrorist opportunity or any particular smuggling method is meaningless, because the opponents in each case will surely find some other opportunity in the end. There is some chance that they will. But reconfiguring their operations and learning new methods is not *costless* for them. It interrupts their business. It forces them to seek out new partners, establish new routes, or acquire new technologies. That makes them more visible to intelligence operations, and vulnerable to insertion of undercover operatives. For all these reasons, it is actually possible to *overestimate* the importance of displacement effects. The more often opponents are forced to make significant adaptations, the costlier and more difficult their business becomes. When the controllers are nimble and adaptable themselves, then their opponents can never settle into a comfortable routine. By never letting the opponents rest, many of them can be hassled out of the game.

In setting the scale for any harm-control project, authorities should always acknowledge and include adaptations which are foreseeable and relatively costless for the opponents, before making any claim to have seriously dented their operations. And if an easy adaptation comes to light, which had not been foreseen at the outset, then the scale of the project should be revisited at that point. The boundaries of the project might be redrawn so that the adaptations themselves can be included and controlled. Alternatively, the intervention plan should be adjusted in a way which makes these adaptations infeasible.

It affects the balance between competing values in harm control operations

Having conscious opposition produces some situations where values normally cherished, particularly in regulatory settings, need to be judiciously sacrificed (to some carefully limited degree) for the sake of effective suppression. For governmental operations, society places a high premium on transparency, predictability, and openness about purposes and methods. Regulations and rules should be clearly written and clearly communicated. The underlying belief is that government agencies, entrusted with the coercive power of the state, ought never to be in the business of delivering nasty surprises. They should announce their priorities, provide clear warnings to violators, and be prepared to explain how they select their targets and allocate their attention. These forms of transparency help protect against the threats of corruption, abuse of power, arbitrariness, capriciousness, and discrimination.

It is perfectly normal, therefore, to have environmental agencies explain up front which harms they will address, and how. Likewise for agencies controlling occupational or transportation safety issues, where there is no brain behind the harm. But where control operations face conscious opponents, revealing too much about your own strategy might give the game away, and render the controls completely

ineffectual. It does not make much sense for police to announce publicly, in advance, where they plan to conduct random breath-testing
checkpoints. It would be foolish for customs agents to reveal the behavioral profiling methods they use to select passengers for search.

During the period of enhanced airport security in the months following 9/11, it was utterly foolish for airlines to stamp the boarding
passes at check-in for passengers who had been selected for higher
levels of security screening. Any passenger carrying a prohibited item
had plenty of time after check-in, and before going through security, to
dispose of it or pass it to a fellow passenger whose boarding card had
not been so stamped. Advance knowledge of the enhanced search made
the enhanced search virtually useless, almost guaranteeing it would
reveal nothing. And violators would actually be attracted to airlines
that operated this system, taking comfort from knowing they would
get advance warning of any extra search.

Should tax agencies reveal the formulas and ratios they use to select
tax returns for audit? If they did, they might facilitate tax evasion
by providing evaders and the professionals who advise them with a
clear map of safe terrain. Should the analytic techniques used for fraud
detection employ the same formulas and score thresholds year after
year? If they do, the opposition will scout out the parameters, and
safely "fly under the radar" with no risk of detection. Predictability in
detection methods seriously undermines compliance.

When facing opponents, operational effectiveness may demand a little less transparency, some artful unpredictability, deliberate incorporation of randomness, an air of mystery, and even the retained capacity
to deliver nasty shocks without any kind of warning. All of these dent,
to some extent, our normal underlying preference for openness. It does
not mean, of course, that these values are simply discarded, or count no
more in this context. These values still remain society's *default setting*
for government operations. But there may be occasions when judicious
sacrifices in the domain of transparency and predictability produce significant gains in compliance management, behavior modification, and
harm-reduction effectiveness. Provided the purposes are valuable, the
sacrifices effective, and the motivations pure, then society gains as a
result.

The Australian Tax Office (ATO), as a matter of course now pub-
lishes its audit strategy, annually, in advance. Their audit strategy lays
out clearly for everyone to see which areas of tax non-compliance

and which sectors will receive the most attention. This practice clearly serves society's expectations in terms of government accountability. But some have questioned whether it actually improves or damages tax compliance. The answer, I believe, would be "it depends what type of taxpayer, and what type of non-compliance." Suppose the ATO has spotted an area of tax law plagued by widespread ignorance, neglect, or error; and their audit plan announces their intention to hone in on that area. They might legitimately anticipate taxpayers would pay more attention to the issues identified, simply as a result of the announcement, and that compliance would improve.

Even in areas involving deliberate and conscious opposition (such as abusive use of tax shelters by the very rich) making such a declaration might, in fact, be a useful tactic. If the abuse of tax shelters were widespread, then announcing clearly to all the violators "watch out, here we come" might have a very positive deterrent effect, and achieve a great deal simply by virtue of the announcement.

What is interesting in this case, however, is that the announcement itself is a tactical choice; and any subsequent action is *another* tactical choice. By all means make an announcement if it will have a significant impact on compliance. By all means follow up with some high profile audits to prove your threat was serious. But bear in mind – given the conscious opponents – that all these actions are problem-specific, *tactical* choices; and they are driven a little less by underlying ideological preferences for transparency. When dealing with cheats, what you *say* might improve their behavior, and what you *do* thereafter might also improve their behavior; but it's a little less important that you *say* precisely what you'll *do*.

That leaves open an interesting ethical question about whether government agencies, facing opponents, should feel obliged to *do* what they *said* they would do. Failure on this count might be construed deceitful, and therefore inappropriate. But many of the tools of intelligence gathering, also brought into play against opponents, are essentially deceitful anyway. Undercover operations are one big lie. Surveillance methods and tools are often concealed or disguised, and disinformation might be used to confound opponents' counter-intelligence operations or erode trust within their organizations. So the use of deceit ought not to be prohibited, provided there is a clear tactical purpose for it. In a game against opponents, a little mystery and unpredictability goes a long way.

The New South Wales police in Australia use road signs on various highways around Sydney that provide motorists with this warning: "Unmarked police patrols operating in this area." For many motorists, this warning probably begs some questions: If the patrols are unmarked, presumably that is so the public cannot recognize them. So why place a sign to announce their presence? Alternatively, if the state police wanted everyone to know police were there (which the presence of the signs suggests), would not *marked* cars be better for the purpose?

I imagine these signs do motivate motorists to drive more carefully, obey speed limits, and buckle-up. They make motorists aware of the *possibility* of police action, but at the same time they artfully preserve some mystery. The sign makes sure motorists consider the possibility that they might be under observation; and the fact that the police cars are unmarked means that motorists can never be sure when they are *not* being observed. This combination – unmarked cars plus the sign – serves to remind motorists about law enforcement, is vaguely suggestive of police omnipresence, and by design keeps everyone guessing.

It did cross my mind, last time I passed one of these signs, that the New South Wales police, having erected the signs, might send all their unmarked cars off to patrol elsewhere, leaving the signs to do the work in these areas. If so, I hope they manage to keep that strategy secret for a very long time!

It is a very useful thing, when facing conscious opponents determined to outwit control systems, to keep them guessing all the time, and to retain the element of surprise.

Notes

1. Jorg Raab & H. Brinton Milward, "Dark Networks as Problems," *Journal of Public Administration Research and Theory*, 13 (2003), 413–439. (pp. 421–422, 430–431).
2. Prior research has shown that smokers do tend to be more broadly prone to risk-taking than non-smokers. They are, for instance, less likely to wear seatbelts, monitor their blood pressure, or even floss their teeth: W. Kip Viscusi, "*Monetarizing the Benefits of Risk and Environmental Regulation,*" Working Paper 06-09 (Washington DC: American Enterprise Institute-Brookings Joint Center for Regulatory Studies, April 2006), available at [www.aei-brookings.org], p. 12. But

a correlation between different risk-taking propensities does not constitute an adaptive response to the removal of one risk by deliberately increasing another.

3. W. Kip Viscusi, *Fatal Tradeoffs: Public & Private Responsibilities for Risk* (Oxford: Oxford University Press, 1992), p. 12.

4. Frances M. Brodsky, "Stealth, Sabotage and Exploitation," *Immunological Reviews*, 168 (1999), 5–11.

5. Ibid. p. 5.

6. Ibid.

7. *"Facts About Drug-Resistant Gonorrhea"* (Atlanta, Georgia: Center for Disease Control, April 2007), available at: [www.cdc.gov/std/Gonorrhea/arg/default.htm#fact].

8. Lawrence K. Altman, "Agency Urges A Change in Antibiotics for Gonorrhea," *New York Times* (Friday April 13, 2007), A10.

9. For a discussion of influenza control strategies, which seek to predict the emergence and transmission patterns for drug-resistant forms anticipated in response to various vaccination policies, see: Roland R. Regoes & Sebastian Bonhoeffer, "Emergence of Drug-resistant Influenza Virus: Population Dynamical Considerations," *Science*, 312 (April 21, 2006), 389–391.

10. For an example of an early alert to developing resistance in influenza viruses, and recommended clinical policies to avoid exacerbating the problem, see: Frederick G. Hayden, "Antiviral Resistance in Influenza Viruses – Implications for Management and Pandemic Response," *New England Journal of Medicine*, 354 (February 23, 2006), 785–788.

11. This particular understanding of the nature of *probability* avoids any conflict between the notion of a physically determined universe and a sense of risk as inherently probabilistic. For a discussion of apparent tension between these two ideas (unresolved) see: Eugene A. Rosa, "The Logical Structure of the Social Amplification of Risk Framework (SARF); Metatheoretical Foundations and Policy Implications," in Nick Pidgeon, Roger E. Kasperson, & Paul Slovic (eds.), *The Social Amplification of Risk* (Cambridge: Cambridge University Press, 2003), pp. 55–56.

12. Ignorance about the details of the dice throw is quite different from ignorance about the system and its underlying probability distribution. The former involves carefully circumscribed areas of ignorance within a system that is generally understood. The latter, as Sunstein puts it, involves "... conditions of *ignorance*, in which regulators are unable to specify either the probability of bad outcomes or their nature – where regulators do not even know the magnitude of the harms that they are facing." Cass R. Sunstein, *Laws of Fear: Beyond the*

Precautionary Principle (Cambridge: Cambridge University Press, 2005), p. 60.

13. The concept of probability (quantified as a number in the range zero to one) was first developed in relation to gambling stakes for mechanically determined games of chance, by Blaise Pascal and Pierre de Fermat in 1654. Peter Bernstein provides a short and illuminating discussion of the effects that the subsequent development of probability theory has had on risk measurement and decision science. See: Peter L. Bernstein, "The Enlightening Struggle Against Uncertainty," in special series, "*Mastering Risk*," No. 1, *Financial Times* (April 25, 2000), 2.

14. In a fascinating discussion of the early development of probability theory, Howard Margolis comments how very quickly, after numerical probabilities emerged in relation to mechanical (e.g. dice-throwing) problems, application of the concept was stretched to cover cases in which there was no physical or mechanical system which might be expected to contribute a set of equally likely outcomes. The modern tendency, of course, is to imagine we can assign numerical probabilities to almost any uncertain prospective event, including the outcomes of other people's thought processes. See: Howard Margolis, *Paradigms & Barriers: How Habits of Mind Govern Scientific Beliefs* (Chicago: University of Chicago Press, 1993), Chapter 6, "The Emergence of Probability," pp. 68–85.

15. Jeffrey Kluger, "Why We Worry About the Wrong Things: The Psychology of Risk," *Time Magazine* (December 4, 2006, Australian Edition), 40–45.

10 | *Catastrophic harms*

This chapter examines the special operational challenges associated with harms that have never happened or happened only rarely, but which might bring extremely serious consequences if they did occur. Examples of such *catastrophic* risks include nuclear terrorism, other radiological disasters such as the meltdown of nuclear power-plant reactors, global pandemics, biological terrorism, genocide, earthquakes, hurricanes, or tsunami powerful enough to cause widespread devastation and casualties on a massive scale.

Some catastrophic risks, such as nuclear power-plant failure or terrorism involving weapons of mass destruction, are man-made. Others involve natural phenomena.[1] Catastrophes might be *unthinkable*, in the sense that they are overwhelmingly depressing prospects to contemplate; but they are not *unimaginable*. Usually we can piece together from prior or related experiences a mental picture of *what it might be like*. But this does not help anyone understand *how likely* it is to happen. And not knowing the underlying probability presents all kinds of operational difficulties. It places us in what Hutter and Power refer to as "an informal "probabilitistic climate" where characterizations of likelihoods are often crude."[2] In this environment, small-probability high-impact risks may often be completely ignored, or equally well "characterize a "space of fear" which can induce hyper-precautionary attention to risk and security."[3]

Some catastrophic risks involve opponents, and the last chapter described how the involvement of *conscious opponents* might render probability assessments especially unreliable because of the variability introduced by their decisions. But even without conscious opponents, the fact that a risk has never materialized, or only very rarely, means that there are not enough incidents available to generate a reliable point estimate of the probability. Very small probabilities are notoriously hard to estimate. Mathematical and statistical modeling helps less than one would hope, because exceptional events lie in the extreme tails of probability distributions, and these tails do not behave well in mathematical terms, failing to conform to well-understood functions or distributions.[4] As a result, estimations of probabilities based on normal or ordinary experience (which is concentrated in the central section of such distributions) are prone to be wildly erroneous. More sophisticated tail-estimation methods, none of which can be guaranteed to reliably reveal the shape of these "tails," have been put to work in a variety of risk-assessment domains. These settings include the forecasting of major stock-market swings, and providing guidance for Dutch engineers on how high to build protective levees for low-lying areas.[5]

In terms of subjective – as opposed to mathematical – assessments, if something has never happened at all, or only once before, then one person might regard the probability of an occurrence within the next ten years as one in a million, and another might say one in a billion. There may be no information available to help determine which is more realistic.

From an operational perspective the seriousness of the potential consequences, should an event occur, makes *prevention* of paramount importance (at least, for any risk that humankind has some control over). Of course, prevention is important for *any* harm. But the basic qualities of catastrophic risks makes the preventive task much more complicated and challenging, even as they make preventive success more critical.

Here are some of the qualities of catastrophic risks that most profoundly affect control operations:

- The very small number of observed instances does not provide a sound basis for probability estimation, nor for detecting any reduction in probabilities resulting from control interventions. No-one knows, therefore, how much to spend on control or whether it is worth spending anything at all.[6] Budget allocations will largely be driven by levels of public attention and concern, which will fluctuate far more widely than the actual level of the risk, particularly around the time that new information or new experiences become available.[7] The budgetary norm in the absence of an event will be significant underinvestment, lurching to over-investment in the wake of a visible incident or scare.[8]
- The short-term nature of budget cycles and political terms-of-office, coupled with the human tendency to discount future impacts,[9]

exacerbates the temptation to do nothing or to do very little, or to procrastinate on deciding what to do.[10] Even if the chance of a catastrophe occurring within fifty years is substantial (as is reportedly the case with respect to the next major earthquake in the San Francisco area), the chance of it happening within a three or four-year political term might seem practically indistinguishable from zero. A succession of short-term political and current cost calculations, therefore, may undermine any sensible longer-term evaluation and response.

- The very small number of observed instances of the harm (in many cases, zero) provides insufficient basis for any meaningful kind of pattern recognition and identification of concentrations. For harms in general, examining patterns of incidents underlies the business of problem-identification and problem-solving, with the fruits of the reactive workload analysis fed back into the control system. Catastrophic risks provide no such fertile dataset, and hence no such opportunity for the normal feedback loop between failures of control and subsequent control enhancements.

- All of the preventive work has to be defined, divided up, handed out, conducted, and measured early in the chronological unfolding of the harm, in the realm of precursors to the risk, and precursors to the precursors. This is intellectually and conceptually challenging work. Given the absence of any discernible patterns of incidents, preventive analysis demands deliberate imagining and dissection of complex scenarios which are, for the most part, unobservable.

- Reactive responses and contingency plans are not operated often enough to remain practiced and primed for action. In order to practice response, authorities must depend on *exercises*, which often lack realism and cannot emulate the scope of a real disaster. Underlying uncertainty about the likelihood of the harm materializing makes the costs and inconvenience associated with exercises difficult to justify.

- In the absence of periodic stimuli, vigilance wanes over time. Response operations, if and when they are genuinely needed, are likely to perform poorly in comparison to other responses oft-deployed and well-practiced.

- Reactive responsibilities are curiously decoupled from preventive operations, and engage quite different agencies or institutions. Response to disasters falls heavily on emergency services, public health systems, civil defense and military resources. By contrast, the work of prevention belongs with intelligence services (in relation to terrorism) or technical and scientific specialists (in relation to major systems failures) who would have only a peripheral role in response should the disaster occur.

- Investments in reactive capacities (public health and emergency response) are more readily appreciated and versatile, having a great many other potential and easy-to-imagine applications. (The fire department gets the new fire engine, the police department gets a new state-of-the-art communication system, the hospital gets a new trauma unit.) Investments in prevention, by contrast, tend to be highly specific to the risk, and difficult to assess in terms of risk impact. Investments in the reactive end of the problem are therefore easier to explain to the public, and easier to justify in terms of their broader utility. The resulting bias may hinder preventive work, despite its pre-eminent importance, even when awareness of the risk is high and resources are available.

- Policy makers at the national level find reactive investments easier to make, as their own intellectual and analytic role is reduced to broadcast dissemination of funds for decentralized investment in emergency services. Investments in enhancing preventive control tend, by contrast, to be highly centralized and much more complex technically. Allocating investments to the preventive end of the problem therefore requires lawmakers to acquire a greater degree of understanding of the risk and its origins and developmental stages, so they can determine the most suitable portfolio of preventive enhancements. That is extremely demanding intellectual work for them, involving complex analysis of imagined scenarios. It is much easier for them, therefore, to distribute the money and push the thinking down to a lower level. The nature of this dilemma at the center exacerbates the bias towards investments in decentralized response capacities, at the expense of centralized preventive operations. Worse, as a practical matter, the decentralized authorities do not really know what to do with the money either, because they cannot relate much to the preventive task, and the probability of this catastrophe occurring *in their area* is even lower than the probability of this catastrophe *somewhere*. So they have the funds in hand, but the intended purposes seem remote. Naturally they use the funding for a broad range of acquisitions peripherally related to the task at hand, fulfilling more general equipment or personnel needs. Everyone pretends these investments enhance control of the risk. The truth, more likely, is that the money ultimately gets frittered away on a vast range of locally determined priorities which are uncoordinated, peripherally connected to the risk, and which neglect the principal imperative: *prevention*.

Creating catastrophic risks, by virtue of partial controls

I referred above to the distinction between *man-made* and *natural* catastrophic risks. *Man-made*, in this context, would normally mean "generated as a result of human endeavor." This description would cover the construction of complex systems with potential for failure (e.g. computer systems with the millennium bug), as well as malevolent acts of terrorists and saboteurs. But there is another sense in which a harm or risk, whether man-made or natural, can be *granted* the qualities of a catastrophic harm, not having had them before, by the construction of a set of *partial* defenses.

The most visible recent example involves the failure of New Orleans' levee system in the face of Katrina – a category four hurricane – in August 2005. Hurricanes are a natural threat to the Carribean and the Gulf of Mexico areas, and occur frequently but with a considerable range in severity. The construction of levees defends the low-lying areas of New Orleans against *all but the most serious* of a continuum of threats. And as the nation observed during Katrina, when levees are finally breached, they tend to collapse and fail completely.[11] Without levees, New Orleans would have faced the whole spectrum of hurricane-related threats, and experienced floods of various magnitudes on a frequent basis. The construction of levees transforms this threat picture into a binary *all-or-nothing* situation, with *nothing* consequential happening most of the time, and a residual threat with very small probability but very high impact.

All of the features of catastrophic risks, listed above, therefore apply to this residual risk. Very few of them would apply if the levees had not been constructed, and New Orleans had continued to face the full range of threats. Frequent incidents with a range of intensities would produce adaptations to the constant threat of flooding, enhance community preparedness, and provide responders plenty of practice and experience.

Does this mean, therefore, that the construction of levees made Katrina more dangerous than it otherwise would have been? And should constructing levees (and all their analogues in other domains) therefore be discouraged?

Presumably the construction of flood defenses protects many residents and much property, most of the time. In fact, the levees successfully protect the city *for the entire lifetime* of many residents. Therefore construction of levees is, on balance, surely a good thing. But if flood-prone cities fortify themselves with levees, then they need to understand the special and awkward characteristics of the *residual* risk, and properly anticipate the consequences. They should anticipate, first, that the protection against lower level versions of the harm will eliminate many ordinary sensible living adaptations that frequent incidents might have produced, like not building houses in flood prone areas.[12] Second, the lack of frequent incidents will dull both the warning systems and the response operations, both of which will be absolutely critical when the "big one" comes. Third, residents may be fooled into believing the city is completely protected, and act accordingly.[13] They may neglect contingency planning, as individuals and families as well as at the city level. Communities will not be conditioned nor equipped for disaster response. When the event finally does happen, it is almost certain to catch everyone by surprise, and to generate a response both sluggish and inadequate.

For all of these reasons, building the levees *might* have made Hurricane Katrina much more dangerous for the city of New Orleans than it would have been otherwise. But the policy failure, if there is one, lies not so much in the construction – which might well be justified and appropriate. Rather, the fault lies in failing to understand the nature of the residual risk, and to deal deliberately and carefully with the dangerous properties it quietly acquires.

Resulting operational imperatives

Dealing with catastrophic risks, however they come to have that particular quality, requires some deliberate attention to the following:

Counteract the temptation to ignore the risk

Understand that the small probability of a disaster, the uncertainty surrounding the probability, the short-term nature of budget and political cycles, and the conceptual difficulty of enhancing preventive controls, all heighten the temptation to neglect or ignore the risk. Some catastrophic risks *ought* to be neglected or ignored – for instance, those against which there is no useful defense (a huge asteroid striking the earth and wiping out human life altogether), or those for which the probability has been determined to be too miniscule to be worth worrying about.[14] Even for these, choosing to neglect them should be a conscious decision; an act of cognitive commission, not omission.

For the remainder, where the probability, though small, is not negligible; where the consequences of an event would be enormous; and where something *could* be done; for these, the temptation to ignore or neglect or put off to another day must be counter-acted. The challenge is to stimulate public and political attention to the risk, and maintain it at a reasonable level and for very long periods. Disaster movies help (the more realistic, the merrier). So do documentaries about the risk and the perils of neglecting it. Such devices can help to confront people with the *vivid data* necessary to provoke action.[15] Incidents involving lower level versions of the harm, whenever they are available, should be fully exploited for the purpose, leading to public inquiry and analysis along the lines of "what could have made this event *much worse?*" What if the tsunami had been another twenty feet higher? What if the earthquake had been two points stronger on the Richter Scale, and the epicenter here rather than there?

In the aftermath of a relatively minor incident, one might deliberately steer the discussion from "how unfortunate for us that it was that bad" to a realization that "we are all quite fortunate it was not much worse." All such events can be used to *help people imagine*, and arrive at clearer judgments about levels of attention and application of resources for enhanced protection.[16] So can similar events, far away. These should be *brought home*. Organize meetings and seminars around the film footage from afar. Invite the distant officials to come and tell their story, after the fact. Provide no escape from these questions: What if that happened here? Are we prepared? What could we do to reduce the probability? How would we know if we had? What is it worth, to us, to cut that chance in half, or to be better prepared?

Define higher-volume, precursor conditions as opportunities for monitoring and goal-setting

Given the nature of these risks, there are not enough incidents to analyze effectively, nor to provide meaningful statistical evidence of any reduction in the risk. It helps, therefore to select precursor conditions that occur with greater frequency as a way of gauging progress over time. When a commercial airliner crashes with hundreds of people on board this is a very serious matter. But it doesn't happen often enough for the Federal Aviation Authority (FAA) to rely on analysis of crashes *alone* to inform their efforts to improve safety. Of course they investigate and debrief each of the (thankfully few) crashes, and they do so exhaustively. As well, they devise and formally define *near misses*, and mandate reporting of these. That produces a richer dataset to serve as a basis for analysis and risk-reduction work.[17] From the database of near-misses and other reportable incidents they can identify patterns, divide up the task, create specific assignments, set goals, implement tailor-made remedies, and monitor their impact on specific problems over time.[18] Then, when the number of near-misses has been driven down to the level at which *there are no longer enough* of these to support meaningful analysis purposes, the FAA then broadens the definition to bring in more data, gaining the opportunity to ratchet safety up one more notch.

The Nuclear Regulatory Commission and the nuclear power industry worked in a similar fashion over the last twenty years, since the failure of controls at the Three-Mile Island nuclear power plant in 1979.[19] The nuclear power industry defines sets of conditions, precursors to a serious failure, where the chronological unfolding of the potential harm reaches certain discrete points. These measurement points might include the moment that pressure in one system or another exceeds or falls below certain thresholds, safety valves open or close, alarms activate, or redundant safety systems kick in. By collating and analyzing data from all these incidents, and analyzing what happened to bring the system to that point, they find ways to drive down their frequency over time. The industry then progressively broadens the range of conditions they monitor, and moves them back further and further in the chronology of the harm. Thus they cut down the incident rates and leave yet more safety systems in reserve, later in the chronological chain, scarcely ever triggered.

The use of such precursor conditions for data gathering, analysis, intervention and monitoring, coupled with insights gleaned through systematic debriefing of near-misses and disasters that have befallen others, gives the preventive control task some *structure*.[20] It provides controllers a way to organize their work and to show others what they have accomplished and how, project by project. It enables them to justify their budgets by showing measurable progress. Focusing only upon the actual number of disasters – typically zero, zero, zero, year after year – does not provide any of these things.

Construct formal, disciplined, warning systems

In the absence of reinvigorating stimuli, *vigilance* wanes over time. Alarm conditions encountered periodically exercise warning systems and make them more sensitive and more discriminating. Absence of alarms, month after month and year after year, degrades their sensitivity over time. Human beings cannot take threats seriously if they have never seen them materialize, and have no related experiences to draw upon which might inform their imagination. And human beings have great difficulty maintaining high levels of alertness when nothing happens for very long periods.

All these factors make it more likely that warning systems will fail, or will not be taken seriously, at the very moment when they count most. Officials might not appreciate the scale of the threat, or be reluctant to acknowledge it, even as a disaster begins to unfold. In extreme circumstances, the ordinary human tendency toward denial may paralyze the response.[21]

To mitigate these dangers, contingency and response planning must take proper account of them. The use of simulations and exercises on a frequent basis can help compensate for the general lack of energizing stimuli. Those with decision-making roles during times of crisis should be asked to watch every disaster movie available, to feed their imagining of what it might be like. Distant experiences should be captured and brought home, providing eye-opening educational opportunities and a chance to test existing contingency plans against real life (but transported) experiences.

To counteract the dangers of denial or misinterpretation of unfamiliar signals, warning systems should trigger response initiation *without* the application of much real-time discretion. Warning signals should be transmitted to multiple sites, so that one crew misinterpreting them or writing them off as false alarms does not impede or delay the broader activation of response.

Vigilance will wane over time if those who have to maintain a state of readiness find themselves in a binary, all-or-nothing, world, facing *nothing* most of the time. On the preventive side of catastrophic risks, we have to find a way to give the work texture and structure, and some sense of progression. On the preventive side, we do that by moving back through the chronology of the harm, dealing systematically with precursor conditions and precursors to the precursors. The response side of catastrophic risks presents a similar challenge. Response operations also need texture and structure and a sense of progression. They need to be stressed, and evaluated under stress, often – not just once in a blue moon. They need a broad range of stimuli that stretch their imaginations in many different directions.[22] If and when these highly unlikely disasters really do occur, then everyone will hope that all of the components of response operations, both human and technical, have actually done something very much like this before, and not too long ago. Maintaining readiness for catastrophic events involves replacing the missing parts of the continuum, artificially filling in the void of less serious but more frequent incidents. This recreates what the catastrophic quality of the risk took away: a practical, short-term process for rehearsal, testing, feedback, and adaptation.

Notes

1. The phenomenon of climate change has successfully muddied this distinction with respect to freak weather events, for which the human race now bears some responsibility. The fact of having contributed to climate change, however, does not give the human race any greater degree of control over each of the specific weather events (cyclones, hurricanes, floods, etc.) that may now occur with greater frequency and intensity. Climate change therefore presents two rather different challenges in terms of control. Climate change at the global level might be slowed or reversed through concerted action. Each devastating weather event, meanwhile, behaves more like an act of nature and is not "preventable" from an operational point of view.
2. Bridget Hutter & Michael Power (eds.), *Organizational Encounters with Risk* (Cambridge: Cambridge University Press, 2005), p. 8.
3. Ibid.
4. Benoit Mandelbrot & Nassim Taleb, "A Focus on the Exceptions That Prove the Rule," *Financial Times*, special series on "*Mastering Uncertainty*" (Friday March 24, 2006), 2–3; Benoit Mandelbrot & Richard L. Hudson, *The (Mis)Behaviour of Markets: A Fractal View of Risk, Ruin, and Reward* (New York: Basic Books, 2004).

5. Such statistical methods include *non-parametric tail estimation*, and *extreme value theory*. For a succinct introduction to the challenges involved in estimating the probabilities of extreme events, see: Paul Embrechts, "Difficult Calls in Judging Risk Extremes," *Financial Times*, in special series, "*Mastering Risk*," No. 9 (June 20, 2000), 8. For a fuller and more technical development, particularly as applied to the financial and insurance markets, see: Paul Embrechts (ed.), *Extremes and Integrated Risk Management* (London: Risk Books, 2000).

6. Cass Sunstein links this phenomenon with the *precautionary principle*, thus: "the Precautionary Principle might well be reformulated as an Anti-Catastrophe Principle, designed for special circumstances in which it is not possible to assign probabilities to potentially catastrophic risks." Cass R. Sunstein, *Laws of Fear: Beyond the Precautionary Principle* (Cambridge: Cambridge University Press, 2005), p. 5.

7. William Leiss & Christine Chociolko, *Risk and Responsibility* (Montreal: McGill-Queen's University Press, 1994), p. 30.

8. Such behavior is not so much irrational as it is Bayesian. Given the range of uncertainty about the underlying probabilities, public estimates of those probabilities are prone to move much more markedly and instantly given a significant new observation than they would have if the available range of plausible probabilities had been narrower and the accumulated mass of prior experience weightier, anchoring the probability estimates more firmly.

9. Future harms should indeed be discounted, but at an appropriate rate. The issue here is the danger of discounting them almost to the point of neglect, particularly when the impacts may be borne by future generations, or may have to be handled by subsequent administrations. For an accessible discussion of the dilemmas surrounding appropriate discounting procedures and rates, see: Lester B. Lave, *The Strategy of Social Regulation: Decision Frameworks for Policy* (Washington DC: Brookings Institution Press, 1981), pp. 41–45.

10. Max H. Bazerman & Michael D. Watkins, *Predictable Surprises: The Disasters You Should Have Seen Coming and How to Prevent Them* (Boston, Massachusetts: Harvard Business School Press, 2004), p. 37.

11. This binary "all-or-nothing" performance of flood defenses was also observed in Northern Europe in 1953 when a severe storm hit the Flemish and Dutch coasts. Several dykes collapsed leading to widespread flooding and over 1,800 deaths.

12. Paul Slovic, Baruch Fischhoff & Sarah Lichtenstein, "Rating the Risks," *Environment*, 21 (April 1979), 14–20, 36–39.

13. Such behavioral responses, when some measure of protection is provided, have been observed in other areas. For example, see: Steven Peterson, George Hoffer, & Edward Millner, "Are Drivers of Air-Bag-Equipped Cars More Aggressive? A Test of the Offsetting Behavior Hypothesis," *Journal of Law and Economics,* 38 (October 1995), 251–264.

14. Scientists have estimated the risk of death by asteroid impact at 1/6,000, which exceeds the average American's risk of death through occupational accidents (roughly 1/10,000). Nevertheless, the latter receives more attention by virtue of being more controllable as well as more accessible and familiar. W. Kip Viscusi, *Fatal Tradeoffs: Public & Private Responsibilities for Risk* (Oxford: Oxford University Press, 1992), p. 5.

15. Bazerman & Watkins, *Predictable Surprises,* p. 92.

16. Deliberately stimulating and organizing available information, and the process of imagination that constructs therefrom plausible scenarios, would minimize what Bazerman and Watkins call *predictable surprises,* defined as "an event or set of events that take an individual or group by surprise, despite prior awareness of all the information necessary to anticipate the events and their consequences." Ibid. p. 1.

17. For a discussion of the importance of capturing, interpreting, and "sense-making" in relation to near misses and other anomalies, see: Hutter & Power (eds.), *Organizational Encounters with Risk,* pp. 15, 18–23.

18. This is precisely the approach prescribed for corporate risk management operations, in (for example): Anthony Carey & Nigel Turnbull, "The Boardroom Imperative on Internal Control," in special series, "*Mastering Risk,*" No. 1, *Financial Times* (April 25, 2000), 6.

19. The US Nuclear Regulatory Commission provides a fact-sheet on the Three-Mile Island incident, available on the NRC website, at: [www.nrc.gov/reading-rm/doc-collections/fact-sheets/3mile-isle.html].

20. The *Risk Management and Decision Processes Center* at the Wharton School, University of Pennsylvania, launched a project in 2000 on "Near-miss Management," with a special but not exclusive focus on the chemical industry. The purpose of the project is to enable organizations to manage and make the best possible use of near-misses, which are "weak signals that illuminate system flaws and catastrophe potential." See the project's website, at: [http://opim.wharton.upenn.edu/risk/projects/nearmiss.html].

21. For a discussion of the role of denial in the process of "risk-incubation" prior to a disaster, see: Barry A. Turner & Nick F. Pidgeon, *Man-made Disasters,* 2nd edition (Oxford: Butterworth-Heinemann, 1997).

22. Even with a constant, deliberate, and energetic process of "imagining" in place, not all disasters will be imagined, or imaginable. My colleague Dutch Leonard distinguishes usefully between *routine emergencies* (those within the normal operating experience of responsible agencies) and *crises,* which are distinguished by a degree of novelty or scale which makes them unprecedented. Response to crises which were unimaginable, and therefore beyond the normal scope of contingency planning, demands a set of managerial and leadership skills special to these contexts. Arnold M. Howitt & Herman B. "Dutch" Leonard, "Katrina and the Core Challenges of Disaster Response," *The Fletcher Forum of World Affairs,* 30 (Winter 2006), 215–221. Other scholars have characterized *crises* in terms of their lack of order due to complex and unpredictable systems interactions, which some have labeled "mess." Ian I. Mitroff, Murat C. Alpalsan, & Sandy E. Green, "Crises as Ill-Structured Messes," *International Studies Review,* 6, 2004, 165–194.

11 | *Harms in equilibrium*

N ormally one expects to be able to chip away at harms, grad-
ually, piece by piece, incrementally shifting the world from a
harmful state to some other, less harmful, state; many small
efforts accumulating to substantial effect. But some harms present an
equilibrium condition, and resist such treatment. They behave like a
ball bearing sitting at the bottom of a depression: give it a little nudge,
and it merely settles back to its original position. The forces of gravita-
tion, coupled with the shape of the terrain, pull it back to where it was.
In response to a perturbation, the ball bearing may wobble around for
a while at the bottom of its hole; but without a substantial shove it will
eventually settle again in precisely the same position.

Equilibrium positions can be either *stable* or *unstable*. A single
domino stood on its end is *unstable*, because a relatively small nudge
will make it fall right over. For the purposes of this discussion, it is the
stable equilibrium positions that concern us, where forces at work naturally tend to counteract small perturbations. In order to move the ball
bearing from a position of stable equilibrium to a different position,
and have it remain there, you first have to deliver a significant nudge,
sufficient to get it out of and away from its current equilibrium position. Then, having escaped the pull of the starting position, you guide
it over the surface, hopefully navigating towards some other position
which is not only *preferred*, but which is also *stable* – in other words,
a preferred state of affairs which will tend to maintain itself, without
constant application of effort or energy.

Some harms behave exactly like this, producing forces that tend to
cancel out any efforts to dislodge them. In such cases, small or incremental efforts will likely fail to produce any lasting impact, because
they don't accumulate in the way one would normally expect. Incremental efforts cannot transform the situation, because they do not
produce momentum sufficient to escape the grasp of the equilibrium
position.

Gang violence in some cities has shown such properties. Gang members carry guns, even though many of them claim to do so only in self-defense. Authorities want the gangs to disarm, and may apply pressure toward that end, prosecuting a few gang members here and there as resources permit. While the majority remains armed, any gang that disarms makes itself especially vulnerable, and may even be inviting attack. If just one gang disarms, that gang will face considerable pressure to rearm very soon (i.e. to restore the original, harmful, equilibrium) or suffer the consequences. In this kind of setting *small* changes are unsustainable, and will tend to be canceled out over time. Small changes do not move the situation beyond the natural gravitational pull of its original starting position. Disarming is unlikely unless *everyone* disarms at around the same time. To make that happen would require a radical intervention concentrated within a short time interval. In other words, the system would need a *big shove*. Once such a radical change had happened, and the bulk of the gangs had disarmed, then authorities could more easily focus their efforts and resources on whoever thereafter stepped out of line. It would take a lot less effort to *maintain* the new, more desirable, state than it took to *reach* it.

For another example, one might imagine an industrial sector largely out of compliance with a certain environmental requirement. All the companies within the sector are supposed to install and operate new technologies for scrubbing their smokestack emissions. For whatever reason, the industry has resisted and the vast majority are now out of compliance. What pressures now act on any company that now leans towards compliance? Presumably the increased costs of the compliant technology will place them at a competitive disadvantage relative to their peers. They might also face opprobrium and sanctions from their peers for "breaking ranks." The widespread non-compliance, therefore, tends to sustain itself, producing forces which counteract and tend to cancel out any gradual or piecemeal shifts towards compliance. Efforts to change the situation either need to be substantial and concentrated, sufficient to alter the prevailing condition, or their effects will dissipate over time.

The same can be true with respect to tax compliance. We know that pervasive and highly visible non-compliance has a psychological impact on taxpayers, making even the normally law-abiding citizens reluctant to pay up when they see the majority of their peers avoiding taxes and getting away with it.[1] Widespread non-compliance with tax law, therefore, begets more non-compliance, and sustains itself as a condition over time. Altering such a condition requires concentrated shocks to the system, and may require strategies designed to change everyone's behavior all at once, in order to break away from the underlying stability of the condition. Useful strategies for this include clear announcement of specific *change dates*. Tax authorities might state publicly that they know a particular form of non-compliance is widespread, and declare a date by which everyone within the relevant sector is expected to come into compliance. This gives non-compliers some time to put their house in order, but the compressed time period relieves them of the sense that they might be the only one complying. The idea is to help them all believe they are part of a much larger movement, and that it would be more costly to be left behind the movement than to be out in front. To be effective, such announcements have to include a threat of concerted and vigorous audits to be launched just after the change date against anyone who fails to alter their ways.

Limited periods of amnesty can also be useful, giving non-compliers a short time frame within which they can repair without penalty. Offers of amnesty, though, are only effective if they have a relatively short time horizon, and where people believe that monitoring and enforcement will be vigorous and sanctions severe after the expiry date. Only then do amnesties produce momentum sufficient to alter the underlying norms.

In relation to the problem of corruption, several commentators have talked of "high corruption equilibrium" and "low corruption equilibrium" to signify relative stability at opposite ends of the corruption spectrum. Michael Johnston suggests specific forces at work which create the equilibrium condition:

The most serious cases – entrenched political and bureaucratic corruption – are equilibria. They are tightly organized and internally stable, creating and being sustained by conditions of weak political competition, slow and uneven economic growth, and a weak civil society.[2]

Commenting on the nature of corruption in Africa, Paul Collier of the World Bank points out the uselessness of gentle interventions: "once corruption becomes normal, reversing the policies that caused it is not enough. The society needs a "big push" to shock it out of a high-corruption equilibrium."[3] Susan Rose-Ackerman points out the importance and difficulties of *sustaining reforms*, and the demonstrated lack of durability in partial or gentle reform programs.[4] Corrupt networks, once powerful and deeply embedded, acquire the capacity to repair themselves. Chipping away at them with a few indictments here and there does not undermine their stability. They have the capacity to recruit new members, and the influence to place collaborators wherever they need them. In a high-corruption equilibrium condition, it is dangerous to be honest, and dangerous to stand in the way of the corrupt enterprise.

At the opposite end of the spectrum, where corruption is the exception rather than the rule, it is the corrupt who are at risk, facing the constant danger of detection and exposure. Different forces operate at this end of the spectrum. According to Johnston,

Supervision from above, scrutiny from without, and structural checks and balances mean that individual officials or small groups do not possess monopoly discretion and find it difficult to organize and coordinate corruption on a large scale. The result is a different sort of equilibrium: corruption may occur but it is kept within limits and does not become entrenched.[5]

In the context of corruption control, the language of equilibria seems quite useful. It helps makes sense of the apparent imperviousness of embedded corruption to minor shocks, the tendency of systems to gravitate towards one end of the corruption spectrum or the other, the daunting challenges and extreme rarity of transition from high corruption to low, and the comparatively small amount of energy required for maintenance once things are mostly clean. It also helps to explain the relevance of a "big-bang approach in which massive changes are introduced all at once," and of designing artful sequences of reform steps which are less likely to suffer reverses because each step builds support for the next one.[6]

In 1993 the newly elected Governor of Puerto Rico, Pedro Rosselló, faced a different kind of entrenched equilibrium. Roughly 75 of the island's 332 public housing projects were under the control of drug lords (and one overarching criminal drug-smuggling organization known as Ñeta), and were considered no-go areas for police and other municipal services.[7] According to some estimates, Ñeta at the time comprised 35,000 armed members, and had access to 250,000 weapons.[8] The power of the drug trade in Puerto Rico stemmed from the special usefulness of the island as a staging point for drug shipments into the continental United States. The island had hundreds of miles of deserted beaches, was close to major drug-producing regions, and (as a US Commonwealth) had no customs controls on flights from the island to the mainland.

Within the public housing estates (or *residencials*) drug dealing was endemic and brazen. Murders were commonplace, and massacres – where groups of people were gunned down on the street – were frequent. In 1994 the murder rate for San Juan, capital of Puerto Rico, was 74 per 100,000 residents, more than double the rate for New York City. The criminal organizations operated their own justice system within the projects, using firing squads to deliver their kind of justice. Fundamentally, the control of the *residencials* by drug lords provided an alternate form of government, an "autonomous state within a state."[9]

Life within the *residencials* could be hellish, with residents deprived of basic services and sleeping on their floors to avoid the bullets that flew in through their windows. Despite the apparent chaos and lawlessness, the situation had its own peculiar stability, displaying the characteristics of an equilibrium. Once the drug lords had gained control of a housing estate, the narrow winding streets and limited points of access made *keeping control* of the area relatively easy for them. Neither cars nor pedestrians could move in or out of the housing estates without the dealers knowing about it. For them, every entrant was in any case a potential buyer, and was scrutinized carefully. Police patrols kept well away, because for them to enter was tantamount to suicide.

This situation was self-perpetuating too. With unemployment rates for residents above 60 percent, children growing up within the complexes automatically went to work for the drug dealers. There was no viable alternative, and their parents had no option but to acquiesce. Objecting, or informing, would bring swift retribution.

Governor Rosselló understood that the deeply-entrenched nature of the problem meant that nothing short of a drastic intervention was likely to have any lasting impact. To begin making any progress, the system needed a huge shove at the outset. Pedro Toledo, head of the Puerto Rico Police Department, suggested one such approach. In the spring of 1993 he asked the Governor to consider a program of military style invasions to retake the housing estates, one by one. Toledo proposed the operations be conducted at night and without warning, using an overwhelming number of police, bolstered by National Guard troops. This combined force would storm a complex using large numbers of military vehicles and landing helicopters on the rooftops. After gaining physical control over the area, the police and guard troops would round up the criminal elements, conduct sweeping searches for weapons and drugs, and use whatever advance intelligence they might have available to guide them to relevant apartments, caches, and other concealment locations. The object of each raid was to regain total control of one complex, clear it of drugs and drug dealers, and re-establish legitimate government – all within the space of a few hours. After that the perimeters of the estate would be sealed with fences, and checkpoints established at the remaining entrances. A handful of police manning each guardhouse, thereafter, could retain control and keep out everyone other than the legitimate residents.

The proposed plan carried enormous operational risks. If the drug-lords were tipped off regarding an impending raid (which was quite possible given the fact that the police department itself was riddled with corruption) and put up armed resistance, the results could be disastrous and casualties heavy. Another possibility was that forces deployed would turn out to be inadequate for the job – as had happened with one failed raid attempt under a previous administration, in 1992. The military-style operations could easily produce civilian casualties. The National Guard troops were not trained in civilian law-enforcement methods. Some believed that poor police morale and eagerness for revenge might lead to a breakdown of discipline, with police acting more like death-squads themselves.

These operations would carry considerable political risk for the Governor himself. He had been elected by a very slim margin, and was not sure how the public would react to the use of National Guard troops in what was essentially a policing context. Any media backlash based on violations of civil rights or cavalier attitudes toward civilian safety could seriously undermine political support for the endeavor. There were plenty of ways the plan could fail, and any one of them would most likely leave authorities in an even weaker position than before.

When dealing with harms in equilibrium, however, there is another failure mode which policymakers should always consider. It is quite possible that in planning and delivering the initial *big shove*, not enough attention is paid to the trajectory with which the system will emerge from its hole, or where it might end up; and if it does end up somewhere better, how to *keep* it there.

NASA knows this, of course, when they want to move a spaceship out of earth's orbit, and set it on a path towards the moon. They know it takes a huge injection of energy (firing the main rockets) to escape the earth's gravitational field. They also know that precise timing is critical, because the resulting trajectory away from earth depends on it. Getting the timing wrong, and therefore the escape trajectory wrong, means a lot of effort will be required later to correct the error. Provided the trajectory is roughly right, then the craft moves on its merry way through space with only minor navigational adjustments to maintain its proper course. The next time the mission will need the main rockets, and critical timing, is when they want to guide the craft into its new, stable orbit; this time around the moon. That stage takes considerable navigational precision and timing, and a lot of energy once again (in this case to slow the craft down). Otherwise the spacecraft merely slingshots off into space again.

Governor Rosselló thought long and hard about the operational risks associated with the large-scale raids. He thought they could be managed. But in the early discussions of the plan, little thought was given to the trajectory of the housing estates, in what state they might end up, and what it would take to find a desirable condition and maintain it over time. One very real long term danger was that any reprieve from Ñeta's control would turn out to be temporary. Maybe, given prevailing conditions in the city, the "state within a state" was the *only* stable equilibrium position. Or, even if there was an alternative condition which was both preferable and potentially stable, maybe the operational and policy interventions might not include a method for getting there, or a safe way of "landing" a community into that new orbit.

The Governor saw this primarily as a crime problem. The plan for massive raids – called *Operation Centurion* – came from the police chief. The operational risks were assessed and addressed through discussions with all the other parts of the criminal justice system. So the deliberations involved the Police, National Guard, the attorney general, the Department of Corrections, and other public safety officials.[10] This was the *crime control* group. What this group *could* do was figure out how to deliver the initial shock to the system, dislodge the drug organizations, and put in place some rudimentary controls like guardhouses in place to try to keep them out. But this particular group could not imagine nor construct suitable long-term alternative states;

nor could they understand the consequences for these communities of chronic unemployment, poverty, neglect of health, inadequate sanitation, deteriorating infrastructure, a history of trauma, a generation of young children already launched upon criminal careers, and families fractured or bereaved through violence.

Fortunately for Governor Rosselló, a quite separate part of his administration was considering options for delivering services and restoring "communities in distress." The secretary of the Department of Housing, Carlos Vivoni, had established a group known as the *Quality of Life Congress* to coordinate the work of sixteen different departments.[11] Members of this group included Housing, Sport and Recreation, Health, Education, Social Services, Youth Affairs, Elderly Affairs, Disabled Citizens, the Women Affairs Commission, and the Corporation of Musical Arts. The Police were also partners in the *Quality of Life Congress*, although they did not regard this work as in any way related to their plans for invading the housing estates. Police thought of their own operation as part of their war against the criminal organizations, rather than as a part of anything to do with restoring communities.

In retrospect, it seems incredible that these two initiatives remained entirely separate – right up to the very last minute. Carlos Vivoni, heading the *Congress*, was not informed about the raids until a few days before the first one was scheduled to take place. The Governor's staff informed Vivoni of the impending raid, purely on the basis that Vivoni's Department of Housing would need to deal with the aftermath of the raids which might include much physical damage. Therefore he should be warned.

But Vivoni, when told of the raids, understood straight away the significance of the coincidence and the valuable connection between the two initiatives. From his point of view, the *Quality of Life Congress* could well imagine a stable state of affairs preferable to the current conditions, and believed they had pulled together a coalition sufficient to make such a state stable, once achieved. With these sixteen agencies on board they could deal with the legacy of trauma, educate the children, provide support to parents, restore services, deliver health care, and support the elderly and disabled. They could, they believed, not only *Restore* communities in distress, but eventually *Re-empower* them to the extent that civility and order could become, once again, a stable norm, and communities would have "the tools with which to retain control of their neighborhoods."[12] The only thing the *Congress* could not do, he felt, was *get in the door.* For these agencies, the most needy estates remained off limits, and so they had no way of *starting.*

Conversely, the crime control team, with its plan, had a way to get in the door, dislodging the ball bearing from its hole; but they had no plan for rolling that ball towards any other sustainable position. Without the *Congress* to follow up, they might have kept that ball-bearing out of its initial hole, but perched precariously on the edge . . . just waiting for some small error of neglect, when all the old forces would reassert themselves, and one housing estate after another might fall right back into its previous condition.

Finally the connection was made, and only just in time. The raids themselves became the first phase of an integrated three-phase plan. Phase 1 was "Rescue." Phase 2 was "Restore." Phase 3 was "Re-empower." Or – for those who like the physical analogy – phase 1 dislodges the ball bearing from its hole. Phase 2 navigates it towards a preferred state. Phase 3 settles it in its new position, and sets up the forces necessary to make that new position stable.

Between June 1993 and January 1996, "Rescue" raids were launched at sixty-seven public housing developments and at seven private developments similarly infested by criminal organizations. There was little public objection to the raids, and no protest against the involvement of the National Guard. The majority of residents approved of the interventions, and only complained later where police in the guardhouses were too permissive in whom they allowed through, or in tolerating drug dealing close by. By the end of 1995, crime in these "intervened" communities had dropped more than 70 percent. Island-wide, serious crimes dropped by 18 percent. The overall murder rate for Puerto Rico stayed roughly constant during this period, so one might surmise that violence was at least partially displaced rather than completely eliminated. Nevertheless the purpose of these interventions was to rescue communities. There is little doubt that the integrated plan achieved that particular result. There is also little doubt that the first phase (the raids) would not have produced sustainable improvements without all the other parts that followed.

Maybe Governor Rosselló was lucky, in this instance, to discover the symbiosis between the two separate initiatives. Hopefully his experience on this front will be useful for others who find themselves confronting harms in equilibrium. They should anticipate all of the following ordinary operational consequences:

- Interventions will involve three distinct phases: (a) *dislodging* from current condition, (b) *navigating* towards new, preferred position, and (c) *resettling* into the new state, establishing the forces or dynamics sufficient to make it stable.
- The initial dislodging phase can require very significant amounts of energy. Small scale, piecemeal, or incremental efforts are likely to fail. Worse, they may increase the system's resistance and bolster the confidence of opponents when attempts to transform the situation collapse.
- *Dislodging*, without serious planning for the subsequent *navigation* and *resettling* can be dangerous indeed. (This is surely the basis for the current wave of criticisms directed against the Bush administration's planning in Iraq). Resulting trajectories can be arbitrary, harmful, and difficult to adjust later.
- The three phases might involve different agencies, policy areas, and competencies.
- It is important to think far enough ahead. One not only needs to *imagine* a better and stable state for the system. One also needs to know what forces would naturally tend to maintain that state, assuming it could be reached. Without clarity up front as to the nature of those forces and how they would operate, there is a real danger that the new state, while imaginable, would take high levels of perpetual effort to sustain. Such a state represents an *unstable* equilibrium, not a *stable* one. In that case the benefits of the intervention may unravel given a momentary lapse of attention or diversion of resources.

When undoing harms in equilibrium, it is vitally important to seek only *stable* equilibrium positions as alternatives, and to have in mind a plan that will get you all the way there.

Notes

1. John Alford & Richard Speed, "Client Focus in Regulatory Agencies: Oxymoron or Opportunity," *Public Management Review*, 8 (2006), 313–331.

2. Michael Johnston, "*What Can be Done about Entrenched Corruption?*" Colgate University. Paper prepared for the Annual World Bank Conference on Development Economics, Washington DC, April 1997. Available at: [http://people.colgate.edu/mjohnston/MJ%20papers%2001/ABCDfinwork.pdf], p. 3.

3. Paul Collier, "How to Reduce Corruption," *African Development Review*, 12 (2000), 191–205.

4. Susan Rose-Ackerman, *Corruption and Government: Causes, Consequences and Reform* (Cambridge: Cambridge University Press, 1999), pp. 219–223.

5. Johnston, "*What Can be Done about Entrenched Corruption?*" p. 18.

6. Rose-Ackerman, *Corruption and Government*, p. 223.

7. For an account of the situation, and the plans developed to resolve it, see: Harvey Simon, "*Mano Dura: Mobilizing the National Guard to Battle Crime in Puerto Rico*," Kennedy School of Government Case Program, Case C109-97-1390.0. (Cambridge, Massachusetts: Harvard University, 1997).

8. Estimates are those of Juan Garcia-Passalacqua, adviser to President Jimmy Carter on Latin American and Carribean affairs. Ibid. p. 3.

9. Description by Juan Garcia-Passalacqua. Ibid. p. 3.

10. Ibid. p. 11.

11. Harvey Simon, "*Mano Dura: Mobilizing the National Guard to Battle Crime in Puerto Rico (Epilogue)*," Kennedy School of Government Case Program, Case C109-97-1390.1. (Cambridge, Massachusetts: Harvard University, 1997).

12. Ibid. p. 4.

12 | *Performance-enhancing risks*

C hapter 9 examined harms involving conscious opponents, where a brain lies behind the threat. This chapter, similarly highlights harms where control efforts confront a form of resistance within an organization, and where those interested in controlling the harms need to understand the genesis and nature of that resistance, lest they be surprised by it. The distinctive characteristic of *performance-enhancing risks* is that the motivation for risk-taking derives from an organization's performance goals, rather than from the personal agendas of individuals or groups. The motivations for risk-taking, therefore, have an organizational origin. Moreover, the resistance to control manifests itself in rather particular organizational behaviors.

Many of the more familiar examples of performance-enhancing risks involve *unlawful* behavior, and have been examined by criminologists and sociologists under the general heading of "unlawful organizational conduct." Obvious examples include:

- the use of torture or other proscribed interrogation methods in order to extract confessions or information from prisoners;
- the payment of bribes by corporations in order to win contracts;[1]
- the use of steroids or other banned substances by professional sports team members;
- aggressive, fraudulent, or abusive billing practices which enable a corporation to maximize profits;
- neglect of safety procedures on construction sites as contractors rush to meet performance targets and project deadlines;
- misrepresenting the financial condition of an organization in order to maintain confidence and drive up the stock price.

In each of these situations, the risky behaviors serve some core purpose of the organization. At the same time, if discovered, they render the individuals involved subject to sanctions as well as exposing the organization to litigation, regulatory, or reputational risks that could ultimately dwarf any short-term performance advantage.[2]

The individuals involved in such proscribed behaviors are drawn in by their peers and socialized by prevailing cultural norms. Individuals vary in the degree to which their personal convictions and values enable them to resist. The moral choice is more about whether to "go along" or whether to resist; it is not so much a question of whether to engage in individual criminal entrepreneurship.

Even though the motivating agenda is organizational rather than personal, the individuals who engage in these behaviors may gain personally from them, in two ways. They may be formally rewarded with bonuses, recognition or promotions for the performance gains they produce, while the organization turns a blind eye or maintains silence on the question of *how* they met their goals. Individuals may also be celebrated informally as heroes or heroines as part of a "star culture" within a work group that knows what must be done, and appreciates those adventurous enough to do it.[3]

The general character of the problem

Previous commentators examining unlawful organizational behavior have pointed to the distinction between means and ends, and the fact that many instances of organizational misconduct involve legitimate ends being served by illegitimate means. Trouble arises, according to Diane Vaughan, when the social context puts greater emphasis on achieving the ends than on restricting the means:

> When the achievement of the desired goals received strong cultural emphasis, while much less emphasis is placed on the norms regulating the means, these norms tend to lose their power to regulate behavior.[4]

In trying to understand unlawful organizational conduct, the adoption of illegitimate means for accomplishing legitimate ends is certainly an important phenomenon to contemplate. It covers and captures *all* of the examples of performance-enhancing risks mentioned above. Nevertheless, it may be useful to include a slightly broader set of risks under the general heading *performance-enhancing* than are normally covered in discussions of illegal or unlawful conduct. In some contexts, the undesirable behaviors provoked by organizational purposes might not be illegal, but merely risky or potentially harmful – either to the organization itself or to others. Furthermore, the choice for individuals or units within the organization as to whether to engage in risky behaviors might not so neatly align with a distinction between means and ends: the choice might simply involve a balancing of two different kinds of risk, just *one* of which is tied tightly to highly visible core performance metrics.

One example of such a *balancing* would be NASA's decision to launch, or not to launch, the shuttle *Challenger* in 1986 in adverse weather conditions. NASA faced considerable pressure to maintain launch schedules and complete the requisite number of missions.[5] The number of missions completed on schedule represented a highly visible metric, closely tied to NASA's budget justifications and congressional support. NASA obviously cared a great deal about safety too, and their engineers had raised serious concerns internally, prior to the launch, about the performance of the O-rings on the main fuel tanks in freezing temperatures. The pressure to launch won out, the O-rings failed, and the craft and crew were lost in the ensuing tragedy. The inquiries and investigations that followed sought to understand the mechanisms through which the organization, perhaps unwittingly, managed to suppress the warnings in favor of the performance imperative.

Another example involves the balancing of efficiency against accuracy in processing operations. In high-volume production settings, the metrics relating to efficiency and timeliness are more tangible and visible than those relating to accuracy. The IRS receives and must process several hundred million tax returns each year. Failure to dispatch tax refunds in a timely fashion leads predictably and immediately to public clamor and congressional scrutiny. Similarly, health care insurers receive and process millions of claims from physicians and other providers, none of whom expect to wait long for payment. The *accounts payable* division within any major corporation, likewise, has to keep up with the flow of invoices for payment, and keep its own administrative costs down.

In these settings the most immediate and obvious pressure is to keep up with the workload. Backlogs are visible and embarrassing, so any failure to keep up with workload volumes is simply unacceptable. Turnaround times for each transaction might also be strictly limited in order to satisfy customer expectations, competitive

pressures, or mandatory timelines. For major processes, the administrative processing costs (normally calculated as cost-per-transaction)
feature prominently as expenses, affecting organizational profitability
in direct and obvious ways. For all these reasons processing efficiency
really counts, and pressures to keep up with the load *and* lower costs
really bite within the organization.

To meet exacting efficiency requirements on the process-side, organizations (or the relevant sub-units) face obvious temptations to cut
corners one way or another, compromising the competing set of values
that relate to accuracy, error-detection, program-integrity, and financial
risk-control. The simplest way to get the tax refunds out on time, when
your processing operation is stretched to capacity, is to suspend audits
and examinations. Better still, *turn off the audit flags* in the system!
That way the returns that would normally be picked out for human
scrutiny simply sail through electronically and without any hiccup.
Now the computers can catch up, the backlog danger is averted; and
nobody can tell for sure how many of the returns processed and refunds
paid *ought* to have been filtered out. Turning off the filters avoids the
embarrassment of anyone having to move piles of work from their in-
box to their out-box without looking at them. There is some comfort
in not knowing how much is being missed. The uncertainty enables
staff to assume a minimal amount of damage.

In my examination of fraud control within the American health care
system, fraud investigators and analysts would complain of instances
where administrators had actually turned off various *edits* and *audits*
built into automated claims-processing systems. These edits and audits
normally perform thousands of rule-based checks on incoming claims,
and flag for inspection any claims that seem to represent unusual,
unorthodox, or unwarranted medical treatment, or which sit outside
the normal confines of policy coverage or price ranges. At first sight it
is hard to imagine an economic rationale for turning such systems off.
The average dollar amount of a claim might be in the order of $100,
where the average cost of processing a claim is closer to 50 cents. Nevertheless these organizations sometimes behave as if they are much more
conscious of the benefits of further efficiency gains (e.g. the chance to
drive the 50c processing cost down to 45c) than of the risks of losing $100 or more, per claim, as a result of failure to detect errors,
fraud, or abuse. Ironically, the edits and audits most likely to be turned
off are the ones that are flagging the greatest number of claims, and

therefore pointing to the most significant financial risks. But these are the ones that can ruin your day if your job-related performance metrics are all about "keeping up." One senior Medicare official, extremely frustrated by the lack of scrutiny exercised by private contractors who process Medicare claims on behalf of the government, told me he had come to understand this relationship and the curious psychology of an efficiency-driven operation.[6] "The cheapest way to process a claim," he explained, "is to pay it *without question*."

Transaction-processing contexts reveal what one might consider to be a clash of purposes, with an accompanying clash of attitudes. One group of staff is concerned with efficient processing of the bulk. For them, exceptions and systems for exception-finding represent an inconvenience and a threat to overall system performance. Another group (usually a separate organizational unit), focused on financial risk and integrity of the payment operation, is mostly interested in detailed examination of the exceptions and anomalies. For them, exception-finding is the starting point for most of their work.

So what is it that ties these last two examples – the shuttle launch dilemma, and the clash of cultures in a transaction-processing environment – to the control of unlawful organizational behavior? Underestimating a safety risk is not unlawful per se. Nor is tilting towards efficiency at the expense of payment integrity, no matter how unwise that may appear in retrospect. Nevertheless these behaviors are produced and sustained by exactly the same set of forces as many of the unlawful behaviors mentioned above, and present very similar difficulties for operational control. In terms of the operational challenges, therefore, these behaviors are worth grouping together under the broader umbrella of behaviors which are both *risky* and *performance-enhancing*. This does not imply that the focus on *unlawful* organizational behavior, which other scholars have chosen, is any less useful. In fact, it suggests their analysis may have broader application than they have claimed because the underlying social structures and cultural contexts which they identify as driving illegal conduct also drive a broader range of risky, but legal, behaviors.

So what is the essential character of, and context for, *performance-enhancing* risks? In a nutshell, they comprise the combination of:

(1) *A core performance imperative* which is unambiguous, tangible, highly visible, and emphasized as critical to organizational success.

(2) *Metrics* related to this performance imperative which are objective, (usually) numerical, and available quickly and easily. These metrics grab and hold everybody's attention.

(3) *A reward system* which recognizes the contribution of individuals or units to this core performance imperative, providing an incentive for them to optimize their own contribution.

(4) *A set of behaviors* which do enhance, or which staff believe may enhance, their contribution to that core performance.

(5) *A set of ancillary risks* produced by those behaviors, potentially harmful to the organization or to others. These might be regulatory or litigation risks (in the case of unlawful behavior), or other classes of risk such as financial risk, reputational risks, or market risks.

(6) *The ancillary risks have uncertain, indirect or longer-term consequences*, which allow individuals to discount potential damage, assume their behaviors will not be detected, hide behind ambiguity about the rules, and derive security from the presumption that the organization itself "doesn't want to know" how they meet performance expectations.

(7) *Inadequate countervailing pressures to control those risky behaviors.*

That may seem a rather elaborate description, but this class of *knots* has a rather elaborate structure. Undoing the knots requires a clear view of the structure and dynamics that produce and sustain such behaviors over time, and some familiarity with their ordinary consequences. Those consequences, which one might reasonably anticipate for *any* such risk, include the following:

- It is not generally wise to rely on line-managers to balance the competing values. The performance objective, for them, is much more tangible and immediate and will tend to dominate their attention.
- In the absence of any visible failure or scandal, staff perceptions of the seriousness of the ancillary risks will decrease over time, and some will therefore drive closer and closer to the edge.[7]
- When a failure does occur (the uncertain dangers actually materialize, or someone gets caught in unlawful or inappropriate behaviors) senior management faces the temptation to sacrifice low level individuals or units, claiming that the behavior of the "rogue unit" is in no way reflective of the organization's broader culture or practices. Senior management will shield itself from culpability in the matter by claiming the behavior, now detected, was hitherto unknowable

and thus beyond their control. By sacrificing low level operatives and admitting no broader problem, the organization's management essentially retains the performance advantages of the improper behavior for the long term – even if these behaviors are temporarily suppressed or suspended in the immediate wake of the scandal.

- If management declares such malfeasance to be isolated, while staff throughout the organization know otherwise, the resulting signal transmitted through the organization can be extremely damaging. Staff assume that management really knows the truth, and actually likes it, and is merely playing a cynical public-relations game designed to minimize cost to the organization even as it minimizes disruption to the prevailing performance model. This tends to confirm for staff what they had always suspected: that management likes the performance advantage and that sanctions applied to the rogues are for getting caught, or for falling off the edge; not for engaging in the risky behaviors themselves.

Given these predictable dynamics and temptations, effective control strategies need to add strength and independence to the constraints on *means,* and to mobilize and increase the influence of individuals principled and far-sighted enough to be guided by a range of values broader than the immediate performance imperatives. Relevant methods include the following:

- Pay attention to the selection of new recruits, and avoid the tendency to replicate the values of the existing workforce. Make sure that interview panels include officials concerned primarily with organizational risk-management (e.g. compliance officers, counsel, inspectors-general) in addition to those gauging a candidate's potential contribution to performance. From the vantage point of risk-control, these officials will be more enamored with the cautious and principled, and a little less gung-ho about "team-players."[8] If the application and evaluation procedure involves opportunities for practical testing and exercises,[9] include within the portfolio of tests a situation where performance on the test would be enhanced by adopting proscribed or risky methods, and where participants might imagine that the chances of detection are quite low.[10]
- Beware the socialization of new recruits. Avoid placing new recruits in a situation where their survival within the organization depends upon their acceptance by a longer-serving and well-established team. Preserve new recruits' sense of belonging to their own cohort. Bring

cohorts of recruits back together again periodically, away from their normal workplace, for candid discussions about their experiences so far, pressures placed on them, and the workplace norms they have encountered.

- Promotion boards, likewise, should include representation by risk-management, compliance, or organizational integrity officers.
- Systems for surfacing, reviewing, and reporting proscribed or inappropriate conduct should include channels independent of line management and outside the chain of command. Otherwise one official, somewhere up the line and overly concerned about the performance imperative, can block effective transmission.
- Establish and publicize opportunities for anonymous reporting, such as complaint systems and whistleblower hot-lines. Establish whistleblower protection policies.
- Mandate the formal recording, investigation, and reporting of all calls received through such systems.
- Establish a direct reporting relationship between officials responsible for organizational risk-control and the Board, or other oversight body. Executives, even up to the rank of Chief Executive, ought not to be able to suppress concerns about methods in their eagerness for performance results. Information about unacceptable risk-taking behaviors needs to be able to flow around them to the highest oversight levels.
- Departments responsible for compliance, risk-management, and organizational ethics need staff within their own units who have credibility throughout the organization and who know the way the organization works, even while holding the right set of values and principles. Selection of staff for these tasks needs to balance knowledge of the organization against the dangers of socialization. Such units would do well to recruit individuals known as high-performers (who thus have credibility within the organization), but who have also demonstrated a broader and more balanced view of what counts – for example, by stepping forward as whistleblowers, or otherwise resisting cultural pressures.
- Even as the organization maintains independent mechanisms for monitoring risk-taking, it should also search for ways to make field staff and line-managers integrate competing values. One useful approach to this involves designing sanctions that translate into the same currency as performance-related rewards. That could mean

loss of any performance bonuses for transgression of means-related constraints. The penalties for paying bribes to win a contract might include loss of any credit, profit, or advantage that came from winning that contract. If a payment processing unit values efficiency too highly, and at the expense of the accuracy or integrity of the payments they make, then find a way to charge them within the organization's accounting systems for measured loss rates (presuming the organization has developed a reliable method for estimating these).[11] The more closely the sanctions can be linked to the performance gains, the more likely it is that lower level staff will be forced to wrestle with the consequences of performance-enhancing risks.

As executives contemplate the nature of performance-enhancing risks, and the control challenges they present, they should understand that these problems, even within their own organizations, also present many of the characteristics of *invisible* risks: The extent and pervasiveness of such behaviors is generally uncertain. Some may suspect a significant problem but lack the means to prove it. Many others have strong incentives to deny or downplay the seriousness of the issue. Staff, even if they assume the boss already knows full well what is going on, will not tell them or talk about it openly because they know any open discussion would put the boss in the awkward position of either having to condone or condemn. The tacit assumption is that the boss cannot afford to do either.

As with other invisible problems, readily available metrics are mostly ambiguous. Cases detected represent the *visible sliver,* and their discovery is quirky and serendipitous. The challenge of control is to expose and deal with the invisible mass. Policy tends to be scandal driven, and lacks longer-term stability and balance. Deliberate and proactive means for determining the extent and seriousness of the problem are a precursor to any kind of effective control. And adopting a passive and reactive stance, resting in the false security derived from *no complaints lately*, becomes a recipe for long-term disaster.

Notes

1. Whether payment of bribes is illegal depends on the location of the deed as well as the country of incorporation for the companies involved. Bribe-paying abroad is prohibited for US-based companies by the Foreign Corrupt Practices Act, 1977. Public Law 105–366.

2. For a discussion of the dominant role *reputational risk* now plays in corporate risk control, see: David Brotzen, "Wise Words and Firm Resolve When Times Get Tough," in special series, "*Mastering Risk*," No. 8, *Financial Times* (June 13, 2000), 10–11.

3. Nigel Nicholson & Paul Willman, "Mastering Risk: Folly, Fantasy and Roguery: A Social Psychology of Finance Risk Disasters," *Butterworths Journal of International Banking and Financial Law*, 15 (2000), 397.

4. Diane Vaughan, *Controlling Unlawful Organizational Behavior: Social Structure and Corporate Misconduct* (Chicago, University of Chicago Press, 1983), p. 55. Vaughan is summarizing the work of Robert K. Merton in "Social Structure and Anomie," in Robert K. Merton, *Social Theory and Social Structure* (Glencoe: Free Press, 1968), pp. 185–214.

5. For an analysis of NASA's decision-making process leading up to the launch, see: Diane Vaughan, *The Challenger Launch Decision* (Chicago: University of Chicago Press, 1996). For a case narrative, see: Oscar Hauptman & George Iwaki, "*Final Voyage of the Challenger*," Cases no: 9-691-037 and 9-691-039, (Boston: Harvard Business School, 1990). For a more general analysis of organizational failures in relation to nascent or emergent risks, see: Diane Vaughan, "Organizational Rituals of Risk and Error," in Bridget Hutter and Michael Power (eds.), *Organizational Encounters with Risk* (Cambridge: Cambridge University Press, 2005), pp. 33–66.

6. Malcolm K. Sparrow, *License to Steal: How Fraud Bleeds America's Health Care System*, 2nd edition (Denver, Colorado & Oxford, England: Westview Press, 2000), p. 35.

7. Hutter and Power describe the progression towards disaster in the case of Barings Bank with their "rogue-trader" Nick Leeson, thus: "The organizational encounter with risk unfolded over a period of time in which senior management denial or ignorance, the overriding of formal controls and a culture of risk taking combined to destroy the organization." Hutter & Power (eds.), *Organizational Encounters with Risk*, p. 14.

8. Robert Simons warns that neglect of these cautions in hiring is most common during periods of organizational success and rapid growth. During such periods, senior executives may also become resistant to bad news and therefore less sensitized to accumulating risk factors. See: Robert L. Simons, "How Risky is your Company?" *Harvard Business Review*, (May 1, 1999). HBR Product no. 99311.

9. For example, the "extended interview" techniques used for recruitment of military officers, and now emulated by other public agencies and by some corporations, involving several days of individual and group exercises closely monitored by a panel of evaluators.

10. Nicholson and Willman, in a discussion of rogue-traders and risk-taking behaviors, emphasize the importance of systematic selection methods to uncover worrisome psychological profiles. This recommendation rests on the assumption that personality profiles are relatively stable throughout professional (i.e. adult) life, and that a specific personality type captures much of the "rogue-behavior" risk. They identify this type as "thick-skinned experimenters looking for excitement without hard work," and state this profile is found much more frequently among men than women. Nigel Nicholson & Paul Willman, "Mastering Risk: Folly, Fantasy and Roguery: A Social Psychology of Finance Risk Disasters," *Butterworths Journal of International Banking and Financial Law,* 15 (2000), 395–397.

11. Integrating efficiency metrics with integrity metrics deliberately undoes the damaging *separation of funds,* whereby a processing operation becomes responsible only for driving down the costs of transaction processing, but bears no responsibility for, and therefore has no interest in, the actual funds being paid out. This situation severely affects the integrity of major public insurance and payment programs, such as Medicare, which employ private contractors to process claims for reimbursement from medical providers. From the point of view of those contractors, the payments themselves are viewed as "government money passing through." For a discussion of this phenomenon, see: Malcolm K. Sparrow, *License to Steal: How Fraud Plagues America's Health Care System,* 2nd edition (Denver, Colorado & Oxford, England: Westview Press, 2000), pp. 135–137.

Conclusion

I t is an odd moment when a brand new book arrives on your desk and as you examine it for the first time, despite the novelty of the content, it immediately feels familiar...because you think you have already met several of its *cousins*.

That just happened to me, only three days before final submission of this manuscript. The book which just arrived is *The Many Faces of Corruption*, edited by J. Edgardo Campos and Sanjay Pradhan of the World Bank. It is quite fat as books on corruption go, with over 400 pages. It has three parts, each organized around a different set of dimensions. The first is organized according to "sectors" (health, education, forestry, roads, water, etc.) and explores the specific types of corruption most prevalent within those sectors. The second part deals with public financial management, and looks in turn at budgeting, procurement, tax administration and customs. The final part examines the money-laundering profession and details strategies for undermining it.

Why exactly does such a book – which amasses a great deal of new information on this one subject – seem nevertheless familiar? Because the authors are deliberately pointing their corruption control colleagues along a new path – at least, a path which is relatively new for the corruption control field. The authors admit up front that their work represents early steps in that journey, but claim that significant opportunities for effective action lie ahead, and *only* along that path. In the "foreword," Danny Leipziger (Vice President of the World Bank) puts his finger on the change in direction that the book signals:

Empirical research on governance and anticorruption has made major strides in the past 10 years, providing increasing empirical evidence that corruption discourages private investment, retards growth, and inhibits poverty reduction efforts. Today, policy makers can use diagnostic instruments to make judgments about priorities for reforms across corruption-prone areas and broadly assess the potential impact over time of reform measures. But the challenge of drilling down to the operational level remains. What and where are the risk points in a given sector? When are they most likely to occur? Which ones, if addressed, might have the greatest impact on a sector's performance? For policy makers, data and information on these queries are what is missing to formulate specific, operationally tractable reforms.[1]

Anyone who was *not* especially interested in corruption, but quite interested in the reduction of other harms, might want a more general translation of this. I would offer the following, more generic, language:

We've done the macro-level analysis and learned a lot from it. We can also use such analyses to monitor aggregate changes in conditions. But the challenge of drilling down to the operational level remains. Now we have to identify the individual knots, and choose those that are most important. Unless we can actually see them clearly, then we will never be able to unravel them.

Jeffrey Sachs' recent book, *The End of Poverty*, feels to me a not-very-distant cousin, at least in spirit and direction, albeit focused on a quite different harm. Sachs too acknowledges what has been learned about the causes and consequences of poverty through macro-level economic analysis. But in introducing his notion of *clinical economics*, he argues that it is time to begin a different journey, exploring the highly variable substructure of the phenomenon of poverty. That exploration, he says, may lead to the identification of actionable projects at a lower level, more tailored focus on specific issues, and the prospect of more immediate gains.[2]

Danny Leipziger finishes up his foreword to *The Many Faces of Corruption* by saying precisely this, with respect to corruption: "This effort represents an initial foray into the deeper crevices of corruption. More work will be required to develop better informed, targeted reform measures at the operational level."[3] What he chooses to label the "deeper crevices," I have referred to earlier in this volume as the "textured middle layers." It's the same idea, and we have for it no standard vocabulary.

Herman Goldstein was pointing down this same path, for the sake of the police profession, as early as the 1970s and described the landscape to be explored fairly thoroughly in his book *Problem-Oriented Policing*, in 1990.[4] He made it perfectly clear that in his view the best hope for effective crime control enhancements lay not at the lowest levels of aggregation (in incident response, which was generally quite well done), nor at the highest levels (where broad categories of crime like "violent crimes" or "thefts" might be considered); but in the messy "in-between" layers, where problem definition and selection becomes an art form.

I am encouraged any time I hear a well respected voice in any one of these fields pointing down this path. Surely practitioners will take notice, I think to myself, when they hear this message from that person. They will listen to him or her, because that person speaks from a deep knowledge of the specific domain, and is a recognized expert within their field. One by one such experts recognize that the analytic and scholarly traditions within their fields have not been sufficiently connected to operational possibilities; and they end up pointing along this path, convinced that this is where the remedy lies.

But then I consider who are "they" who might listen to these experts, and I worry that the audience is too small. For Goldstein, *they* are police officers and criminologists, and virtually nobody else. Sachs will surely be read widely by those interested in poverty reduction. But will his work be read by environmentalists, or by those interested in controlling human trafficking, or by counter-terrorism officers? Would police executives or transportation safety officers read a book on poverty reduction, and understand the significance of the departure being made within that field from the analytic traditions of the past? And if they did, would they grasp the relevance of that departure for their own profession?

I would venture a guess that neither Sachs nor many officials at the World Bank have read Goldstein. And if poverty experts read about corruption, or anti-corruption professionals read about poverty, it is not so much because these two fields are making the same important step to begin the same important journey. Rather it is because the problems of poverty and corruption are known to be linked, especially in the context of the developing world. The connection is about the *harms,* not about the shared challenges of *harm-reduction.* I applaud all of these authors, and others who have provided similar guidance in other domains. But I deeply regret the fact that each discipline seems to have to learn these rather general lessons by themselves, in isolation; and when they do, the message then spreads predominantly within the confines of each discipline.

This book is intended to reach right across the spectrum of harms, and make plain to all that the harm-reduction task involves a more general art, which can be codified and taught. I trust that Part I has adequately demonstrated the importance of separating the destruction of bads from the construction of goods; and provided some guidance on how to tell which model is appropriate in different circumstances. I trust the early chapters also firmly established the importance of navigating the middle layers – which sit above the level of individual incidents, but below the level of broad generalities. I trust the two chapters on defining problems conveyed the extraordinary range of choices practitioners face as they consider at what *size* and in *what dimensions* to define a problem, and how many to take on at one time. I trust that Chapters 5 and 6 clarified the critical role that analysis must play at different stages of the problem-solving process, and the nature of the *performance account* that becomes available to organizations once they actually learn the operational harm-reduction *performance*.

I do hope this book helps move practitioners beyond the first few steps of their new journey, as indicated variously by Goldstein, Sachs, Campos, Pradhan, and others. As is the manner of experts in any one domain, these scholars have presented rich descriptions of the middle layers, full of knowledge and detail and copious examples from their fields. They demonstrate the possibility of slicing and dicing their general harms in different ways, and lay out the insights gleaned from specific decompositions or disaggregations they have used. What they each do, for their fields, is present a map of the terrain more detailed than anyone has seen before; and they invite others, later, to provide even richer detail and to fill in the parts as yet uncharted.

But mapping the territory, while clearly essential, is quite a different thing from actually *stepping into that territory and beginning work on it*. The accumulating knowledge base that constitutes and further refines the maps will ultimately count for nothing unless practitioners jump in and start working on the objects that the maps reveal. To make that leap, they need more than just the maps. They need a method of working. They need relevant decision frameworks. They need authorization. They need an organizational theory. They need forms! They need to know the relationship between harm-reduction projects and other types of work, such as functional and process-based. They need to embrace the concept of portfolio-management, and apply it to actionable harm-reduction projects. Then they have to find the Nigels within their organization, or recruit them, and learn how to commission them appropriately. They need to understand the profound changes for managerial decision making that occur once they actually start picking and choosing among candidate risk-concentrations, resolving conflicts over definitions, and selecting the right partners for each enterprise. They also need to decide how much time and effort to spend scanning for emerging problems never seen before, and to devise the means for conducting and sustaining such scanning operations.

I hope that Part I of this book actually takes practitioners beyond having or holding or appreciating the maps, and gives them the confidence to jump in. Once they do, and when they start picking up particular knots and studying their structure, only at that stage will they discover how strangely some of these objects behave and how awkward they are to unravel. At that point, Part II of this book may help, as it describes some of the most common and most troublesome properties that objects within this landscape exhibit. And whether these "knots" have these properties or not has little to do with which professional domain they belong within. It would be really quite sad, and an awful waste of time, if each discipline had to discover all of these properties and their operational consequences by themselves, in isolation, without any sharing of such insights across the broader harm-reduction community.

I would be delighted if experts in specific domains found the first part of this book useful to them as they examine the analytic traditions of their fields. They might test the extent to which macro-level analyses have historically dominated their policy discussions, and whether the literature has systematically picked apart and provided mappings of the lower-level texture of their harms. They might examine which dimensions have most often been used to define problems, and which ones have never been used at all. They might determine whether or not the domain-specific literature reveals a tendency to define problems in a way that makes them align nicely with existing organizational structures and methods, or with the interests of certain parties. Or does the analysis that has been done reflect a genuine respect for (and therefore an eagerness to discover) *the natural shape and size of the harms themselves*? In the design of operational interventions, has enough attention been paid to the particular structures of different knots; or do the major debates within the field still revolve around preferences among tools? Are conference agendas mostly hatched in the *field*, with a focus on specific problems; or are they hatched in the *toolshed*, with a focus on specific methods and the contributions of specific actors?

I would also be delighted if practitioners and researchers alike found *qualities of harms that present distinctive operational challenges* a useful and important way of categorizing harms. Developing this focus might better connect the study of risk and risk-control to the practical and organizational challenges of risk-mitigation. I hope practitioners across a broad range of harm-reduction activities will continue to tell those of us in academia which classes or properties confound them most often, and what particular puzzles those classes present.

Hopefully practitioners will take from this a little courage, either grasping more clearly what they have already begun to do, or recognizing opportunities they have not seen so clearly before. I hope this book helps them resist the ever-present temptation to relax back into familiar methods, to rely upon well-engrained theories of operations, to rejoice in familiar forms of functional expertise, to champion their favorite tools, or to be satisfied when they simply manage to keep pace with established processes.

I hope this book eases the pain of jumping into the textured, middle layers, where everything has an awkward shape, and multitudes of unfamiliar choices have to be made and then defended. Surely it is here that the bulk of the important work of harm-control really lies.

Notes

1. J. Edgardo Campos & Sanjay Pradhan (eds.), *The Many Faces of Corruption: Tracking Vulnerabilities at the Sector Level*, International Bank for Reconstruction and Development (Washington DC: World Bank, 2007), from the "Foreword" by Danny Leipziger, Vice President, World Bank. p. xi.
2. Jeffrey D. Sachs, *The End of Poverty: Economic Possibilities for Our Time* (New York: Penguin Books, 2005), pp. 74–89.
3. Campos & Pradhan, *The Many Faces of Corruption*, p. xiii.
4. Herman Goldstein, *Problem-Oriented Policing* (New York: McGraw-Hill Publishing Company, 1990).

Index